The Politics of
Interdisciplinary Studies

The Politics of Interdisciplinary Studies

Essays on Transformations in American Undergraduate Programs

Edited by
Tanya Augsburg *and*
Stuart Henry

McFarland & Company, Inc., Publishers
Jefferson, North Carolina, and London

LIBRARY OF CONGRESS CATALOGUING-IN-PUBLICATION DATA

The politics of interdisciplinary studies : essays on transformations
  in American undergraduate programs / edited by Tanya Augsburg
  and Stuart Henry.
       p.   cm.
     Includes bibliographical references and index.

     ISBN 978-0-7864-4168-6
     softcover : 50# alkaline paper ∞

     1. Education, Higher — United States.   2. Interdisciplinary
approach in education — United States.   I. Augsburg, Tanya.
II. Henry, Stuart, 1949–
LB2322.2.P68   2009
378.1'990973 — dc22   2009018369

British Library cataloguing data are available

Cover image ©2009 Shutterstock

Manufactured in the United States of America

McFarland & Company, Inc., Publishers
  Box 611, Jefferson, North Carolina 28640
  www.mcfarlandpub.com

September 18, 2009

Acknowledgments

There are a few people whom the editors would like to acknowledge for their help with this volume. In particular we thank: William H. Newell who provided early encouragement and strong support for the project, and for his lifelong dedication to furthering the development of interdisciplinary studies; and Rick Szostak for his insight and optimism that enables him to see change as opportunity, rather than as challenge and defeat. Both Bill and Rick's collaboration in analyzing the core themes of the various chapters has made our conclusion more valuable than it would otherwise have been. We would also like to thank Allen Repko for his enduring faith in searching for the common core of interdisciplinarity and for reminding us all how giant oaks can indeed grow from little acorns, provided that the soil in which they are sown is ripe for sustainability. Behind all of our thoughts is the foundational influence of Julie Thompson Klein whose pioneering work has expanded and continues to expand the boundaries of knowledge through interdisciplinary thinking. We are thankful for her support and invaluable feedback. Finally, we would like to thank all the contributors for bringing this project to fruition.

Table of Contents

Preface

The focus of this book is primarily on undergraduate interdisciplinary studies degree programs (e.g., bachelor's in interdisciplinary studies) and the politics that has led to their transformation from experimental innovations in higher education to a variety of different manifestations that depart significantly from their original objectives. In particular, we argue that the field of undergraduate interdisciplinary studies has reached a critical juncture. At a time when the idea of interdisciplinary studies has entered the mainstream of research and academic discourse, programs that explicitly deliver undergraduate interdisciplinary degrees seem to be under attack, with several being closed down or dispersed. Michael Moran, in his 2006 article in *Politics*, invites us to explain "why, in a world where almost everyone speaks approvingly of interdisciplinarity, disciplinary identities are if anything strengthening their hold over the academic mind.... What accounts for the apparent paradox that interdisciplinarity is simultaneously hugely popular but unable to make serious headway?" (Moran 2006, 73). He argues that this is because the very idea of interdisciplinarity is "only possible in a disciplinary world. The notion only makes sense as a reaction against, or an attempt to unify, modes of knowledge presently separated into disciplinary domains" (Moran 2006, 74).

Our book tries to explain this paradox from the inside and from the ground up. In doing so it provides: (1) an overview of the political economy of higher education shaping these changes, (2) concrete case studies of the changes that have taken place at a variety of colleges and universities, and (3) a review of the new directions that significantly engage undergraduates in interdisciplinary thinking. In the process we are centrally concerned with how to sustain viable interdisciplinary studies programs.

Martin Trow's extremely influential 1984 article "Interdisciplinary Studies as a Counterculture" conceptualized program viability in terms of failure and survival, and argued that those programs that find complementary niches

1

are more likely to survive than those that present themselves as radical alternatives. We have since learned, as William H. Newell has argued in this volume, that rather than being a linear development there is clearly something of a cyclical nature to the field of interdisciplinary studies; analysis by James W. Davis, Raymond C. Miller and Helen Goldsmith of San Francisco State University's experience with interdisciplinary studies shows, while some interdisciplinary programs close, others may be born even in the same institution. Allen F. Repko, in his contribution to this volume, reframes the politics of interdisciplinary program survival in terms of the ecological discourse of sustainability, and there is much to commend this approach.

While we agree with Julie Thompson Klein's (2005) observation in *Humanities, Culture and Interdisciplinarity: The Changing American Academy* that the discourse of interdisciplinarity has often been one of conflict, and while we may claim that we live on the margins and in the interstices of more established fields of knowledge, we also suggest that interdisciplinarity is a discourse of uncertainty and change and, therefore, its future may remain as contested terrain. Our book then moves us from the prevailing rhetoric of struggle to reveal the politics and intrigue involved in how major changes in the direction of interdisciplinary programs occur in ways that depart significantly from the ideals of academe. We show that it may not be enough to have excellent pedagogy, student-centered learning and effective student outcome assessment measures, without also having a "politics of interdisciplinary studies." Without a political awareness of the disciplines' resilience in the face of educational administrators' attempts to control disciplines; without a realization that interdisciplinarity can be but a temporary tool in the wider politics of university power struggles; without reflecting on the reality that university administrators can indulge interdisciplinarity without being committed to its fundamental principles; without realizing academic administrators can throw it over the side as just so much ballast; and without recognizing that many senior administrators did not get to govern universities because of their accomplishments as interdisciplinarians; indeed, without an understanding of these political realities, sustaining interdisciplinary studies will be much more difficult.

This volume was several years in the making. In 2005 Stuart Henry assembled a conference panel on Administration and Interdisciplinary Studies Programs (IDS) for the annual meeting of Association for Integrative Studies (AIS) that was held in Fairfax, Virginia. At the time Henry was chair of the Department of Interdisciplinary Studies at Wayne State University. The other panelists included: James Hall, the director of the New College, University of Alabama, Tuscaloosa; Janette Kenner Muir, associate dean for New Century College of George Mason University (and the 2005 AIS Conference organizer); Paul Burkhardt, who was the newly appointed dean of Graduate Studies at Prescott College but who had overseen the closure of Arizona International College in Tucson, Arizona; Rick Szostak, former associate dean of the Office of Interdisciplinarity at the University of Alberta; and Kevin H. Ellsworth, the director of the Bachelor of Interdisciplinary Studies (BIS) program at Arizona State University (ASU). Tanya Augsburg, who at the time was senior lecturer in ASU's BIS program, served as both panel moderator and discussant. Henry's contribution to the panel was subsequently published in the 2005 volume of the official publication of AIS, the academic journal *Issues in Integrative Studies* (*IIS*). Responses by several of the panelists and the discussant (Szostak, Burkhardt, and Augsburg) were published in the 2006 volume.

In 2006 we conducted a survey on IDS faculty teaching at public universities to establish how widely this trend was affecting undergraduate interdisciplinary studies and reported their findings at the AIS conference (Augsburg and Henry 2006). In all, 74 institutional representatives were surveyed. However, the survey resulted in only 11 responses to the questionnaire representing a 14.9 percent response rate. In addition, 5 responses were received from respondents who were unable to complete the survey but offered views/opinions on the issues. Clearly the response rate was insufficient to make any representative claims about the population surveyed, and even less about the general population of IDS in public universities. Thus we were unable to draw any definitive conclusions.

However, the paper incited a lively response indicating further exploration was in order. Our cautionary tone regarding the future of undergraduate interdisciplinary programs and the lack of security of faculty positions in the field was generally viewed as too pessimistic despite the challenges that several long-standing programs, such as those at Wayne State University, Miami University of Ohio, and Appalachian State University were facing at the time.

Many things changed not long after we delivered our presentation. Stuart Henry left Wayne State University for San Diego State University in 2006 not least because he saw the "writing on the wall" for the future of that program, and Tanya Augsburg left Arizona State University for San Francisco State University in 2007. The existing programs at Wayne State University, Miami University of Ohio, and Appalachian State University all were significantly transformed in 2007, being either completely closed (WSU) or being absorbed into other administrative structures (Appalachian State and Miami). In contrast, two undergraduate interdisciplinary programs, the Interdisciplinary Studies Program at University of Texas at Arlington and the Liberal Studies Program at San Francisco State University, added multiple tenure-track lines for the first time in their long histories. All these changes were the topic of much discussion among those associated with undergraduate interdisciplinary programs, which was particularly evident among the participants of the Fall 2007 AIS conference at Arizona State University. Among the questions that arose were: "Whither interdisciplinarity?" "What has changed about IDS programs?" "What is the future of IDS programs?" "Where are they going?" and "What is happening to their resources, particularly their faculty"? More generally, "Is there a national trend occurring that is affecting long-standing undergraduate interdisciplinary programs?"

We found these questions intriguing. We were interested in identifying emerging patterns and trends among undergraduate IDS programs and were encouraged by various colleagues in the field, including the AIS Board, to explore further this phenomenon. The challenge was locating the data from which patterns, trends, and common core themes could be identified. We decided that a volume of collected essays, in which contributors would provide rich, in-depth institutional histories, insight on program internal politics, and salient concepts for the future sustainability of interdisciplinary studies, seemed like the most feasible and valuable approach. Our selection of faculty and institutions included both those whose programs we knew had closed completely, others that had undergone major changes that diminished their operations and others that had expanded or were interested in starting new programs. Clearly not every IDS program could be included, and some who were invited declined our invitation. In the end those who accepted and whose programs are represented here provide a rich array of insights with a set of common themes that emerge and that are drawn out in the concluding chapter.

A few comments on methodology are in order. Interdisciplinarians as a group are naturally open to the use of multiple methods. By design, the book is based on what Rick Szostak, who coauthors our conclusion, calls "the 'insider observations' of those dedicated to the development of interdisciplinary programs." On many occasions, personal memories are supplemented by interviews with others or faculty surveys or reference to textual materials regarding program development. While such an approach runs the risk that contributors will be too positive in their assessment of the value of interdisciplinarity in general, and the value of their programs in particular, the trajectories of many programs has encouraged a soul-searching that should at least severely limit, if not completely eliminate this sort of bias.

Interdisciplinarians are always on guard for scholarly bias. And authors are generally careful to provide supportive evidence for the key arguments they put forward. Given the complexity of program histories, let alone political realities, the possibility exists that some crucial information may have been left out. We acknowledge too that there is always more than one side to any story. Nonetheless, this volume does in our opinion provide a sound basis from which to develop hypotheses regarding the historical trajectory of interdisciplinary programs and what works and what does not work in sustaining interdisciplinary programming administratively. These hypotheses in turn can be evaluated in practice in a variety of ways. We believe that the varying analyses of the micro-politics of university decision making captured in the contributors' histories and explanations for local structural and curriculum changes will provide those in interdisciplinary studies with a valuable resource for sustaining a more viable future for the field.

REFERENCES

Augsburg, Tanya, and Stuart Henry. 2006. Faculty on the margin? The state of the profession in undergraduate interdisciplinary programs. Presentation at Bridge-Building: Connecting Hearts and Minds, Arts and Sciences, Teaching and Research, Academy and Community, The 28th Annual Conference of the Association for Integrative Studies, October 5–8, Atlanta, Georgia.

Klein, Julie Thompson. 2005. *Humanities, culture and interdisciplinarity: The changing American Academy.* Albany: State University of New York Press.

Moran, Michael. 2006. Interdisciplinarity and political science. *Politics* 26(2): 73–83.

Trow, Martin. 1984/85. Interdisciplinary studies as a counterculture. *Issues in Integrative Studies* 3: 1–16.

Introduction

Undergraduate interdisciplinary studies programs have reached a crossroads in their development. At a time when the idea of interdisciplinary studies has entered the mainstream of research and academic discourse, those programs that explicitly deliver generic undergraduate interdisciplinary degrees seem to be under attack, with several longstanding programs being closed down and their faculty dispersed, often to disciplinary departments. This development has been true of leading undergraduate interdisciplinary programs at Miami University of Ohio, Wayne State University, and Appalachian State University, to name just three. While this development might be unremarkable if it were only occurring in a few isolated cases, there seems to be a pattern in universities across the United States, as evidenced by the contributions to this book. As one scholar remarked during the 2004 Association for Integrative Studies conference, "How different is the current 'crisis' from others in our history? Being interdisciplinary means living on the edge. We are always in crisis. That's what energizes us!" The provocative question is whether this current "crisis" marks a significant turning point in undergraduate interdisciplinary education and if so, what does it mean for undergraduate education, disciplinary knowledge production and interdisciplinary studies? Have we come of age, in the sense that interdisciplinary studies is so dispersed across disciplinary fields that it is "the air we breathe," or does the latest development represent a cooptation of its ideals? As Katz (2001) stated in "disciplining interdisciplinarity": "As interdisciplinary programs have gained a degree of relative institutional comfort, they have had a tendency to become "disciplined" themselves; that is, to establish their own canons and to defend against the very sorts of incursions and invigorations that might rework them in the ways they did the traditional disciplines" (Katz 2001, 521). Indeed, she argues that while "interdisciplinary studies programs have 'settled in'" they "continue to exist within an environment where unrelenting disciplinary claims to knowledge hold sway" (Katz 2001, 522). Vasterling et al. state that

"Recent fortunes in institutionalisation may have mainstreamed interdisciplinarity, but they have not provided material and conceptual support for its development. These factors make interdisciplinarity as a radical research or pedagogic position difficult to sustain" (Vasterling et al. 2006, 66).

In an article in *Liberal Education* entitled "Interdisciplinarity at the Crossroads" Ethan Kleinberg (2008) raises some of these important questions, particularly about the paradox of growth, normalization and "disciplinary" conformity that he describes as a "pact with the devil" entered into by undergraduate interdisciplinary studies programs in the first decade of the 21st century:

> In today's competitive college market, "interdisciplinary studies" are a major selling point for colleges and universities. These once marginal sites for innovative scholarship are now prominently displayed in brochures and Web pages, and they are viewed as necessary for attracting the best students.... At one level, it is a testament to the success and viability of the many interdisciplinary departments, programs, and centers that they have gained institutional status. One could even claim that the twenty-first-century university marks the ascension of interdisciplinarity as the dominant educational paradigm.... And yet, on closer examination, it is apparent that the academic structure and place of the majority of these programs, departments, and centers are not substantially different from the academic disciplines, departments, and divisions they were originally designed to challenge ... interdisciplinary studies became complicit, if not responsible, for the fragmentation of the university into a series of localized specializations isolated from, and in competition with, one another to attract niche customers/students. Thus the interdisciplinary departments, programs, and centers found willing partners but at a price: their interdisciplinarity. Far from marking the dawn of an interdisciplinary era, this pact with the devil has marked the end of real interdisciplinarity [Kleinberg 2008, 6].

While Kleinberg argues that the success of interdisciplinary studies has undermined, or is in danger of undermining, its own ethos, others have questioned whether the widespread dispersal of interdisciplinary studies in the academy has led to a liberal arts backlash that has seen disciplines use their hegemonic power to re-colonize some of the interdisciplinary innovations that led to its 21st century ascendancy (Henry 2005). It is toward an exploration of these issues in the context of real-world developments in undergraduate education that this book is directed.

The primary focus of this book is on the history, politics and paradox that has led four-year undergraduate interdisciplinary studies degree programs in the United States to their apparent downfall early in the first decade of the 21st century, several after 30 or more years of growth and success. The book also focuses on the ways that some interdisciplinary programs have weathered the storm and in some cases have emerged stronger and more resilient, and at what cost. Have we, in the process moved from strong interdisciplinarity to weak interdisciplinarity as Ray Miller argues in this violume?

Moreover, while specific content-based interdisciplinary programs of the kind Kleinberg refers to (such as environmental studies, urban studies, women's studies, communications studies, area studies, Africana Studies, gay and lesbian studies) have been allowed to flourish, successful generalized interdisciplinary programs have been increasingly curtailed. We ask why this development is occurring at this point in time. Is there something fundamentally flawed about the enterprise of interdisciplinarity as Moran (2006) argues, or does the problem lie with the particular form: the generic undergraduate interdisciplinary studies degree? Has the interdisciplinary studies degree become redundant having been replaced by a proliferation of interdisciplinary subject-focused degrees, and is its future survival destined to be a degree completion mechanism, designed to improve retention rates by passing through students who are unable or unwilling to make it in traditional disciplinary fields? Alternatively, has undergraduate interdisciplinary education grown so large and from a disciplinarian's perspective "out of control" that its wings are being clipped to stifle further ascendancy? Before we can answer these questions we need to describe what we mean by the undergraduate interdisciplinary degree and its place in the growth in interdisciplinary undergraduate education.

Undergraduate Interdisciplinary Degrees

As Klein (1990, 156) has shown, since its emergence interdisciplinary education has taken a number of forms, from whole universities designed to deliver interdisciplinarity, through core curricula, general education and clustered courses, to individual courses and graduate and professional studies. But it is the proliferation and demise of the four-year interdisciplinary degree that we are concerned with here. Klein explains,

> The curriculum in most interdisciplinary degree programs is centered on issues of national experience, or major ideas in Western culture, important social topics, and scientific issues that are regarded as socially and intellectually important. The courses themselves are usually organized around a particular subject: a theme, problem, topic, issue, region, cultural period, institution, figure, idea, or in some cases a given field of study. The usual procedure is to organize them around three clusters of disciplines: the social sciences, natural sciences, and humanities. In general there are two types of courses: courses promoting breadth to a wide spectrum of knowledge ... [and] courses examining disciplinary and interdisciplinary methods, concepts and

theories, either within different modes of inquiry or applied to particular problems and issues [Klein 1990, 163–64].

Klein points out that these courses move toward increasing synthesis or integration at their upper levels and help students balance depth specialization and breadth integration. Indeed, she says, "it is synthesis that distinguishes 'disciplinary' and 'multidisciplinary' education from 'interdisciplinary' education (Klein 1990, 166). She reports the most common methods of instruction include "core seminars, individualized study, workshops, colloquia, projects, and theses" (Klein 1990, 166). More recently, Klein and Newell have defined interdisciplinary studies not as a distinct subject area of knowledge but as "a process of answering a question, solving a problem, or addressing a topic too broad or complex to be dealt with adequately by a single discipline or profession.... IDS draws on disciplinary perspectives and integrates their insights through construction of a more comprehensive perspective ... interdisciplinary study is not a supplement but it is complementary to and corrective of the disciplines" (Klein and Newell, 1997, 393). Others (Augsburg 2006, 15; Repko 2007, 130–35) have since broken down this definition into five constitutive elements of interdisciplinary studies that include: (1) addressing a complex problem that cannot be resolved using a disciplinary focus (Klein and Newell 1997, 393; Boix Mansilla and Gardner 2003, 3); (2) drawing on a variety of insights and knowledge bases regardless of disciplinary or non-disciplinary source (Klein 1996; Repko 2008a); (3) creatively integrating knowledge and insights (Haynes 2002; Repko 2008a); (4) producing a comprehensive interdisciplinary understanding of the problem, that is (5) a cognitive advancement over a single disciplinary understanding (Boix Mansilla 2004; Repko 2008a). Clearly, as Klein was first to observe, the concept of "synthesis" or "integration" is the central distinguishing feature of interdisciplinary studies. While the value of interdisciplinary integration has been nationally recognized by leading figures in higher education (Boyer 1998; Gregorian 2004) as a means of addressing the complexity of major contemporary issues, the field may not have demonstrated this through conventional measures of assessment, not least because its core dimension, synthesis, has proven to be difficult to achieve and even more difficult to measure. However, before we get ahead of ourselves, we need to briefly discuss how, and to what extent, undergraduate interdisciplinary bachelor's degree programs rose in popularity, and how interdisciplinarity ascended.

The Growth and Ascendancy of Interdisciplinary Studies

In the 1930s, following American University's mid-nineteenth century reorganization along the lines of the German research university (Swoboda

1979), and merely a generation after the formation of academic disciplines, we saw the formation of the first programs in interdisciplinary studies: "many so called 'traditional' academic disciplines are not much older than some interdisciplinary programs — in effect the founding of modern disciplines preceded the emergence of interdisciplinary programs by roughly seventy years" (Augsburg 2006, 9). Interdisciplinary studies programs were partly a reaction to the fragmentation and professionalization of knowledge produced by disciplinary proliferation, and partly a response to the need for a more coherent general education for undergraduates. As a result of increasing disciplinary specialization some universities created general education curriculum along the lines of "Great Books" seminars. In the 1930s American Studies and other "area" studies developed that provided knowledge integrated across disciplines about a particular area (Klein 1990). At this time, too, the first interdisciplinary arts programs in the U.S. were created. By the 1940s experiments in interdisciplinary education and research became "commonplace" (Sherif and Sherif 1969, 3).

The emergence of interdisciplinary studies programs was also tied to a growing critical movement in higher education. Hendra and Harris (2002), for example, have documented how interdisciplinary studies degree (IDS) programs are associated with the history of experimental progressive education. Colleges including Antioch, Bard, Bennington, Black Mountain, Goddard, and Sarah Lawrence had begun to experiment with student-centered learning in the 1920s and 1930s as a reaction to the emergence and growth of the modern research university. Influenced by John Dewey and the Progressive Movement in education and the liberation movements of the 1960s, these colleges

> emphasized individualized or interdisciplinary programs and the fine arts; independent study along with greater student responsibility for the educational process; the development of a community of learners; experiential learning, whether work or service related; small, seminar style classes; and mentoring relationships with faculty. They tended to de-emphasize "such traditional practices as grades, examinations, degree criteria and entrance requirements" [Rudolph 1962, 476]. Their commitment to a philosophy of educational experimentation and "learning how to learn" as a foundation for such non-traditional practices marked these colleges as a distinct new type on the higher educational scene [Hendra and Harris 2002].

Hendra and Harris (2002) state that by the 1970s, 17 of these experimental colleges, including such notable institutions as Antioch College, Bard College, the New College of Hofstra University, Monteith College of Wayne State University, Northeastern Illinois University, Goddard College, the University of Massachusetts/Amherst, the University of Minnesota, New College of Sarasota, and the University of Wisconsin/Green Bay had formed into a "University without Walls" with a set of principles that expanded higher education beyond traditional age cohorts and valued pragmatic and experiential learning, and collaborative curriculum design that involved students and administrators, as well as faculty. They also valued independent learning, flexible course delivery modalities and students taking classes at more than one institution.

However, it was the cultural changes and protest movements of the 1960s, led by reform-minded academics in leading universities that thrust forward the reality of change. There was a growing critique from radical educators and philosophers such as Ivan Illich and Michel Foucault who viewed education as social control, at the same time as educational reformers and the student movement called for radical educational change. As Katz says,

> Interdisciplinary studies blossomed in the United States beginning in the late 1960s through the 1970s. Programs, concentrations, and even departments were established in response to demands stemming from the larger political climate when civil rights, anti-imperialist, antiracist, and women's movements burgeoned on campuses and beyond, riding upon as much as interrogating enlightenment thinking and the dominant universalist assumptions that held it in place, and — with struggle — opening up the university to all kinds of hitherto marginalized publics.... These classed, raced, and gendered groups (both students and faculty) demanded curricular and other changes not only to reflect their presence in the academy but also to uncover, recover, and even celebrate their diverse histories in the world [Katz 2001, 519–520].

It was at this time that several of what would become the longstanding generic programs in interdisciplinary studies were founded. Several of these began as "colleges within colleges" such as Fairhaven College at Western Washington University, which formed in 1967 as "an innovative, interdisciplinary, liberal arts laboratory for student-centered, collaborative teaching and learning" (Newell et al. 2003). Wayne State University's precursor to its interdisciplinary studies degree, the University Studies/Weekend College Program, formed in 1973 directly from the faculty and students in its Montieth College, and became The College of Lifelong Learning, carrying with it many of its "University without Walls" principles. Others, such as Miami University's School of Interdisciplinary Studies, formed in 1974, was housed in its Western College, and yet others also adopted this college-within-a-college model including New College at University of Alabama, Tuscaloosa, formed in 1971. (George Mason University's New Century College also followed this model but much later, in 1995.)

From these experimental roots the rise in enrollments of multi- and interdisciplinary studies degree programs began slowly. The National Center for Educational Statistics (NCES) gathers information on bachelor's degrees awarded. NCES defines multi- and interdisciplinary studies as "instructional programs that derive from two or more distinct programs to provide a cross-cutting focus on a subject concentration that is not subsumed under a single discipline or occupational field" (NCES 2002). Data from NCES reveal that in 1970-71 there were a mere 6,200 students graduating with degrees in multi/interdisciplinary studies per year. By 1991-92 that number had risen to over 17,000, and since 1994 interdisciplinary graduates averaged around 26,000 a year. In 2005-06, 32,012 bachelor's degrees in multi-/interdisciplinary studies were awarded, an increase of 79 percent over 1991-92, an average growth of 5.6 percent per year (NCES 2008); indeed, this is the fifth fastest rate of growth among the 22 bachelor's fields listed by the NCES. A recent study of the growth in interdisciplinary studies degree fields reveals that "the total of interdisciplinary fields in our sample institutions grew by nearly 250 percent between 1975 and 2000: from 674 programs in 1975–1976 to 1,663 in 2000–2001" (Brint et al. 2009, 170).

Correspondingly, there has been a rise in literature in the field (Haynes 2005, 1; Klein, 2005), and in 2005 the first textbooks in interdisciplinary studies were published (Augsburg 2005, 2006; Repko 2005, 2008a), which as Castellana (2005, 1) says, "has political significance marking a coming of age." Indeed, in 2009 the first encyclopedic volume, *The Oxford Handbook of Interdisciplinarity* appeared (Frodeman, Klein, and Mitcham 2009).

Nor is this growth surprising, given that leading educational policy makers such as Ernest Boyer (1998) and the Carnegie Foundation's Vartan Gregorian (2003) have lamented the myopia of disciplinary undergraduate education that produces barriers to knowledge rather than bridges to problem solving. Indeed, Dr. Elias Zerhouni, head of the National Institutes of Health, said in 2003 that we need a new roadmap of interdisciplinarity and integration of knowledge to understand society's complex problems. Similarly, the American Association for the Advancement of Science's CEO, Alan Lashner, stated in a 2004 *Science* magazine article: "interdisciplinarity characterizes so much of today's most exciting work." Lashner's greatest fear is that "our scientific institutions are not well positioned to promote the interdisciplinarity that characterizes so much of science at the leading edge." In addition, and consistent with this shift in policy, federal funding agencies began favoring interdisciplinary-designed projects in their funding decisions (National Academies 2004).

Given these accolades and successes, why is it that several interdisciplinary studies programs in the United States have, in the past few years, seen their resources cut and their innovative and experimental programs diminished, or in some cases, merged into conformity with the traditional disciplines? We know of at least six: WSU (closed down completely, faculty dispersed to disciplinary departments), the University of Alabama-Tuscaloosa (moved from the autonomous New College, into a College of Arts and Letters), George Mason University (whose New Century College was considerably diminished in size), Appalachian State University (closed as a department and moved into a University College, with faculty dispersed into disciplinary departments), Miami University of Ohio (closed and merged into Liberal Arts with faculty dispersed into disciplinary departments), and Arizona International (which was closed down completely). Perhaps there is something more political, if not exactly sinister, going on here? Is this development a reflection of the disciplining of the field; regularizing it, normalizing it, limiting it, into traditional categories of higher learning? If so, who is doing this and why? What are the causes of this trend? Is the field of interdisciplinary studies, as we know it, sustainable?

Explaining the Paradox/Crisis/Change

Martin Trow (1984/85) was one of the first to address the issue of the sustainability of interdisciplinary studies programs although he framed it differently. He argued "the success and failure of interdisciplinary studies programs are a function of their relation to the rest of higher education, in their own institutions and elsewhere" (Trow 1984/85, 3). He said that in the tradition of the experimental colleges their survival or demise is tied to whether they stand fundamentally critical of American higher education or are prepared to find their own place in its richness and diversity. Trow pointed out that the former have failed while "those that have claimed a place in the spectrum of higher education to serve that segment of the student population which wants and can profit from what interdisciplinary programs and colleges can offer, have on the whole, survived and flourished" (Trow 1984/85, 3). However, as we have argued, what is significant about the first decade of the twenty-first century is that "even long-standing interdisciplinarity programs, that have become departmentalized, institutionalized and routinized, are ultimately still vulnerable to the power of the disciplines" (Henry 2005, 3). In an analysis of the possible explanation for these changes Henry (2005) argues that a significant issue in this paradoxical situation of growth, success and demise, is institutionalized disciplinary power, or what Ben Agger (1991), applying Gramsci, labeled "disciplinary hegemony." Disciplinary hegemony, as Michael Moran points out, is embodied in disciplinarity:

> Disciplinarity — the systematization of knowledge into discrete, specialized, hierarchical domains — was "strengthened in the Enlightenment, both by the emergence of modern scientific specialisms, and by the Enlightenment mania for the classification and codification of knowledge into encyclopedic sys-

tems.... Disciplines, therefore are about power, hierarchy and control in the organization of knowledge" [Moran 2006, 74].

Indeed, the argument has been made that "disciplinary parochialism," "disciplinary imperialism" (Sayer 1999) and the "politics of disciplinary advantage" (Rogers, Booth and Eveline 2003), have conspired to attack the vulnerabilities of interdisciplinary studies, programs, departments and colleges (Henry 2005). Disciplinary power seeks to discipline interdisciplinarity from its position of control, regulation and selection that is embedded in the institutional structures of power of the university: "Discipline positions itself as a prototypical model for generating authority and thus sets the standards for judging what counts as knowledge and determines who will be afforded access to resources and influence. Deviance from its strictures can lead only to marginalisation" (Rogers, Booth and Eveline 2003). In the process of regularizing, normalizing and incorporating, the very distinctiveness of interdisciplinary studies as a pedagogically sophisticated attempt to integrate knowledge across disciplines becomes, instead, just another isolated Department, defending its turf while resisting others' attempts to claim its space. In such an environment links and bridges to disciplinary Departments may become dilutions, if not invasions, that reduce the transcendent possibilities of interdisciplinarity to mundane replications of established fields of knowledge that can then claim to be deeper, richer, more focused and precise. As Ted Benson (1982) pointed out over 25 years ago, the remarkable breadth that interdisciplinarity claims can be redefined as shallow; its bridge building as a confused blurring of distinctions; its experimentation as expendable, and its own concepts as borrowed from the disciplines; where original, interdisciplinary theory can be proclaimed as conceptually "lite," and its methods seen as lacking standards, its courses, trading rigor for excitement. Interdisciplinarity, Benson said, is logically inverted, since disciplinary study should precede interdisciplinary study, and if not, interdisciplinarity impedes disciplinary development. Especially during times of scarce resources interdisciplinary courses can be seen as costly, while ignoring their embodiment of best practice pedagogy. As Jerry Petr said in 1983, "Interdisciplinary studies programs appear to many as expendable frills in higher education, in part at least due to the predominance of the Benson arguments in the court of public opinion" (Petr 1983, 21). Most recently Michael Moran says that while disciplinarity has been highly successful at creating hierarchies of power that have resisted managerial-administrative power in higher education, "Interdisciplinarity must be understood ... as a strategy that potentially solves problems faced by many different interests opposed to these disciplinary elites. The fact that it can be used for so many different purposes explains its popularity, but it also reveals its fatal weakness" (Moran 2006, 82).

Given this kind of critique of its integrity and value, how is interdisciplinarity disciplined? According to Rogers, Booth and Eveline, the purity of disciplinary work is contrasted to the "dirt" that is interdisciplinarity, a dirt that threatens to undermine disciplinarity. To manage and disarm this threat disciplinarity devalues interdisciplinarity as inferior, ineffective and/or insignificant, through defining interdisciplines as derivative of, and hierarchically inferior, to the disciplines; placing interdisciplinarity in a support role to disciplines, valuable for filling in the gaps, serving as a resource, but denying its own autonomous existence; excluding interdisciplinary work as, at best, a distraction from disciplinary work; and portraying its practitioners as outsiders the mainstream, as the "other."

Moreover, Kleinberg (2008) argues that because of the disciplinary critique, emerging interdisciplinary fields, whose faculty needed professional legitimation and economic security, have reacted by adopting the mantle of the traditional disciplines:

> As these previously marginalized fields grew and legitimized themselves through sound scholarship, curriculum, and teaching, they took on the characteristics of the traditional disciplines they were designed to challenge. Many of these fields now boast journals, monograph series at university presses, and professional associations with annual meetings. Some have control of, or a say in, the hiring and tenuring of faculty and thus have developed institutional networks of senior scholars who serve as referees. These are all developments that mirror the preexisting structure. This is not surprising, considering the need for institutional support, in terms of both funding and staffing, and the ways this support appeared to promote the project of interdisciplinary work and teaching. The professionalization of interdisciplinary studies was also necessary to blunt criticism from the more traditional disciplines and departments that interdisciplinary scholarship and teaching lacked sufficient disciplinary depth, that they could not be sufficiently rigorous, and that there would be no basis upon which to judge the quality of the scholarship and teaching [Kleinberg 2008, 8].

So why has this challenge to interdisciplinary studies occurred now, when interdisciplinarity as a concept and as a cluster of fields is on the ascendancy? Part of the reason is precisely the success of interdisciplinarity at a time when some traditional disciplines, especially in liberal arts education, are languishing, in what Stanley Katz (2005) and Bill Readings (1996) have called "a project in ruins"; when major funding agencies have switched gears, along with leading educational policy makers, to decry the divisional separation among disciplines, and to extol the virtues of interdisciplinary connectedness. The initial tentative struggle of interdisciplinary work that could, in earlier years, have been dismissed as a marginal experimental practice — alright for those who have not been able to succeed in the disciplines, has given way to a substantive body of research, practice, and students, that we describe as "interdisciplinary ascendancy."

This promise of transcendence has emboldened some interdisciplinarians to attack the disciplines at the very time when they have been challenged by shifting priorities, sinking state (and, therefore, state university) budgets (down 10 percent between 2000 and 2003), and pressure of enrollments, with increased applications and improved retention, making campus space scarce. The early jousts at the disciplines as "tribes and territories" from those like Becher (1989), has been expanded by others. Indeed, indicative of this posture Stephen Rowland (2003) states, "Disciplines are an increasingly irrelevant mode of knowledge production, more geared to the concerns of academics to create and solve their own problems, than to engage with the world outside." In contrast, interdisciplines are seen as "geared to the solution of practical problems, by overcoming disciplinary boundaries and drawing upon different fields of expertise" (Rowland, 2003).

Interdisciplinary critiques have grown to sufficient strength to challenge the disciplinary academy at the very time at which the academy feel most vulnerable, a position that has quelled much internal oppositional critique. As Cindi Katz says, unlike the expansive 1970s:

> The present academic context is one of budgetary restraints and cutbacks, shrinkage, and closure are linked to a consumerist model of education with increased calls for accountability, "excellence," and a market orientation in the production of both graduates and knowledge. This situation has "disciplined" many members of the academy and sobered anybody with even a stray oppositional thought. As resources become scarcer and the calls for accountability more shrill, the administrative and scholarly tendency to police the borders between disciplines has sharpened [Katz 2001, 519].

Finally, and particularly in times of economic consolidation, some university administrators have sought to use "interdisciplinarity" against the disciplinary power of traditional university departmentalized structures, as a legitimating mechanism to consolidate several departments into larger, but more economic units (Moran 2006). Nor is this administrative challenge to the disciplines new. Kleinberg describes a presidential plan, the first moves to establish interdisciplinarity at Wesleyan College in 1958, that "called for doing away entirely with the traditional departmental structure of the American university system" and for establishing interdisciplinary colleges that was a clear challenge to traditional disciplines: "Perhaps most striking is that this plan sought to destabilize the authority of the faculty and the disciplines themselves by asking instructors to move away from disciplinary pronouncements based on past success and formulations and, instead, to extend themselves beyond the areas of their authority and expertise in pursuit of innovation" (Kleinberg 2008, 8). Not surprisingly, these kinds of developments represent a major threat to traditional disciplines. The result has been a closing of ranks by traditional liberal arts disciplines against the most vulnerable of the interdisciplinary studies degrees, which are those generic undergraduate programs that are the focus of this book. Interestingly, as Ray Miller points out in this volume, the most vulnerable here are not those programs that offer "weak" interdisciplinarity but those that offer its "strong" version, in that they are pedagogically sound, rigorous and thus represent a real threat to the disciplines. This backlash has occurred in a number of ways and at different institutional levels.

Undergraduate interdisciplinary programs have been de-clawed by: (1) cutting interdisciplinary program budgets, (2) starving them of faculty resources, (3) removing class size caps, and (4) moving them into larger colleges, typically liberal arts and/or sciences. Here it is claimed, they can serve the functionally catalytic role of stimulating traditional disciplines to talk with each other, providing an in-house model for effective teaching and active learning, which avoids the cost of faculty development. One of the ultimate ironies faced by undergraduate interdisciplinary units is that, since they are interdisciplinary, and typically taught by disciplinary converts, any other faculty members, with a little training, can be seen as capable of teaching in their programs. Therefore, increased faculty lines for interdisciplinary studies programs, at a time of economic and demographic pressure, are less likely to follow increased enrollments, although there have been instances where tenured faculty, like students, who do not fit traditional departments after reorganization are "dumped" into interdisciplinary ones. More likely, since interdisciplinary faculty are disciplinarily rooted, they are required to teach in their disciplinary fields as a substitute for new faculty hires; thus they can become a reservoir of reserve faculty labor.

If the field of interdisciplinary studies reacts to these attacks, it is threatened with being dispersed. If it does nothing, it will either be absorbed to become another "disciplined" interdisciplinary field of study, like women's studies or African American studies, environmental studies or area studies. Indeed even if, as some have advocated (Repko 2006; 2008b), it defines its core concepts, theories and methods, and vigorously polices its boundaries by making clear distinctions between itself and the disciplines, it will surely also become, for all intents and purposes, a discipline. The very processes it uses to fight those who are trying to absorb or disperse it will have again disciplined interdisciplinarity. In contrast to Trow, then, "perhaps contesting the terrain will ultimately prove to provide greater long-term resilience than finding an ecological niche" (Henry 2005, 3).

Clearly a variety of short-term tactics of resistance (such as protest, political campaigns, media exposure) are available to sustain individual departments or programs; longer term preventative tactics that engage disciplines without dismissing them, might be more helpful in building bridges without losing what interdisciplinary autonomy has been accrued. Whether these kinds of tactics will be sufficient to enable the long-term sustainability of interdisciplinarity within academia, or whether they mark the dawn of cooptation, absorption and regularization, remains to be seen. If we accept Michel Certeau's (1984) insight that tactics can never overthrow the strategies of disciplinary hegemony, we will have to make do with "getting around the rules of constraining space." Although Vincent Leitch may be correct when he states that, in spite of their striving to be different, in the end interdisciplines "submit to modern disciplinarity, its requirements, standards, certifications as well as its methods (exercises, exams, rankings, supervision, norms)" (Leitch & Ruiz III 2005). Indeed, as he cynically observes, rather than bringing about significant change in pedagogy, theory, or organization of academia,

> the departmental structure of the American college and university looks pretty much today the way it did a half century ago. So too does the job market, a great respecter and enforcer of established disciplines.... [I]nterdisciplines are generally housed in underfunded and nomadic programs or institutes, not departments. So we live in a time of limited and constrained interdisciplinarity. Postmodern implosion thus far has been a partial, a limited phenomenon: nation-states and borders continue to operate; private and public spheres are distinguishable still; the arts remain distinct and recognizable; traditional disciplines retain autonomy and power [Leitch and Ruiz III 2005].

Prospects for the Future

Given the limitations to autonomy/elimination or integration/cooptation what, if any, are the indicators for a sustainable future for undergraduate interdisciplinary studies? One of the first observations is that bigger programs need not necessarily be better or for that matter more sustainable. Some of the largest, such as those at Wayne State University, Appalachian State and George Mason University have either been closed or raided, with some of their programs or most of their faculty dispersed to disciplinary departments in other colleges. Large interdisciplinary studies programs can be inherently unstable and vulnerable to disciplinary hegemony. One reason for this is that disciplines organized by department see generalized interdisciplinary studies students as potentially their own majors, the logic being: "If these students were not taking interdisciplinary studies they'd have to choose one of our majors." A second reason for instability is that the generality of interdisciplinary studies can lead to an influx of undecided students rather than genuinely interdisciplinary students, which fuels the view that these programs are a catch-all or dumping ground for those who either can't make it, or can't decide. Third, because of their generic nature, some large programs, such as Arizona State University's 2400 student undergraduate Bachelor's in Interdisciplinary Studies (BIS) are viewed by university administrators as adequately staffed by full-time lecturers (rather than core tenure-track faculty) employed primarily as teaching staff who are not expected to publish and are thereby effectively rendered immobile. At a major research university these characteristics make interdisciplinary programs second-class operations, and also cheap ways of doing business. As nonprofit colleges and universities become increasingly more corporatized, running programs without core tenure-track faculty can be construed as innovative (Bousquet 2008). Such "innovation" can be attractive in the context of the competition with for-profit universities with their rolling semesters, "accelerated" programs, and their obsession with "enrollment management," "student retention," and "graduation rates," but this is at the expense of quality education. Indeed, these structures may be better suited to the changing student demographics that include more working students, part-time students, and older/returning non-traditional students. As a result, there may be something more sustainable for interdisciplinary studies in relatively small, high quality programs such as Emory University's, which are inherently non-threatening.

A second observation about the future direction of generic undergraduate interdisciplinary studies is that it invests in its own professionalism, regardless of the dangers of becoming "disciplined" in the ways we have described above. Indeed, Repko (2006) has argued that this is critical for its future sustainability. This would involve more attention to concepts of integration, theory and methodology. Also important is that its practitioners increasingly publish in its journals, and that they also establish more literature based on empirical and evidence-based evaluation of the effectiveness of what they do. Not least, there should be advances in student outcome assessment for interdisciplinary studies, to demonstrate effectiveness and improve pedagogies to make its methods more effective. Indeed, some have implied that the relative underdevelopment of its outcome assessment may be a factor in the current demise of interdisciplinary degree programs:

> The rapid growth of these programs is accompanied by an often-warranted concern about the quality of learning taking place: What constitutes quality work when individual disciplinary standards are inappropriate or inadequate. Greater emphasis on evaluation and accountability across the academy ... accentuates the ambiguity surrounding quality assessment work. Faculty and programs remain ill equipped to advance students' understanding of complex issues or to evaluate the impact of interdisciplinary programs on firm grounds,

making interdisciplinary programs vulnerable to reduction and closure [Boix Mansilla and Duraising 2007, 216].

Certainly there have been major efforts to move in new directions in establishing firm criteria for assessment (Wolf and Haynes 2003; Repko 2008b; Boix Mansilla and Duraising 2007).

A third observation on the sustainability of the field of interdisciplinary studies has to do with the very dialectical nature of its relationship to the academy. On the one hand, as Cindi Katz points out, it is a harbor for marginal critics of mainstream academia, who would be unlikely to survive in the mainstream. At the same time it is a very difficult enterprise to sustain:

> It is far easier to consume interdisciplinarity than produce, maintain, or make a living from it. When we read, study, or attend conference presentations that work across disciplines, we provide the integrative interdisciplinary leaven. Interdisciplinarity is hard but pleasurable work at the moment and site of reception. Its production can be a bit more contentious and far more difficult to sustain. As interdisciplinary fields grow along with their constitutive parts, their sheer bulk makes even consumption hard. Journals proliferate, edited collections abound, conferences and workshops mushroom. Interdisciplinary studies is nothing if not an industry. Keeping up with it all is impossible but nevertheless causes anxiety about what knowledge matters, which methods are appropriate, whose theories are most timely [Katz 2001, 524].

In the end we may be faced, as Newell argues in this volume, with a cyclical process. In Kuhnian terms (Kuhn 1970), as new knowledge forms on the margins and interstices of the disciplines challenging their dominance, authority, methods and logic, and its advocates fight to establish themselves as a recognized field of inquiry with their own vibrancy, synthesis and alternative approaches, so they become more established and have less need to be defensive. As they become normalized, the need for a generalized critique from interdisciplinary studies subsides. As they become the established "normal science" of academe, so anomalies and increasingly difficult and more complex questions arise. These cannot be answered from within the now normalized frameworks, and once again the need for critical breakaway inter-interdisciplinary inquiry is needed. At this point the margins are again volatile as the now established interdisciplinary fields are challenged by those breakaway elements on their margins, and so the cycle begins again. Perhaps, as Katz observes, the role of the interdisciplinarian is most effective on the outside challenging the boundaries, whosever boundaries these are:

> I am drawn powerfully by and to Robyn Wiegman's call that we who are located in established institutional spaces for interdisciplinarity use those spaces to rethink and rework radically the "relationship among identity

knowledges, institutional resources, and the organization of disciplines." To do so would be to alter the grounds of knowledge and the troubled and troubling structures that hold them in place; to make good on the incomplete project of interdisciplinarity by using its logics to continue to disrupt the academy as a realm of power and knowledge. This is not a "minor" project [Katz 2001, 524–525].

The Organization of This Book

The book is organized into two parts. Part I focuses on the history of longstanding interdisciplinary studies programs. Here the contributors describe the significant changes that have occurred to their programs. They offer case studies of interdisciplinary studies programs that range from those that have been completely shut down, to others that have been substantially transformed, reorganized, or reconfigured. The contributors to this section explore the processes whereby these changes occurred and the challenges that they faced. The authors then draw lessons about the things that could have been done differently that might have made them more sustainable. It is important to note, however, that at the present time some programs such as those at Miami University and Appalachian State may "rise from the ashes" reincarnated in different forms, but so far these new lives have yet to be fully known or realized. In the case of San Francisco State University we see, from three different perspectives, how and under what conditions some interdisciplinary programs have been closed whereas others have emerged to create new beginnings. Here we had the unique opportunity to provide depth analysis for one institution from several vantage points and layers. San Francisco State has a long tradition of interdisciplinarity, with several programs shutting down in recent years, while another has been revitalized with the addition of new tenure-track lines. Part I, therefore, concludes with two case studies from San Francisco State, which bridge into a third article from San Francisco State in Part II describing innovations that are currently underway. Part II, New Directions, then explores new programs in undergraduate interdisciplinary studies that have either grown in recent years or are on the threshold of launching and that display new possibilities for the future.

The concluding chapter of the book identifies common core themes drawn from these locally situated, contextually unique case studies. Here we provide an overview of the political economy that provides a context for the specific developments discussed earlier and summarize what worked and what did not. From this analysis we provide insights into the pathways and avenues that point the way to interdisciplinary sustainability.

REFERENCES

Agger, Ben 1991. *A critical theory of public life: knowledge, discourse and politics in the age of decline.* London: Falmer Press.

Augsburg, Tanya. 2005, 2006. *Becoming interdisciplinary: An introduction to interdisciplinary studies.* Dubuque, IA: Kendall/Hunt Publishing.

Becher, Tony. 1989. *Academic tribes and territories.* Milton Keynes, UK: Society for Research into Higher Education and Open University Press.

Benson, Ted C. 1982. Five arguments against interdisciplinary studies. *Issues in Integrative Studies* 1: 38–48.

Boix Mansilla, Veronica. 2004. *Assessing student work at disciplinary crossroads.* Interdisciplinary Studies Project, Project Zero, Harvard Graduate School of Education, http://www.pz.harvard.edu/interdisciplinary/pdf/assessingstudentwork.pdf (accessed October 6, 2008).

Boix Mansilla, Veronica, and Howard Gardner. 2003. *Assessing interdisciplinary work at the frontier: an empirical exploration of symptoms of quality.* GoodWork Project Report Series, Number 26. Also published in *Interdisciplines.* http://www.interdisciplines.org/interdisciplinarity/papers/6 (accessed October 6, 2008).

Bousquet, Marc. 2008. *How the university works: Higher education and the low-wage nation.* Foreword by Cary Nelson. New York and London: New York University Press.

Boyer Commission. 1998. *Reinventing undergraduate education: A blueprint for America's research universities.* Washington DC: The Boyer Commission on Educating Undergraduates.

Brint, Steven G., Lori Turk-Bicakci, Krisopher Proctor, and Scott Patrick Murphy. 2009. Expanding the social frame of knowledge: Interdisciplinary, degree-granting fields in American colleges and universities, 1975–2000. *Review of Higher Education*, 32: 155–183.

Castellana, Richard. 2005. Becoming interdisciplinary: Pioneer text on IDS has political significance. *Association for Integrative Studies Newsletter 27(2)*: 1–4.

de Certeau, Michel. 1984. *The practice of everyday life.* Trans. Steven F. Rendall. Berkeley: CA: University of California Press.

Frodeman, Robert, Julie Thompson Klein, and Carl Mitcham. 2009. *The Oxford Handbook of Interdisciplinarity.* Oxford: Oxford University Press.

Gregorian, Vartan. 2004. Colleges must reconstruct the unity of knowledge. *The Chronicle of Higher Education*, June 4, 12–14.

Haynes, Carolyn, ed. 2002. *Innovations in interdisciplinary teaching.* Westport CT: Oryx Press.

_____. 2005. Mapping the past for the future: Klein tracks long-term evolution of IDS in U.S. *Association for Integrative Studies Newsletter 27(3)*: 1–3, 7.

Hendra, Rick and Ed Harris. 2002. *Unpublished results: The University Without Walls experiment.* http://www-unix.oit.umass.edu/~hendra/Unpublished%20Results. html (accessed October 8, 2008).

Henry, Stuart. 2005. Disciplinary hegemony meets interdisciplinary ascendancy: Can interdisciplinary/integrative studies survive, and if so, how? *Issues in Integrative Studies* 23: 1–37.

Katz, Cindi. 2001. Disciplining interdisciplinarity. *Feminist Studies* 27(2): 519–525.

Katz, Stanley N. 2005. Liberal education on the ropes. *The Chronicle of Higher Education.* Chronicle Review, April 1: B6–B9.

Klein, Julie Thompson. 1990. *Interdisciplinarity: History, theory and practice.* Detroit: Wayne State University Press.

_____. 1996. *Crossing boundaries: Knowledge, disciplines and interdisciplinarities.* Charlottesville: University Press of Virginia.

_____. 2005. *Humanities, culture and interdisciplinarity: The changing American Academy.* Albany: State University of New York Press.

Klein, Julie Thompson, and Newell, William H. 1997. Advancing interdisciplinary studies. In *Handbook of the Undergraduate Curriculum,* ed. Jerry G. Gaff, James L. Ratcliff and Associates, 393–415. San Francisco: Jossey-Bass.

Kleinberg, Ethan. 2008. Interdisciplinary studies at a crossroads. *Liberal Education,* 94(1): 6–11.

Kuhn, Thomas. 1970. *The structure of scientific revolutions.* Chicago: University of Chicago Press.

Leitch, Vincent B., and Nicholas Ruiz III. 2005. Theory, interdisciplinarity, and the humanities today. An interview with Vincent B. Leitch. *InterCulture,* http://www.fsu.edu/~proghum/interculture/VBL%20Interview.htm, (accessed October 3, 2005).

Leshner, Alan. 2004. Science at the leading edge. *Science* (February 6): 729.

Moran, Michael. 2006. Interdisciplinarity and political science. *Politics* 26(2): 73–83.

National Academies of Sciences, National Academy of Engineering and Institute of Medicine. 2004. *Facilitating interdisciplinary research.* Washington DC: National Academies Press.

National Center for Educational Statistics (NCES). 2002. *Classification of instructional programs (CIP 2000)* http://nces.ed.gov/pubs2002/cip2000/ciplist.asp?CIP2=30 (accessed October 8, 2008).

_____. 2007. *Digest of educational statistics, 2006,* Table 254. Washington DC: U.S. Department of Education.

Newell, William H., James Hall, Steve Hutkins, Daniel Larner, Eric McGuckin and Karen Oates, 2003. Apollo meets Dionysius: Interdisciplinarity in longstanding interdisciplinary programs. *Issues in Integrative Studies* 21, 9–41.

Petr, Jerry C. 1983. The case for/against integrative studies. *Issues in Integrative Studies* 2, 20–23.

Planty, M., W. Hussar, T. Snyder, S. Provasnik, G. Kena, R. Dinkes, A. Kewal Ramani, and J. Kemp. 2008. *The condition of education 2008* (NCES 2008-031). Washington, DC: National Center for Education Statistics, Institute of Education Sciences, U.S. Department of Education. http://nces.ed.gov/programs/coe/2008/pdf/39_ 2008.pdf (accessed October 8, 2008).

Readings, Bill. 1996. *The university in ruins.* Cambridge, MA: Harvard University Press.

Repko, Allen F. 2005. *Interdisciplinary practice: A student guide to research and writing.* Boston: Pearson Custom Publishing.

_____. 2006. Disciplining interdisciplinary studies. *Issues in Integrative Studies* 24: 112–142.

_____. 2007. Interdisciplinary curriculum design. *Academic Exchange Quarterly* 11(1): 130–137.

_____. 2008a. *Interdisciplinary research: Process and theory.* Thousand Oaks, CA: Sage Publications.

_____. 2008b. Assessing interdisciplinary learning outcomes. *Academic Exchange Quarterly* 12(3): 171–178.

Rogers, Steve, Michael Booth, and Joan Eveline. 2003. The politics of disciplinary advantage. *History of Intellectual Culture,* 3(1). http://www.ucalgary.ca/hic/issues/vol3/6 (accessed September 30, 2005).

Rowland, Stephen. 2003. Seeing things differently: the challenge of interdisciplinarity. http://www.ucl.ac.uk/cishe/colloquium/papers/rowland.html (accessed October 2, 2005).

Sayer, Andrew. 1999. Long live postdisciplinary studies! Sociology and the curse of disciplinary parochialism/imperialism. Lancaster, UK: Lancaster University: Department of Sociology. http://www.lancs.ac.uk/fss/sociology/papers/sayer-long-live-postdisciplinary-studies.pdf (accessed October 2, 2005).

Sherif, Muzafer, and Carolyn W. Sherif. 1969. Interdisciplinary coordination as a validity check: Retrospect and prospects. In *Interdisciplinary Relationships in the Social Sciences*, ed. Muzafer Sherif and Carolyn W Sherif, 3–20. Chicago: Aldine.

Swoboda, Wolfram W. 1979. Disciplines and interdisciplinarity: A historical perspective. In *Interdisciplinarity and higher education*, ed., Joseph J. Kockelmans, 49–92. University Park, PA: Pennsylvania State University Press.

Trow, Martin. 1984/85. Interdisciplinary studies as a counterculture. *Issues in Integrative Studies* 3: 1–16.

Vasterling, Veronica, Enikő Demény, Clare Hemmings, Ulla Holm, Päivi Korvajärvi, and Theodossia-Soula Pavlidou. 2006. *Practising interdisciplinarity in gender studies*. York, UK: Raw Nerve Books.

Wolfe, Christopher, and Carolyn Haynes. 2003. Interdisciplinary writing assessment profiles. *Issues in Integrative Studies* 21: 126–169.

PART I. THE HISTORY OF INTERDISCIPLINARY PROGRAMS

CHAPTER 1

The Political Life Cycle of a Cluster College: The Western College Program at Miami University

William H. Newell

Introduction

This chapter tells the political and organizational story of the birth, maturation, and death[1] of a nationally prominent interdisciplinary studies program. While the story is of some interest in itself as a tale of academic intrigue and of note because it relates to a well-known interdisciplinary experimental college program, my chief motivation in writing it is to extract lessons that can help other interdisciplinary programs thrive and spare them the fate of the program to which I have devoted so much of my academic career.

It is rare to witness first-hand the entire lifecycle of a thirty-four-year-old institution. I was the first external faculty member hired by the newly formed Western College of Miami University in 1974 and will be the last faculty member to offer a course (the year-long senior project workshop) in 2009-2010 to the final cohort of students still in the pipeline after the closing of the School of Interdisciplinary Studies (Western College Program) in 2008.

The Birth of the Division

Miami University bought the adjacent campus of the Western College (known throughout most of its existence as the Western College for Women) when it folded financially and disbanded in 1973 after 120 years of continuous operation. The librarian and one student stayed on to become part of whatever academic program the University would establish in its stead, and a few faculty members and administrators were absorbed into the main campus; the acquisition was viewed bitterly by most of its departing faculty, its students and its alumnae. Miami University President Shriver and Provost Brown solicited suggestions widely for what to do with the campus (which ranged from a law school to a golf course to general University expansion), but they preferred to use it to establish a new academic program (one that could serve as part of their legacy).

The committee they formed examined a number of models for the new program, and after thorough ventilation in university governance, Miami settled on a four-year interdisciplinary, living-learning, experimental cluster college that would incorporate what they saw as the best elements of the educational experiments of the 1960s. That decision was warmly (if somewhat cautiously) embraced by younger, innovative, or left-leaning faculty members. However, the characterization "experimental" proved to be a two-edged sword that was viewed skeptically or with hostility by faculty members with vivid negative memories of campus unrest (including a student sit-in at the naval ROTC building just before the shootings at Kent State in 1970) and by those with more traditional educational values. Indeed, that clash of political and educational values would resurface from time to time throughout the life of the program.

After the conceptual model was adopted by Miami governance, an Interim Committee sketched out a curricular and organizational structure. While the six newly hired faculty members and two administrators of the Western Program (as I will refer to it hereafter for simplicity's sake) were free to treat this structure as a suggestion (Annual Report 1974-75), we embraced the underlying vision whole-heartedly and made few basic changes, instead focusing our attention on implementation. Nonetheless, the initial view of the emerging Western Program by the rest of the University was perhaps clouded by the fact that only one (Curt Ellison) of the original faculty members, and neither of the administrators, was hired from within the University. On the whole, we were perceived as outside agitators and that perception was correct.

The curriculum and academic and social policies of the Western Program were hammered out by a very young faculty, most new to teaching. Among the first group hired, I was the only full-time faculty member with prior experimental college experience, having taught in the Paracollege at St. Olaf College during its first four complete years of operation. Our college-building discussions were led by Dean Mike Lunine and Assistant Dean Allen

Davis, both of whom came to Miami from Hampshire College. Mike provided visionary leadership for a faculty considerably younger than he was, and he mesmerized (and frequently challenged) the University with his articulate and inspirational presentations on the new program. At Western, our discussions were interminable and carried out with messianic fervor; we weren't just creating a cluster college, we were setting up an educational utopia.

The 154 first-year students whom we would start teaching in the fall of 1974 had been recruited during the University's summer orientation, before the faculty even met in July to settle on a first-year curriculum and start designing courses. Since the students were sold on a vision glowing in its vagueness, and since daily reality can never consistently rise to the ideal, it is not surprising that almost half (45 percent) of those students left at the end of the first year (Annual Report 1975-76), nor is it surprising that those who remained four years to graduate exhibited a genuine pioneering spirit.

The reality of the first year, in fact, was far from ideal. In some instances, courses were designed too late to order books for the start of classes, and the faculty was lucky to stay even a week ahead of the students in the books when they finally arrived. The two-person faculty course teams met several times a week, often along with residence hall staff and students who were encouraged to participate in shaping their own education, to plan what should take place next week in their sections of the multi-sectioned interdisciplinary core courses; to plan second-year courses for the following year; and to debrief what happened in classes last week. Peabody Hall, which held classrooms, the women's residence hall, and faculty and administrative offices, was undergoing extensive renovation (necessitated by years of deferred maintenance) so we dodged construction workers in corridors draped with plastic to protect us from plaster dust, and had to talk loudly in class over the noise of skill saws and hammers. Faculty and their families attended a weekly community dinner with all the students, and some faculty mixed socially with students on weekends in the Rathskeller next door. Corridor meetings and community meetings were the forums at which divisional social policy was set. It was chaotic, hectic, exhausting, and exhilarating — a powerful bonding experience (for those who stayed) that produced a close-knit community fostering both group identity and individual growth, nurtured a collaborative approach to learning, and forged life-long friendships — giving real meaning to the concept of learning communities.

That bonding experience affected how the students and faculty in the Western Program perceived not only themselves but also the rest of the University, and those perceptions in turn contributed to how we were viewed by those outside the program. Many Western students, abetted by administrators and faculty (including myself), soon developed an "us and them" mentality. We were special, different, and yes, better. We were innovative, the vanguard of a curricular and pedagogical future we were designing together; we stood for civil rights, women's rights, and the environment; we were democratic and fiercely egalitarian; and we were interdisciplinary. The contrast was stark. The rest of the University offered no environmental majors and few environmental courses, the few women faculty members it hired did not feel well treated, and it had one of the lowest proportions of minority students (2.1 percent) in the nation. It was nearly a decade later that the University appointed its first (part-time) faculty development person (on the recommendation of an all-university committee I chaired); pedagogical innovation was not a high priority. The University was unapologetically hierarchical (and remains so today). And the interdisciplinary courses offered throughout the rest of the University in the mid–70s could be counted on the fingers of one hand. In short, at the time there seemed to be some justification for making invidious distinctions between us and "across the street" (referring to Patterson Avenue, which constitutes the dividing line between the Western campus and the "main" campus).

During those formative years of the late 1970s, our students ruffled plenty of feathers across the University. One of the members of the first class was elected president of the Miami University student body (the first of four Western student body presidents in a five-year stretch) on a co-education platform. He succeeded is getting Peabody Hall designated as the first coed-by-floor residence hall, and its successful operation led to the (begrudging) acceptance of fully coeducational residence halls. A later student body president from Western, however, ran successfully on the Seven Dwarfs ticket, mocking the lack of student power in governance. Another student activist founded the Oxford Tenants Association (for all Miami University students living off-campus). But in the early days, few or no Western students at that time joined a fraternity or sorority (which form the basis for much politically-influential student culture at Miami), feeling that the community at Western already provided everything those organizations could offer.

The administration of the Western Program inadvertently but routinely challenged a wide range of University rules and procedures, simply because the activities of the Western Program cut across administrative lines (academic and student affairs, disciplinary departments, even physical plant). Each new phase of the development of the program necessitated requests for exemptions and special treatment or to rethink the rules for everyone. An endless string of such requests was bound to upset not only the enforcers of bureaucracy, but also those trapped by bureaucracy who would like an exemption or two for themselves.

The faculty had little time to participate in the life of the rest of the university; we had so many demands on our time getting a cluster college under-way that we were lucky to do any research, much less engage in university service. Still, the Western Program was a full-fledged division of the univer-sity with all the perks that go with divisional status, including a guaranteed seat on a number of all-university committees. Faculty members in other divisions might wait decades for an opportunity to sit on committees that Western junior faculty members reluctantly joined their first year at the uni-versity; in general, faculty perks in governance were few and meager at the university, since all real power was retained by central administrators. Not only that, but Western Program faculty got to teach small classes, something other faculties would love to do at the lower division. A certain amount of jealousy was the inevitable result.

The effect of student activism and ill-disguised feelings of superiority within the Western Program, combined with ruffled feathers, bureaucratic irri-tation, and faculty jealousy, raised serious problems when the university came to determine the long-term status of the Western Program. The program was granted only provisional status when it began operations, with the understand-ing that it would be evaluated in the fifth year, at which point the Univer-sity Senate would vote whether to grant it permanent divisional status or to terminate it. The rationale was to wait until the full curriculum was in place, which would take four years since we admitted only first-year students, and thus in the first four years added only one level to the curriculum each year as the first cohort moved through it. But on the grounds that each year the Western Program was in operation, more money was being squandered on a costly program (as Miami's original and unrealistic projections of enrollment at Western had not materialized), the provost was pressured into moving up the evaluation to the fall of 1978, the fourth year of the program (before the first class was even graduated).

The provost was heavily politically invested in the Western Program and intent upon securing its permanent status. Believing in the high quality of the program, he appointed a blue ribbon panel of a dozen prominent faculty members known to be fair-minded but skeptical of Western to examine it and make a recommendation to the University Council, which would in turn make a recommendation to University Senate. The blue ribbon panel voted unanimously (after serious debate) to recommend approval, but University Council (chaired and influenced, but not controlled, by the provost) issued both a favorable majority report and a dissenting minority report. The Uni-versity Senate meeting attracted hundreds of faculty members, filling the largest auditorium in the university. After the majority and minority reports were presented, the tide of debate shifted back and forth between those who insisted the program could not be approved (because it did not contribute its share to overhead even though it covered its marginal cost) and those who urged its approval in spite of its modest financial shortfall. The debate was quieting down and the tide of sentiment seemed to have swung towards the nays when a stocky white haired man I'd never seen before strode to the front of the room. He said (as close to verbatim as I can manage): "My name is Harry Weller and I teach zoology. As I was walking to this meeting I promised myself I wouldn't say anything because I don't know anything about the Western Program, but I can't stand it any longer. I have yet to hear anyone make the case that Western is anything less than an excellent program. Miami University stands for excellence. Let's vote the damn thing in!" The provost immediately called for a vote and the Western Program was approved by more than 60 percent.

The Evolution of the Division

Three years after the Western Program was approved as a permanent part of the university and shortly after Curt Ellison replaced Mike Lunine as dean and started his seventeen years in that position, new Miami University President Paul Pearson, facing a budget crisis, came to see Dean Ellison in his Western office and asked the him to explain why the Western Program shouldn't be closed. Ellison described the kind of education that takes place in the program and showed him just how little money the university would save by closing it. President Pearson was so impressed that, from then on when he encountered potential donors who questioned why Western should exist, he told them that he wished the entire university could offer the kind of education that the Western Program provides.

Continuing challenges to the Western Program from some Miami faculty, staff, and alumni focused on what would come to be referred to as Western's "insularity," even though there was a highly visible presence across campus of Western student leaders. Most Miami students were aware that something called "Western" existed, but knew almost nothing factual about it beyond rumors. The name itself ("Western College of Miami University" or the "Western Program") offered no clue, and the subsequent name, the "School of Interdisciplinary Studies (Western College Program)" — arbitrarily assigned by the Board of Trustees upon agreeing to the permanent status of the program after four years — frankly didn't communicate much either. The program was tiny (less than 300 students in a university of 15,000) yet its campus was large and quaint (no lines of red brick buildings). The rumors were plentiful and quite diverse — from a program for slackers or a remedial program, to an honors program for eccentrics, or a program for radical activists. (Those rumors help explain why the university campus tour never included the Western campus, and why student tour guides, if asked what happens on the Western campus, tended to say things like "They're pretty weird; you wouldn't want to go there.")

What all rumors had in common was the contention that Western students were different. That contention would be affirmed should they actually meet one, given the prevailing "us and them mentality" among Western students, or should they encounter one in an upper-division course, since Western students invariably talked in class, acted self-assured, and seemed intellectually engaged. And a few Western Program students were highly visible at the university beyond student body presidents or other leaders in student government; they were leaders of social justice, political, community service, or environmental organizations. In later years, they became presidents or officers of fraternities or sororities (often promoting community service), and most recently, outspoken advocates for gay, lesbian, and bisexual rights. What these Western student leaders had in common seemed to be left-wing, altruistic, activist agendas that were out of step with the dominant student culture, which after the "Reagan Revolution" tended toward social and political conservatism. They weren't "normal" Miami students.

A closer examination of the Western Program helps explain why President Pearson so admired it, most Miami students dismissed it out of hand, and the university's admission office never figured out how to market it to high school students. The curriculum dealt substantively with the environment (natural sciences), social justice (social sciences and humanities), multimedia (humanities), computer and quantitative literacy (social and natural sciences), writing (all fields), and self-designed concentrations and individual senior projects that went off in every conceivable direction. In short, there was no specific content focus to the Western Program but rather an eclectic variety of approaches to a diverse set of topics or issues. Pedagogically, the faculty made significant use of lectures (the traditional banking model of education), seminars (discussion-based learning), group projects (collaborative learning), experiential learning, inquiry-based learning, writing across the curriculum, service learning, living learning/learning communities, peer mentoring, advising, writing revision, multicultural learning, and of course interdisciplinary studies. Thus, if anything, the Western Program was characterized by its very diversity of pedagogies (Newell 1984). Socially, the Western community was equally concerned with individual development and group cohesion. Again, no focus was evident. Indeed, what characterized the Western Program was that it seamlessly integrated almost every educational innovation explored in the 1990s, and it had been pioneering many of them for the previous decade and a half.

In a sense, then, even though the name "School of Interdisciplinary Studies" was added in front of "Western College Program" in the 1980s, interdisciplinarity was just another educational innovation to the faculty and not its primary characteristic. But to the students, interdisciplinarity was the key to the coherence of the program. Western students, I finally came to appreciate, generalized and internalized the interdisciplinary approach, applying it to everything they did. Instead of drawing on the perspectives of various academic disciplines alone (encountered systematically in the required core curriculum) and integrating their insights into a complex problem, they drew as well on perspectives of other students (seminar discussions, collaborative learning, living-learning), other senses (experiential learning), other cultures (multicultural learning, study abroad), other religions and political ideologies (service learning), etc. Through "integrative learning," as I termed this generalized interdisciplinary approach, Western students had found a way to integrate pretty much the full range of innovative pedagogies as well as the substantive areas of the curriculum and the community. Because all their college experiences were, thus, mutually reinforcing and synergistic, their combined effect was multiplied and the effect transformative. I didn't stumble upon this understanding of programmatic integration until the mid–1990s (Newell 2001), and to the best of my knowledge it was never adequately communicated to the admission office or central administration, perhaps because they were operating on a different educational paradigm. Even had we done so, I doubt marketers or administrators would have seen much significance to it, any more than they saw that self-conscious integration was key to how interdisciplinary studies at Western was distinct from interdisciplinary studies as practiced in most of the rest of the university. Indeed, when I laid out the difference between interdisciplinary and multidisciplinary studies to one provost, he airily dismissed it as "words, words, words." President Paul Pearson may have appreciated that the integration of diverse innovations was key to the high quality of the Western Program, but if so, he was probably the last president or provost at Miami University to do so. This remained the case despite the well-reported testimony of alumni, who in cycles of program reviews repeatedly returned extremely positive evaluations of the utility of their Western education to their lives after graduation.

High quality alone, however, was not enough to provide institutional security for the Western Program, especially when it seemed to defy "normal" institutional categorization. For eighteen years, however, it was backed by the political prowess of Dean Ellison. He was brilliant at academic politics, and having spent four years at Miami before Western became part of it, was well connected with administrators and faculty leaders in other parts of the university and especially in central administration. One strategy he used was to make himself indispensable to central administration by taking responsibility for major new initiatives, the most visible being the revisions of the university-wide general education requirements and of the University honors program. Both activities resulted in the adoption of comprehensive institution-wide programmatic changes (e.g., the Miami Plan for Liberal Education, which attracted some national publicity), and the creation of new administrative units (e.g., the Office of Liberal Education) and positions (e.g., Director of Liberal Education). He also chaired a number of major all-university dean searches. Upon stepping down as dean of the School of Interdisciplinary Studies (at the time the senior dean in the university) he was promptly asked to serve several years as interim dean of the School of Education and Allied Professions and then as interim dean of the School of Fine Arts. Whether they understood or even liked the Western Program, no president or provost during those years was willing to question its existence while Dean Ellison was solving their other problems for them.

Since the philosophy and structure of the Miami Plan for Liberal Education and, to a lesser extent, the Honors Program were clearly indebted to the Western Program, Dean Ellison was able to convince central administration that Western served not only to educate its students but also as a well-spring of innovation for the rest of the University. Programmatic, curricular, or pedagogical innovations could be field tested in the Western Program, and the successful ones disseminated throughout the university. That strategy for making the Western Program seem more central to the mission of the university seemed quite benign at the time and I (and all my colleagues as far as I know) warmly supported it, but it would come back to haunt us later.

Enrollment had always been an issue for the Western Program, in part because of our difficulty in succinctly stating the focus of the program. When we were able to talk at some length with prospective students, however, as we did each year during summer orientation to those students already accepted at Miami University who chose to seek us out, we were able to paint an attractive picture of life at Western and the range of opportunities it opened up. A few high school students applied directly to the Western Program (often based on recommendations by program alumni, their former high school teachers, or guidance counselors), but most of our first-year students were picked up at summer orientation. A series of bureaucratic and political decisions in other parts of the university, however, made it virtually impossible to attract more high school students directly to Western, to recruit from the ranks of undeclared major students in each year's entering class at Miami University, or to attract Arts and Science majors to our lower division general education offerings. The admission office felt it must recruit for the university as a whole, and was unwilling to undertake special recruiting for a particular division. It also was unwilling to permit Western alums (many of whom were eager to recruit for the program) to go into high schools and recruit only for our division; indeed it viewed them as competitors with its own recruiters. Nor did it see that it had any obligation to address central administration concerns about our enrollment. By tradition (based, apparently, on a unilateral decision by a middle-level administrator decades ago), all entering students with undeclared majors were assigned to the College of Arts and Science, and the dean of that college was unwilling to let Western recruit from their ranks (even if some students might be best served by the Western Program); nor was the provost willing to revisit that decision. While the lower division courses in the Western Program (which constituted the majority of our offerings) were all approved by the university as fulfilling requirements of the Miami Plan for Liberal Education (that is, the general education requirements of the university), the curriculum committee of the College of Arts and Science refused to approve our courses as fulfilling the liberal education requirements of the College. In a few cases, that refusal was based on legitimate differences in educational philosophy, but mostly it reflected nothing more than turf protection. Since no Arts and Science majors were willing to fulfill College and University liberal education requirements separately when they could "double dip" using liberal education courses offered in the College, no College of Arts and Sciences majors took our lower division courses. These decisions by the office of admission, the dean's office of the College of Arts and Science, the provost, and the Curriculum Committee of the College of Arts and Science combined to box in the Western Program and keep it from attracting more students. However, that didn't keep a succession of provosts from criticizing the Western Program for its low enrollments.

A strategy that emerged early in Dean Ellison's tenure addressed the enrollment challenge by working collaboratively with the Department of Architecture. The chair of architecture, Hayden May, devised a plan for all architecture majors to fulfill their university-mandated general education requirements in their first two years by completing the interdisciplinary core courses offered by the Western Program. The plan was first given tacit approval by University Council in their refusal to merge the Western Program and the College of Arts and Science in the spring of 1981, and was formally approved by the University Requirement Committee in April of 1981 (Annual Report 1980-81). Hayden May was quite familiar with (and supportive of) the Western Program since one of his daughters had graduated from it and the other was enrolled in it at the time, but he was responding primarily to concerns expressed by his faculty about the fragmented liberal education experienced by their majors. The two faculties endorsed the plan on purely utilitarian grounds: increased enrollment and educational integration respectively. I felt that there is a natural affinity between interdisciplinary studies and architecture, which can be understood as an applied interdisciplinary study, but few of my colleagues and none of the architecture faculty looked at it that way. They saw it as a marriage of convenience.

The honeymoon was blissful: the enrollment of the Western Program was doubled overnight, a respectable faculty cost/expenditure ratio was achieved, the Department of Architecture earned accolades from an accreditation team for its innovative approach to the general education of its majors, and the clustering of general education courses for architecture majors in morning hours eased constraints on expanded studio requirements for first-year students, seen at the time as highly desirable. But problems quickly surfaced as advisors worried about the large number of required credit hours (16–17/semester) for architecture majors (May 2008) after the architecture Bachelor of Environmental Design program required an additional 7–8 semester hours of studio courses each semester. Professionally-oriented architecture majors couldn't readily understand why they were forced into a determinedly nonprofessional liberal arts program for their first two years. Western staff worried that the living-learning program was being undermined by some hard-partying, disaffected architecture majors, and a few members of the architecture faculty had second thoughts about the experimental nature of Western Program courses. Curricular integration was limited to the occasional architect teaching in a Western Program core course, one joint appointment (2/3 architecture, 1/3 Western) of a popular faculty member initiated by Western, and scattered examples drawn from architecture in some Western courses. Consequently, the two-year requirement gradually eroded to a one-year requirement, and exceptions to that were granted to honors students and then to other students as well.

Developments in the years that followed never overcame the overall effect of these decisions, which was a significant lower level of enrollment in the Western Program after the early 1980s. As the once-young faculty from the formative years of Western received annual raises and eventually approached retirement, and provosts allowed a senior faculty member to move into Western and approved new hires while enrollment was not expanding, the cumulative effect was a substantially greater salary burden on the program. With revenues decreasing and costs increasing, Western inevitably became more expensive on a per capita basis. Its budget was tiny in absolute terms, it was still not the most expensive program in the university even on a per capita basis, and costs were soon to drop considerably as senior faculty retired and entry-level faculty took their place early in the 21st century — indeed, the program was about to become rather inexpensive. Critics, not surprisingly, ignored these factors and pointed out how expensive the Western Program had become.

The Demise of the Western Program[2]

At their April 23, 2003, meeting, the Miami University Board of Trustees approved a new budget strategy proposed by President Garland based on 9 percent annual tuition increases. This increase was part of a novel attempt to shift Miami University to a "single tuition plan" that collapsed the difference between in-state and out-of-state tuition, raising all tuition charges but, at least initially, providing financial awards to in-state students to offset increases. The plan for that budget was developed in the President's Executive Committee (which consisted of the president, the vice president, and "several other individuals") without vetting by, input from, or even the awareness of the rest of the university, until it was approved by the Board of Trustees.

The plans to offset increased charges to in-state students were hard to explain to the public, and tuition increases of that magnitude at a state institution were politically unpopular. It wasn't long before the state legislature responded by putting a much lower cap on tuition increases. The Miami University annual budget was at that point several million dollars in the red, with built-in deficits looming from debt service on a major construction program for professional schools and student facilities. The trustees, predominantly business people familiar with downsizing, directed central administration to cut costs until the budget was balanced. The board directed its finance committee to come up with rough ideas of how to achieve those cuts. On the list they produced were the generic statements "close divisions" and "close departments." The trustees made it abundantly clear to central administration that trimming around the edges would not be acceptable; they wanted to see major cuts, including entire programs, departments, and divisions. The President's Executive Committee went to work and brainstormed a single-spaced list a couple pages long of possible cuts. The Western Program was on that list. After the trustees had a chance to look over the list, they engaged in a fairly generic conversation with central administration about the possible location and magnitude of cuts within the university. The trustees identified the Western Program as one that ought to be looked at pretty carefully when central administration prepared its short-list of possible cuts. The Western Program was in jeopardy and its faculty and administrators remained unaware of its plight.

It was not surprising to anyone in central administration that the President's Executive Committee had included Western on its initial list of possible cuts, because they knew that there were two divisions the president intensely disliked: the School of Education and Allied Professions, and the Western Program. There were several reasons for his antipathy to the Western Program. One was based in educational philosophy. The president had repeatedly expressed in public his displeasure with two of the four goals of the Miami Plan for Liberal Education — engaging with other learners and teaching critical thinking. Those principles pretty well characterized the educational approach of the Western Program. Another reason was based in administrative style. The president had chided the faculty of the Western Program for permitting students to participate in the governance process, and the dean for permitting faculty to be involved in decisions that he saw as the dean's responsibility. The Western Program was highly democratic and the president was highly hierarchical if not autocratic. A third reason was that he saw Western Program students and faculty as troublemakers. Mostly recently, when Students for Staff campaigned in 2004 for a "living wage" for classified staff, and actively supported a strike on campus by classified employees, prominent among the speakers at the public rallies were several students in the Western Program, and a few Western Program faculty members were present as well. Their immediate target was President Garland (who, in light of the budget shortages, was in no position to accede to their demands), and the Board of Trustees, who Students for Staff held responsible for Miami's wage structure. Garland appeared to take the attacks personally.

All of the reasons the trustees latched onto the Western Program in their discussions with central administration are more inscrutable, since I have no informant recently retired from the Board of Trustees to reveal what was said and by whom when central administration was not present. However, it is well known that the board relies heavily on the president and provost to inform them about the workings of the university, so it is reasonable to surmise that over the preceding decade the president had communicated his reservations about the Western Program. Also, for members of the board who had graduated from Miami University since the mid–1970s, their impressions of the Western Program were already shaped during their undergraduate years. Finally, it should be noted that a member of the Board of Trustees, who had made a seven-figure donation for the Richard T. Farmer School of Business, amassed his fortune as head of the Cintas Corporation, which had been embarrassed recently by a Western student. At a Miami University career fair, the student dumped a basket of dirty sheets on the Cintas table (their main business is uniforms and laundry) and read a flier about Cintas labor abuses over a bullhorn ("airing their dirty laundry in public"); he was escorted out by security and, at later career fairs, the Cintas table was protected by one or two guards.

When central administration took a closer look at the Western Program as they were preparing their short list of proposed cuts and closures, they relied heavily on program reviews. They saw what they considered to be a "very damning" pattern going back three program reviews. For instance, the most recent external reviewers said in their private debriefing meeting with central administration that the program was in trouble, and if serious changes weren't made, the program would die. Unfortunately, what they wrote in their January 2005 public report was dramatically different in tone, asserting that the Western Program was "valuable and unique" and that it should be "valued, preserved, nurtured and developed" (Winkler 2006, 1). Even so, the external reviewer report identified a number of areas of concern, specifically the alleged "insularity" of the Western Program, its low and declining enrollment and consequent increasing cost, lack of innovation in recent years, and problems with mentoring junior faculty. Variations of those issues had been raised with central administration in the private debriefing meeting of the previous external reviewer, but she never wrote a report stating them. And the recollection of central administrators who had been around for the external review before that was that they too had raised all those issues in private as well (except the mentoring junior faculty), but central administration never checked on those privately-expressed concerns with Dean Ellison and the written report was even more positive than the most recent one. Of course, it is impossible to know to what extent central administrators heard what they expected to hear or placed undue weight on concerns they already shared. Nevertheless, the secret perception of central administration in the Garland era was that external reviewers had shown a pattern over the last fifteen years or so of serious concerns that called into question the viability of the Western Program. By the time this perception of non-viability became public it would be too late politically to correct it.

In contrast, the perception of the faculty and administration of the Western Program was that two of the last three external review teams submitted very positive reports and the third one had submitted no report. Granted, the external reviewers had identified concerns already known by those in the Western Program, but we viewed those concerns very differently. Enrollment and costs, we felt, were driven by external factors beyond our control. Assistant deans had sunk a lot of time and thought into doing everything possible to maximize enrollment within those constraints — designing a new brochure and redesigning the website, hosting groups of high school guidance counselors, calling all admitted students who had expressed an interest in the Western Program and setting up teams of current students to make follow up phone calls, etc. We thought it ironic that the previous provost had granted us an additional tenure track position (as had another provost a few years earlier), yet we were being criticized because our costs were too high. The charge of insularity didn't ring true, since a number of faculty were involved in joint research or grants with faculty in other divisions, several faculty were teaching courses in other divisions or in the university honors program, our faculty were visible members of a number of major all-university committees, one of my colleagues directed the university's faculty development program for senior faculty, and some faculty members were working with graduate students in other divisions. Many of our students were highly visible leaders in a wide range of all-university student activities (and a disproportionately high number of them ironically received Presidential awards for their service). Moreover, all Western students took fully half their coursework over four years in other divisions of the university, a degree of curricular reliance on the university as a whole quite atypical of other Miami divisions. We acknowledged, though, that we had made some questionable hiring decisions and had not been able to establish a solid third generation of Western faculty.

The charge that we had not been sufficiently innovative since the 1980s took us totally by surprise. We felt we had one of the most innovative programs in the country — certainly it featured just about every "alternative" bell and whistle in higher education over the last fifteen to twenty years — and the Western Program was widely recognized in the literature on innovative programs as one of the leading interdisciplinary undergraduate programs in the country. Again, the problem was that our perceptions conflicted with those of the central administration, and there was no opportunity, forum or occasion, to find this out, much less talk through our differences. We presumed that our mission was to construct an excellent innovative program and then continue to implement it well. Central administration presumed, they now said, that our mission was to *keep* innovating. In part, that presumption may have been grounded, ironically, in our earlier claim that Western could serve as a testing ground of innovations for the rest of the university. For example, the new provost (a political scientist brought to Miami from Princeton who, in his first year as a university administrator, would preside over Western's demise) cleverly devised a political argument that, in a way, the Western Program had "won," because we had advocated interdisciplinary studies for years, and now that everyone was doing it, we were no longer needed as a division. Since we had never taken the time or made the effort to clarify for ourselves, much less publicly articulate for others, how our approach to interdisciplinary studies was different from its practice in the rest of the university, we were in no position to rebut his contention.

By March of 2005, central administration had made the decision to give the Western Program (in John Skillings' words) "one last chance" to address the set of damning concerns (as they saw them) revealed through the program review process. This decision reflected a shared recognition by the Board of Trustees and central administration that there would be "some kind" of Western Program. "I think everyone wanted to have something [at Miami] that was Western-like, a Western presence at Miami University, but it wasn't clear that what we had, a separate division, was the way to go. We have strong support from the Western alumnae, and wanted to hold true to what we agreed to back in the '70s when Western College closed." So central administration told the Western Program dean to "come up with a plan for what the future might look like." Central administration proposed that an all-university committee convene first to come up with a proposal to which the Western Program could then respond, but the dean argued vehemently that the Western Program should be permitted to come up with its own plan first, and he prevailed.

What remains murky is what the dean was told about the requirements of the plan and about the predicament the Western Program now faced. Everyone agreed that the plan was to reflect a "bold new vision," and that it should address a number of long-standing concerns about the division, such as insularity, enrollment, cost, innovation, and mentoring. Central administration was utterly convinced that it was brutally clear that the Western Program was about to be closed unless it came up with a plan focused on those five points, and that several members of central administration individually "hit" the dean with those messages on multiple occasions. The dean was equally convinced that he was kept in the dark about the severity of the situation and could never get central administration to explain what they were really after in the plan — indeed, he tried unsuccessfully many times in the fall of 2005 to get even a meeting with the provost to find out.

The supporting evidence is mixed. On the one hand, it may be difficult for a gentle soul (especially a literary scholar, not a politician, as Dean William Gracie is) to internalize a painful message when he is repeatedly "hit" with it. On the other hand, when the president and provost finally met face to face with the Western Program faculty in January of 2006 they were unclear about what they disliked about the plan that had been devised by the faculty under Gracie's direction and submitted to them as well as publicly released — indeed, they made almost no mention of either that plan or the impending fate of the Western Program. At the January 2006 encounter with the Western faculty, the president spent most of the meeting humiliating us, telling us we were shoddy scholars, irresponsible teachers, etc.; and the provost barely opened his mouth, merely glaring angrily.

No matter which perspective on these events is correct, central administration incorrectly assumed that the Western Program faculty knew where things stood all along, and knew precisely what they were required to achieve as they developed a new plan for the future. In retrospect, it is clear that the faith of central administration in hierarchy and the chain of command was ill-suited to this situation. They needed to have a direct discussion with the Western Program faculty and do it before heels were dug in and bitterness precluded any give and take (as was the case after the president lambasted the faculty). The meeting needed to be candid but collegial. Unfortunately, a very different kind of meeting took place.

Given this lack of communication, it is not surprising that the long-range plan produced by the faculty was not as radical a departure from the status quo as central administration expected, nor was it as focused on the five concerns (which the faculty viewed quite differently anyway). Consequently, the plan was "very badly received" by central administration; indeed, John Skillings characterized their reaction as, "For God's sake, weren't you listening? We had five key things that we needed you to address. We looked at your report and, frankly, it hardly addressed any of them. What the heck are you people doing over there?"

As if the situation were not murky enough, it seemed evident to others in central administration that the president had made up his own mind that the Western Program should be closed *before* the faculty was give a "last chance" to come up with a plan. It also appeared to them that the Board of Trustees was ready if not eager to approve a proposal to close the division. (It didn't help that, at this time, the Architecture Department had unilaterally chosen to end its collaboration for student enrollment in the Western Program — an act that did not occur, curiously, until well after the controversy over Western's future surfaced, and one that, unlike all former actions about the collaboration, was never discussed between the two programs.) Even if the faculty had come up with a plan that the rest of central administration viewed as excellent, it is John Skillings' assessment that it would have been an up-hill battle to convince the president of its value and for him to persuade the Trustees not to close the division. The president wanted blood and the trustees wanted a major closing (and conceivably some blood as well).

The next step was to form an all-university committee (the so-called "Winkler Committee," chaired by Miami Distinguished Professor of History Allan Winkler) to come up with the bold plan that the Western Program faculty had allegedly not produced, one that addressed the five concerns. A secondary objective of the Winkler Committee was said to be to keep together as many of the Western Program faculty members as possible. The committee was also informed that central administration was seeking to restructure the University Honors and Scholars Program. The Winkler Committee came up with a proposal that they felt would address both matters while "articulat[ing] how the values of Western College might be preserved within a framework that might be better integrated into the entire university" (Winkler 2006, 1). Their strategy was to "figure out a way in which Western might be integrated into the larger Miami University honors program," and their solution was to propose "a model that would incorporate the Western College Program into the Honors and Scholars Program while still preserving a measure of autonomy and maintaining many of the features that we believe have long made Western distinctive" (2). I suspect that the wording of this proposal may have been meant as a sop to the faculty of the Western Program, since it suggested that the current program would be moved, not closed, and any changes would be modest, but it proved to be unacceptable. In fairness, the committee was given only two months to deliberate, so it was difficult to think through such a complex issue. Nonetheless, when the University Senate deliberated the proposal, it was quickly pointed out that the honors program and the Western Program had different, and somewhat incompatible missions so placing the two programs under the same umbrella (the metaphor used by the Winkler Committee) was not feasible. Yet since by that time the provost had already endorsed the proposal, it appeared that central administration was willing to move not close the Western Program, letting it remain largely intact.

In retrospect, it seems to me that the provost should have given the Winkler Committee sufficient time to vet its proposal, and the Winkler Committee should have said something like the following: The current Western Program should be closed, and members of its faculty should be invited to join with faculty from other parts of the university currently teaching in the University Honors and Scholars Program to come up with a proposal for a Western Honors College that would have many of the characteristics of the present Western Program. The Western Program faculty would have been understandably dismayed that their program was being closed but most if not all would have been willing to contribute to the development of an honors college with prominent Western features; the proposal would have withstood close scrutiny by University Senate; central administration would be assured that its five concerns were met and there would still be a visible Western presence at Miami University; and the Board of Trustees would have been happy that the division was being closed and that the honors program would gain visibility (since The Ohio State University had recently beefed up its honors program and was attracting the kind of students that Miami wanted).

With the rejection of the recommendation of the Winkler Committee in the spring of 2006, the University Senate established what became known as the Momeyer Committee to come up with another plan, one that might keep the program intact although eliminate its divisional status. This committee, which was much more favorably disposed to the current Western Program because it was set up and charged by the faculty-controlled University Senate instead of central administration, came up with a proposal to close the Western Program as a division and move it as a department to the College of Arts and Science. That proposal was endorsed by the University Senate with virtual unanimity. However, Dean Karen Schilling of the College of Arts and Science told the Senate that she would not accept that move, and instead would establish another interdisciplinary program, still with some Western-like features, inside the College of Arts and Science. The recruitment of students for the Western Program, and admissions to it, would end. Western faculty members were to be dispersed to their disciplinary "home" departments, though a few might be selected to participate in designing the new program.

At this point friends of the Western Program had run out of options: central administration had decided to close the division, any link to honors was now not politically viable; and the College of Arts and Science would not permit the current Western program to move in. Then yet another committee, co-chaired by Chris Myers (a Western Program faculty member highly respected in the College of Arts and Science) and including various Arts and Science faculty members, sketched out a design for a future new program with Western-like features. An interim director (Mary Jean Corbett from the English Department) was appointed by the dean of the College of Arts and Science, beginning fall 2008. The interim director will identify the faculty members who will then come up with the precise design for a new program, and commence its implementation. Meanwhile, the School of Interdisciplinary Studies (Western College Program), one of the most outstanding interdisciplinary studies programs in the country, is being phased out and will cease offering courses in 2010 when the last cohort graduates. At this writing, any plans for hiring a faculty, developing a curriculum, or creating a residential program are still not public.

Lessons from the Lifecycle of the Western Program

I believe a number of political and organizational lessons can be extracted from the experience of the Western Program that can be generalized to other cluster colleges and, with attention to institutional context, to other broadly or generically interdisciplinary programs. Those lessons would need to be rethought, however, before they could be applied to interdisciplinary programs with a clear substantive focus, e.g., an environmental studies program.

First, interdisciplinary programs are *always* at political risk. Even when an interdisciplinary program is warmly embraced and strongly supported by all relevant institutional leaders, it is still at risk by its very nature. Budget crises can erupt with the speed of 9/11 or key supporters can unexpectedly move on or be moved on, and interdisciplinary programs (especially of the experimental college variety) inherently run against the grain of the hierarchical, discipline-based structure of the institution and thus stand out, as the Western Program did, as "low hanging fruit."

Second, the best strategy for minimizing the chances of being plucked from the vine is to so thoroughly integrate the program with the rest of the institution that it cannot be plucked without pulling down the entire vine. The integration of individual students, faculty members, or administrators is not enough — the Western Program had a myriad of such individual ties; rather, what is required is structural integration, and where it exists, constantly pointing out the benefits for the entire institution. For example, the novel curricular integration that characterized the structural fusion of Western's lower-division interdisciplinary core curriculum with upper division courses taken across the university to complete a unique degree for self-selected Miami students, thereby adding appeal for the entire university, could and should have been consistently promoted. For example, instead of developing two new environmental majors at Western as the penultimate dean did (with my endorsement), which then prompted the College of Arts and Science to immediately develop its own competing co-major, the dean of the Western Program would better have approached the dean of the College of Arts and Science about setting up a joint task force with faculty representatives from both divisions charged with designing an environmental major that drew on the distinctive strengths of both faculties. The goal would be to come out with a major that required courses in both divisions, which would then give a large minority of the faculty of Arts and Science an organizational and curricular stake in the continuation of the Western Program. (It might even have led them to be more receptive to approving Western courses as fulfilling the College's liberal education requirement, which would have had profound implications for total enrollment in Western Program courses.) For example, the structural integration of the architecture (and later, interior design) majors with the Western curriculum and residential college that lasted well over two decades would have been continuously reviewed, refined, and improved. Such appropriate innovations as systematic joint appointments and curricular offerings that featured more regular team teaching might have occurred. Conceptually, structural integration could be seen as a "merger" of kindred interdisciplinary programs, one theoretical, and the other applied. As it was, the arrangements at times seemed mostly tolerated by two faculty cultures that rarely interacted, leaving integration of the two areas mostly to students who were expected to figure it out for themselves.

Third, since broadly interdisciplinary programs, especially experimental cluster colleges, run counter to the presumptions and experience of most senior administrators, it is important to find ways to expose them directly to selected aspects or features of the program that they are likely to appreciate. It is risky to rely on the administrator of an "alternative" program to serve as the only information conduit between an interdisciplinary program and central administration. Program heads chosen for administrative attributes more than commitment to interdisciplinarity may be ill-equipped to sell the program to leaders of the institution, and those chosen for their commitment to interdisciplinarity more than their administrative skills may be ill-equipped to discern the concerns and intentions of institutional leaders and to convey them to the faculty of the interdisciplinary program. Central administrators were often invited to participate in public or ceremonial events, including student presentations, of the Western Program over the years, but such figures tend to allocate their time selectively and in any event that kind of engagement alone will not secure their understanding of the program. Other, more integrative ways to involve key decision makers must be constantly pursued. And the time to arrange such experiences was long before the program was in jeopardy.

Fourth, a high premium should be placed on the political skills of candidates seeking to administer an interdisciplinary program. The last two times deans were hired, the Western Program faculty backed candidates who were, in the first instance, adept at thinking structurally, and in the second instance, well-networked across the university. In neither instance were they chosen primarily for political skill, under the presumption that the program was not at risk.

Fifth, it turns out to be unwise to attack politically the most powerful leaders of the institution in which one's interdisciplinary program is located, especially on issues that are not central to the well-being of the program.

Sixth, in an era when interdisciplinary studies programs have become the latest academic fashion, it is imperative that interdisciplinary programs (especially long-standing ones) reexamine the nature of their distinctive contribution to the institution. If an interdisciplinary program approaches interdisciplinary studies the same way everyone else in the same institution does, then our provost was correct: that program is no longer needed. My observation is that interdisciplinary programs such as the Western Program tend to be more fully interdisciplinary, especially more committed to interdisciplinary integration; also, they (especially the ones of the experimental college variety) tend to generalize the interdisciplinary way of approaching the world and extend it to include innovative pedagogies (e.g., collaborative learning), programs (e.g., service learning), and curricula (e.g., problem-based courses)—

what I call "integrative learning." Yet these are, in most programs with which I am familiar, still little more than tendencies. I believe the most viable strategy for preserving these interdisciplinary programs is for them get serious about interdisciplinary studies. They need to become self-conscious and intentional about interdisciplinary process. They need to immerse themselves in the recent literature on interdisciplinarity, e.g., Allen Repko's (2008) *Interdisciplinary Research: Theory and Process*. They need to redesign their courses accordingly and communicate their revised intentions to their students. And only then are they in a position to articulate a theory-based and curriculum-implemented distinction between the interdisciplinary studies they do, and "interdisciplinary studies" carried out in the rest of the institution. The alternatives are to settle for a single substantive focus (e.g., the environment) and drop their broadly interdisciplinary approach, or to die.

NOTES

1. For the classic study of the life cycle of interdisciplinary programs, one written with the Western Program in mind, see Martin Trow (1984/85).

2. The end of this narrative would be based on unsupported speculation were it not for the courageous cooperation of Vice Provost (formerly Interim Provost) John Skillings, who agreed to a remarkably candid formal interview immediately upon his retirement in July 2008 that revealed key internal details about the decision of central administration to close the division.

REFERENCES

Annual Report of the Western College of Miami University, 1974-75.

Annual Report of the Western College of Miami University, 1975-76.

Annual Report of the School of Interdisciplinary Studies (Western College Program), 1980-81.

May, Hayden, personal communication, August 27, 2008.

Newell, William, H. 1984. Interdisciplinary curriculum development in the 1970s: The Paracollege at St. Olaf and the Western College Program at Miami University. In *Against the current: Reform and experimentation in higher education* ed. Richard Jones and Barbara Smith, 127–147. Cambridge, Mass: Schenkman Press.

_____. 2001. Powerful pedagogies. In *Reinventing ourselves: Interdisciplinary education, collaborative learning and experimentation in higher education* ed. Barbara Leigh Smith and John McCann, 196–211. New York: Anker Press.

Repko, Allen F. 2008. *Interdisciplinary Research: Theory and Process.* Thousand Oaks, CA: Sage Publications.

Skillings, John, interview July 8, 2008, Oxford, OH.

Trow, Martin. (1984-85). Interdisciplinary studies as a counterculture: Problems of birth, growth, and survival. *Issues in Integrative Studies* 3: 1–16.

Winkler, Allan M. 2006. Report of the ad hoc committee on the Western College Program, March 6.

CHAPTER 2

The Devolution of the Individualized Degree at the University Without Walls/University of Massachusetts–Amherst

Rick F. Hendra

The individualized degree was one of the more successful innovations of the progressive college movement, having survived into the 21st century. Pioneered by Arthur Morgan's curricular reform at Antioch College in early the 1920s, it was embraced by Goddard and other Dewey-inspired, experimental colleges that arose in the 1930s. The individualized degree later became an article of faith for the dozens of University Without Walls programs that popped up across the United States in the early 1970s — central to their mission of empowering students to become lifelong, self-directed learners (See Eldridge 1984; and Harris and Hendra 2002, for a brief history of the University Without Walls). Its future (and theirs), however, seems clouded in the increasingly corporate climate of 21st century higher education.

The defining characteristic of the individualized degree is the individual student's role in helping to define and design it, assuring that the course of study addresses that student's learning goals and obstacles while meeting broad institutional standards instead of standard major requirements. Like the interdisciplinary degree, it was in part a reaction to the strictures of the departmental major; but it was more fundamentally a shift from a faculty-centered to a student-centered instructional approach, a shift in focus from *teaching* to *learning*. If one goal of an undergraduate degree is to prepare learners to dispense with their teachers and become lifelong, self-directed learners, then the inmates must one day be given the keys and taught to use them — to set their own learning goals and design their own courses, even their own field of study. Designing one's own degree is thus a form of meta-learning, of learning how to learn — in this case, how to organize one's learning projects cumulatively and sequentially towards an academically sound undergraduate degree.

The individualized degree should not be confused with the interdisciplinary degree. Though the individualized approach to designing the major often leads to an interdisciplinary course of study, and its products are often defended by similar arguments, its possibilities are broader. An individualized degree plan may be more narrow in scope, elevating what might seem a sub-field or specialized concentration within an existing major — like jazz in the standard music major — into a full-fledged, individualized major of its own, perhaps even with its own minor concentration in, say, jazz education.

Or the individualized degree might be broader — "transdisciplinary" rather than interdisciplinary. A degree plan in robotics might encompass three disciplines (computer science, electrical engineering, and mechanical engineering); a degree in gerontology, four (think biology, psychology, sociology, and community health education). Or a degree might be problem-focused, "concentrating on a theme such as aging or racism."[1] These degrees typically make no pretense to in-depth study in all the component disciplines, settling instead for broad overviews and working vocabularies for each, establishing academic depth in the problem or task to which they've been mutually applied rather than in the disciplinary methods and foundations of the more traditional interdisciplinary major. This depth — and the specific title to the degree it enables — distinguishes the individualized degree from the less respected, more widely available general studies or liberal studies degree, which combines maximal flexibility with only minimal structure. Though not as tightly structured as an interdisciplinary degree, the individualized degree raises the same questions as to the capacity of any one discipline to comprehend or address the complex, holistic nature of the subjects in life's curriculum.

Because the interdisciplinary and the individualized degrees offer overlapping challenges to the hegemony of the departmental major, the advance or decline of either approach in the marketplace of academic options is likely to redound upon the other. And so I offer this history of the individualized degree at the University Without Walls at the University of Massachusetts/Amherst as a cautionary tale, addressed not only to the diminishing number of University Without Walls programs still hanging on around the country[2] but to non-traditional majors and degree programs everywhere.

Development of the Individualized Degree at UWW/UMass

The University Without Walls entered UMass–Amherst through its School of Education, admitting its first students in 1971. It was one of the original 20 sub-grantees for planning funds given to the Union for Experimenting Colleges and Universities by the Office of Education and the Ford Foundation to develop UWW's nationally. The School "had become a Mecca for those interested in innovative education" (Harris 1985, 7) at the time, under an enterprising and progressive young dean, Dwight Allen, oft quoted (perhaps apocryphally) as saying "let a thousand balloons rise."

Appropriately, UWW at UMass was researched and developed through the collaborative efforts of 75 graduate and undergraduate students and a group of interested faculty from around campus, brought together in a course called "Innovation in Higher Education" under the leadership of School of Education faculty member Tom Clark. They operated through a town meeting format with numerous task forces tackling the hard issues of admissions policies and procedures, prior learning assessment, faculty resources, and governance. Similar planning groups were underway at the 19 other institutions that had received funding, and they were encouraged by the UECU to communicate, to support each other, and to share ideas. They did, and they continued to stay in touch and share resources through the early years of the UWW movement (Harris 1985, 8).

What defined the UWW movement and enabled much fruitful collaboration were the eight organizing principles to which all the participating programs were required to subscribe to become an approved UWW under the UECU umbrella. These required the inclusion of a broad age range of students, the use of adjunct faculty from the community, the development of seminars to prepare students to learn on their own, etc. Another stipulation, according to the UECU's *UWW: First Year Report*, was that "[p]rograms were to be individually tailored by student and advisor. There would be no fixed curriculum and no uniform time schedule for the award of the degree" (Union of Experimenting Colleges and Universities 1972).

How these individually tailored degrees would be structured and what they would look like was left to the local UWW's operating within their different institutional environments. Some UWW's (Friend's World College was one) devised and required a written plan for each coming semester or year's learning activities, to be approved by the learner's advisor. At UWW/UMass, we devised a single, rather elaborate, six-page form requiring learners to define in a page, more or less, the proposed area of concentration and its principal areas of study; and then, in the five pages following, to lay out their entire college curriculum, all 120 credits of it. These were divided between those within the "Area of Concentration" (UWW's title for the individualized major) and those that were simply "Other Learning;" and again within each division, between credits completed and credits proposed.

This "UWW Degree Plan" was prepared with assistance from both a UWW staff advisor and a "faculty sponsor" with relevant disciplinary expertise, chosen by the student from any of the UMass campuses. The faculty sponsor's signature on the degree plan attested to the soundness of the conception and the adequacy of the coursework and other learning proposed for the learner's area of concentration. The advisor's signature signified that it met both university and UWW degree requirements. Faculty sponsors were more or less actively involved in the degree planning process, depending on their interest and availability. The UWW advisor, however, was always centrally involved. The advisor was responsible for helping the learner work out the degree as a whole — helping to clarify career and educational goals, to brainstorm possibilities and identify workable areas of concentration, to research those most worth the learner's while, and to define a field of study the learner would be motivated and able to finish. The product of those efforts, often going through several drafts as early hopes and ideals ground against the whetstones of practicality, was a reviewable degree plan.

Advisors were responsible for getting this degree plan properly worked out in all its elaborate detail (identifying not only the titles of courses and their credits, but the dates of courses planned or completed, crediting institution, general education designation or none, etc.) on the degree plan form, and then shepherding that degree plan through UWW's even more elaborate review and approval process. In addition to gaining the approval of the student, the faculty sponsor, and the advisor (together known as the "Degree Committee"), the degree plan had to be finally approved by UWW's Academic Assessment Policy and Assessment Committee (APAC). While the faculty sponsor's approval generally rested on expectations rooted in a vague understanding of curriculum coupled with intimate knowledge of the coursework in their own discipline, UWW's review centered on general principles of good curriculum design drawn from both traditional and progressive sources.

Because the learners' constraints were so often intractable — and this by design, as one of UWW's criteria for admissions was that the applicant's circumstances made more traditional programs inaccessible or impractical — UWW presented its principles in terms of broad goals rather than specific credit requirements, to ensure flexibility. Still, there was a strong program push against settling for expediency. Going beyond the tick sheet of usual university requirements, the program set forth its own curriculum requirements in the "UWW Degree Plan Criteria Sheet," which served from the early years through the early 80s to guide the student and advisor in preparing, and APAC in reviewing, the learner's degree plan (University Without Walls 1979, 38).

First, an unspecified "balance" was required between breadth and depth in one's area of concentration credits, and between theory and practice in one's learning modes (prior learning credits often filled that requirement). In those early years, it was also required that learners' degree plans reflect on "self in society" and address "the "social/historical context" of their fields, through their coursework and portfolios. As the prior learning portfolio course developed to meet the university's writing across the curriculum requirement, skill in written communication was added to UWW's curriculum goals.

There was no requirement that the area of concentration be interdisciplinary in any clear way. It was required only that the first page narrative defining the area of concentration also identify and provide some rationale for the "components"—the main "skill or knowledge areas"—that made up the area of concentration. Students were encouraged to identify three to five main skill and knowledge areas for their area of concentration, each area comprising at least nine credits in some combination of coursework, independent study, and prior learning.

The components were a point of confusion for students and even for staff, at times. Students would often list ethics or business law as a component of their area of concentration, though they only had a single course in the subject and no stated intention of writing about either topic in their portfolio. Advisors were generally clear that one course did not a component make. But naming those components was another matter. Some advisors recommended using the names of any academic departments from which students might be taking nine or more credits, making these degrees look more like interdisciplinary degrees, or more accurately, multidisciplinary degrees. The robotics degree described earlier, drawing on electrical engineering, mechanical engineering and computer science would be a good example. Other advisors would steer learners to identify different components within a single academic discipline, so long as there were nine or more credits in each. Thus, an area of concentration in information management might include components in general management, accounting and finance, and business technology, all from the School of Management. The staff never framed a policy to circumscribe the definition of "components," perhaps wisely deciding not to tie their own hands — or their students' hands. The profusion of possibilities for an individualized area of concentration made possible by this loose approach to components was one of the selling points of the program, essential to making it work for so many learners.

These same ambiguities, however, made it necessary to present the program's requirements in a clear way to students, provide some rationale for them, and guide students in meeting them. The bulk of this responsibility fell on the UWW advisor, and was accomplished primarily through a series of one-to-one meetings with individual learners in their first semester. The advisor was assisted in this task by the *UWW Handbook* that every new student received. This was a longish document — 74 pages of mostly single-spaced prose — organized under general headings like "Curriculum," "Steps in the Program," "The Development of the Degree," "People and Paper Resources," and so on (University Without Walls 1979, 1983). These broad headings were intended to organize dozens of freshly written short essays and existing program handouts (such as the "Degree Plan Criteria Sheet") into a well-ordered resource. The *Handbook* explains the mission of UWW, the philosophy behind its curricular requirements, and the steps to completing successfully one's UMass degree through UWW.

For the student of alternative higher education, The *Handbook* is a fascinating document. When it was written, the staff included the founding director; three early graduates of UWW, now with their master's degrees and hired back as full-time advisors; along with several regular staff and graduate teaching assistants pursuing graduate degrees through the UMass School of Education. It is clearly the work of several staffers, though none are credited. The *Handbook* is thick with educationist jargon and principled reasoning, some of it sounding dated now. But it suggests a staff both well informed and still passionate about the purposes, principles, and methods defining their alternative bachelor's degree program. The chapter titled "Curriculum: Goals & Components" goes beyond the stated UWW degree requirements to propound the purposes of the program and the "themes" of interdisciplinary study, critical thinking, experiential learning, "cultural relativism," and lifelong "autonomous" learning that pervaded the curriculum and identity of UWW then. And it insightfully notes that

> [T]he minimal structure of the curriculum necessitates that the student, sponsor and advisor who work together as the degree committee infuse the degree planning process with the same purposes and themes. Such a thematically coherent advising and degree-planning process provides an important link between the various components of the curriculum [University Without Walls 1979, 6–7].

In other words, what UWW lacked in the way of specific credit and course requirements could be replaced by the clarity and coherence of the program's curriculum goals, if applied thoroughly and consistently in the creation of each individualized degree. Not all students even read the *UWW Handbook*, of course, let alone pondered its philosophical coherence. For students, it was mostly a reference guide to the UWW requirements, though a few always found it intriguing and enlightening. It was left to the advisor, once again, to coax students into reading the *Handbook* and to convey or reinforce its contents and inspiration as needed in advising sessions.

Ideological as well communal support was provided in the early years through UWW's "Introductory Seminar," a six-credit course "designed to provide students with an intensive introduction to the UWW educational philosophy and learning process and to a core of values, perspectives, and modes of thinking defined as central to the program" (University Without Walls 1979, 13). The course was centered on readings and discussions rather than the actual tasks of degree planning, which were still left to the learner's own devices with the assistance of one-to-one meetings with the advisor and, less often, the faculty sponsor.

The review of the degree plan by the Academic Policy and Assessment Committee (APAC) enforced and reinforced the degree plan criteria, both for the students and the advisors. APAC, soon divided into several working subcommittees renamed "Academic Review Teams" (ART) to manage the workload, would debate among themselves how much depth or breadth was enough for this one-of-a-kind area of concentration, and whether there was enough theory or firsthand experience or engagement with the social implications of the field. The credits were added up and checked against university requirements as well. The team's decision and recommendations would then be written up and explained to the learner in a letter from the advisor, and followed up if necessary with an advising session. I've no statistics on the rates of approval over the years, but I'd say that two thirds of the degree plans submitted were typically approved on first review, or found "approvable" pending a faculty sponsor signature or some minor correction to the credit lists (a missing general education designation, a wrongly categorized course, etc.).

Students whose degree plans were sent back for revisions were grateful for specific instructions on how to get their degree plans approved, but often mystified by the curricular concerns behind them. Degree plans might be denied approval and returned to the student because the "components" were misidentified or not identified at all. The title of the area of concentration might be deemed inappropriate. The rules of thumb for distinguishing between breadth and depth among the courses and in the degree often seemed subjective to students, as did the means for demonstrating a grasp of the social/historical context of one's field, and the number of credits awarded for prior learning. The advisor typically tried to clarify and justify the ARTeam's assessment, appealing to the *Handbook*, which the student was supposed to have read; but the process remained more opaque than not to many students whose degree plans were not approved on first review. Some never completed their degree plans, or never found a faculty sponsor to approve them, or simply gave up on the process for their own reasons, uninspired by a process they found vague and frustrating. There was a high attrition rate in the early years. The relationship with the advisor was most often the deciding factor in whether these students finally finished or disappeared.

To better guide and motivate students in the degree planning process, and to avoid repeating the same information in meetings with each individual advisee, some instructor/advisors began setting aside time in the Introductory Seminar to address the more practical aspects of degree planning. By 1984, the six-credit Intro Seminar had been reduced to three credits and paired up with a new course, the Degree Development Seminar, which was dedicated to the task of helping learners prepare a degree plan which would pass muster with the ARTeam.

The Intro Seminar kept its focus on critical thinking, social justice, and reflecting on one's own experiences. It was re-titled "Perspectives on Learning" and over time it became attached more to the prior learning portfolio process than to degree development. The Degree Development Seminar was then charged with providing the overlay of theory and context for the tasks of degree planning as well as with guiding those tasks themselves. The *UWW Handbook* became a class text. Different instructors taught the Seminar differently, but most sections looked at what it means to be "educated," at the relationships between liberal and professional education, theory and practice, pedagogy and andragogy, and UWW in the University. Through such simple devices as using first names, acknowledging the university's shortcomings, and putting learners' needs at the center of the curriculum, the Degree Development Seminar recast the relationship between teacher and student. Students, given tools and responsibility, became learners. Teachers, focused on their students' priorities instead of their discipline's, and became mentors and facilitators.[3]

Learners were required to research their areas of concentration as fields of both study and employment in order to create a degree plan likely meet their needs while gaining the requisite approvals from their faculty sponsor and the internal UWW Academic Review Team. We hoped that along the way they'd learn to make better use of the University and of community based learning resources, become more efficacious learners, and gain skills and enthusiasm for directing their own lifelong learning beyond graduation. And indeed, there was considerable anecdotal evidence of success in these efforts.

UWW staff came to understand the Degree Development Seminar as a "process" course as opposed to a "content" course, meaning that its focus was not on mastering some established body of knowledge or skill set as defined by a discipline and imparted by an instructor, but on helping learners understand and navigate the academic environment and use the tools UWW provides to clarify, pursue, and achieve their own educational goals.

The Seminar was a defining innovation. It doubled the number of courses offered and required by UWW, strengthening the emphasis on teaching in the program. It led to a second process course just a few years later, "Writing About Experience," to support the prior learning process. Over the course of their first year in UWW, these courses led students to examine their pasts and chart their futures, a powerful and empowering model of an integrated student-centered curriculum. Students embraced them. By bringing students together around their common needs as UWW students, the Degree Development Seminar promoted community and peer support. By bringing theory and practice together to serve learners' own educational needs, the Seminar put UWW's own principles into practice, and managed the uncommon feat of raising standards while increasing retention.

The introduction of the portfolio-writing course in 1986 brought UWW's original, fifteen-year curriculum development effort to fruition, and brought UWW itself a level of success and acceptance that had long seemed elusive. At its peak in 1989, the teaching staff included three lecturers and nine professional staff, teaching UWW courses as adjuncts in the School of Education, where UWW was administratively housed. Since 1971 it has graduated more than 3,000 alumni. Its student body was 292 in 1987, with peak enrollment years being between 1984 and 1989.

The Decline of the Individualized Degree at UWW/UMass

It's been said that every success carries the seeds of its own demise. UWW had given the individualized degree the attention it deserved only by devoting very considerable time and resources to it. The evolution of the individualized degree had begun with a form, which led to a handbook, which then became a text in a three-credit course dedicated to completing that form. ARTeams met regularly to review the forms, often sending them back for revisions. Students and advisors both invested considerable time in the degree planning process, and as the ARTeam raised standards (requiring a well polished narrative and clearly identified components), the time commitment only increased. We began a long search for ways to streamline the process.

The first pushback on the Degree Plan form, sometime in the mid 80s, was to limit the first page narrative discussing the area of concentration and the student's background for it to one page. The constraint was eased by no longer requiring students to address the UWW criteria in these statements. Paragraphs addressing the criteria had often been formulaic ("I will address the theory requirement with class work, the practice requirement with my portfolio...") and unconvincing. So in the interests of brevity and readability, the student no longer had to explain how the degree plan met UWW's curriculum goals, so long as the advisor and ARTeam could see that it did.

Around this same time, the staff agreed to drop the requirement that students address the social/historical context of their field from the curriculum goals. In part, this reflected the changing political climate, affecting staff as well as students; and in part it reflected the awkwardness of finding social issues courses in fields like accounting and technical writing.

The de-emphasis on UWW's curriculum goals in writing up the degree plan reflected a widening split in how the Degree Development course was taught. Those instructor/advisors whose graduate degrees were in education typically required readings and discussions on professional vs. general education, theory and practice, adult learning, how a university works, and other articles providing context for the issues in degree design. As new advisors were hired from other disciplinary backgrounds, they tended to require fewer readings in education, focusing more on the actual tasks of degree development: researching one's area of concentration as a field of work and study, finding a faculty sponsor, and preparing the degree plan. Educational theory was neither their interest nor that of most of the students in their classes, after all. A good degree plan could be produced without it.

Soon, the *UWW Handbook* also began to be edited down and refocused more on the tasks of degree planning and less on the theory that supported those tasks. Chapters on "Curriculum: Goals and Components" and the "Area of Concentration" were pared down, and the "Degree Plan Checklist" was dropped from its pages as it was from general use.

This process of streamlining and deracination picked up steam with the departure of the founding director, Ed Harris, and several veteran staff in the late 80s, following major budget cuts, brought on by the recession of the late 80s. This reduction initiated two decades of stagnant and declining budgets, during which UWW moved from a state funded to a self-sustaining program. By the year 2000, UWW's teaching/advising staff had declined to 10. UWW managed the decline in state funding by developing workforce education programs in collaboration with public and private sector agencies and appropriate academic divisions at UMass. Initially, these were funded by grants and contracts. By the year 2000, UWW was funding these programs through the tuitions they generated, running them through Continuing Education for a percentage of the net. As UWW became tuition driven, teaching and advising loads inevitably increased. The pressure for streamlining led to a further shortening of the degree plan narrative, to two paragraphs (a description of the area of concentration and a list of its component areas of study) accomplished by removing the student's account of how the proposed area of concentration built on her experience and shaped her future plans.

Program development, however, posed an even greater challenge to the individualized degree. UWW's workforce education programs were designed to provide professional degrees in fields the university didn't, though it might offer some relevant courses. To provide solid professional degree programs for human service workers, for paraprofessionals looking to become teachers in the schools, and for other occupations, UWW developed courses for those fields at times working adults could take them, even delivering them onsite, as with the Organizational Leadership program at MassMutual Financial Group in Springfield, MA. UWW's individualized degree made these programs possible, though providing such ready-made degree tracks more or less precluded students, depending on their program, from individualizing the degree for themselves. In the Teacher Licensure Program (TLP), for instance, there were 48 required credits of coursework which we provided, so the area of concentration for each student looked virtually identical.

The standardization of the degree in these programs posed problems for the Degree Development Seminar as well. Students in these tracks didn't need to come up with a title for their area of concentration, find (or design) their own courses, or even find a faculty sponsor. The degrees were so similar within the TLP and Early Childhood Education programs that standard templates were drawn up, describing these areas of concentration and their components, that all the learners in those programs used. The Degree Development Seminars for students in these tracks began to look very different from those for the "individualized" students. The context of educational philosophy and values that had supported the tasks of degree design no longer seemed relevant in "track" programs where those tasks were no longer necessary.

The ARTeams also found the degree plans from these programs challenging. We soon agreed that there was no point in reviewing a dozen TLP degree plans that all looked the same. They'd be approved en masse, with individual review provided only to those with an additional concentration or minor. More awkward were the individualized degree plans submitted by the MassMutual students, who weren't obliged to use a standard area of concentration title. These sported a disconcertingly wide variety of area of concentration titles for essentially the same coursework. That coursework was essentially pre-approved since UWW, the faculty, and the sponsoring organization had designed and approved the program; so the ARTeams were reduced to critiquing the learner's attempts to present these as different fields of study. The new staff hired to manage these workforce development programs were understandably unimpressed with the whole degree planning and reviewing process.

It was symptomatic of the growing disconnect between theory and practice when, in 2005, an issue arose in the ARTeams over what came to be called "... and ..." degrees. These appeared to be multidisciplinary degrees but without any unifying overlap — e.g., "business, human services, and art." While a connection might somehow have been found to tie those very different fields into one coherent, coordinated course of study — some social issue or professional enterprise, perhaps — these areas of concentration were instead simply assembled out of previous coursework and experience. Their reason for being was expediency in getting students graduated. So long as they had forty-five credits in the different fields covered under the title and other UMass requirements were met, there was nothing more required of them. One of the three ARTeams was routinely approving these. The question of curricular integrity was raised in terms of our depth as well as breadth criterion and our policy against the award of general studies degrees. UWW staff agreed to reject these catchall concentrations. But the issue wasn't obvious to everyone, especially to recent hires, perhaps reflecting the extent to which staff discussions of program goals and philosophy had been displaced by a more practical and pressing agenda since the budget cuts in 1989.

The corporate management ethos[4] that Chancellor Lombardi brought to UMass–Amherst in 2002 brought these pressures to a head. Having demonstrated its ability to generate income, UWW was told in 2004 that the university would be withdrawing all its remaining state funding from this program by 2006. UWW was expected to become self-supporting (and pay over a third of its revenues in overhead to UMass and its Continuing Education Division as well). We were now forced to run all our courses through Continuing Ed for the revenues they generated. Several staff retired.

Faculty and departments were also under pressure. Faculty sponsors became increasingly hard to find and less likely to contribute. Departments began to demand a share of the revenues for the courses their faculty taught for us. A new associate provost for our Outreach Division was hired in 2004. The following year, UWW's director of 15 years stepped down and a new interim director (previously the manager of our MassMutual program) was soon leading UWW in a major revision of its curriculum and business plan.

In the new curriculum initiated in the fall of 2007, the Degree Development and Perspectives on Learning Seminars were consolidated into one course, titled "Frameworks for Understanding." Four new courses leading students to reflect on their experiences in light of theory in key aspects of professional life were added to the curriculum (on leadership, organizations, public policy, and technology). The prior learning portfolio has been streamlined, from a minimum of four essays down to three maximum in the "Writing

About Experience" course. The new courses are part of the new Professional Studies curriculum, designed to be the primary route for students through UWW. Starting in 2008 UWW's courses will only be offered in online and blended formats.

Professional Studies students can choose among forty different area of concentration titles, whose descriptions and components are laid out for students to copy onto their degree plans.[5] A faculty sponsor is no longer required, as the difficulty in obtaining them is compounded by the impersonality of the online environment. The advisor's role has been scaled back too, as the student is now spared most of the tasks that once attended degree development and the degree development aspects of the new Frameworks course have been pared back accordingly. There is little reason now to discuss issues in education and explain UWW's philosophy. There is less involvement in career planning because there is less planning for the degree.

Because the titles of these areas of concentration were chosen from among those most often seen in the past, and because each student's program of studies is inevitably unique, if only in their prior learning credits and their choice of electives around the university, UWW still considers these to be individualized degrees. They are no longer student conceived and designed to the extent they were, but they allow even greater flexibility. To make these 40 tracks attractive to the widest number of students possible, the official descriptions of their component studies are quite inclusive. The health advocacy concentration, for instance, says, "Academic components can include coursework in political science, health, communication, sociology, psychology, intercultural studies and public policy." If a student can't find forty-five credits under all those headings from the courses he or she's already taken or plans to take, the student can shop around for another area of concentration that works better. As there are no longer faculty sponsors to insist on the necessity of certain key courses, students have more latitude to take what they want (or can find), so long as they meet the numerical benchmarks of the university (120 credits, 15 graded, etc.) and UWW (45 credits in the area of concentration, 15 upper division credits, etc.) for graduation.

Though UWW's Academic Review Teams still review Professional Studies degree plans to make sure the coursework matches the area of concentration title and components and meets the criteria for balancing depth/breadth and theory/practice, the time it takes to review them has been cut back considerably — as intended. The student's ideas and their expression are no longer an issue for ARTeams. Most students are simply choosing a degree now instead of designing one. The degree plan form itself has been reformatted into an online Excel form, which automatically totals credits, enters required UWW courses, and notes general education requirements.

Advisors, instructors, and students all spend less time and energy on degree development now. There are still some students who design their own areas of concentration in fields outside of Professional Studies (which covers health and human services, education, and management); but these students are becoming fewer as there is no longer a Degree Development Seminar to support them in that process and finding a faculty sponsor (as these students still need to do) is still a daunting challenge. For most students now, the UWW degree is a welcome compromise between the regular, rigid, university major and a general studies degree, offering all the title specificity of the former with nearly the flexibility of the latter. It's not a project they need to grapple with. The educational value of taking a semester to research and structure future educational and career plans has been lost. And for most UWW students now, that's not an issue. They're there to get a good degree with as little hassle and cost as possible. While some still come to UWW for the opportunity to design their own degree, for most students the challenge to take on more responsibility for their learning was never more than an acquired taste, a taste UWW no longer cares — or can afford — to cultivate.

It remains to be seen whether UWW can hold on to the student-centered teaching model that the Degree Development Seminar initiated. The degree planning process no longer finds its larger purpose in helping adult students become more self-directed, lifelong learners. Other curriculum tools giving students more responsibility for their learning, such as independent learning contracts and practica, are also much less used now than they were in earlier years. The erosion of oral and written conversation in UWW on the philosophical legacy of ideas and values connecting it to its roots in Progressive Education and the experimental college movement has sapped meaning and support for these alternative curricular vehicles. But in the new UMass, where "money matters" and "time is the enemy," philosophy seems puerile and individualization seems labor intensive. If UWW is going to grow into the revenue engine UMass wishes, it needs to scale up its numbers. In the fall of 2008, UWW boasted over 500 students, still with only 10 teaching/advising faculty. More students means more standardization, more streamlining, less personal relationships, and courses that adjuncts can teach without taking on major advising responsibilities. It means a very different UWW than the one originally envisioned by the UECU — operating in a very different university as well. It would be worth researching whether this decline in the vitality of the individualized degree has been replicated in other UWW's. Sadly, the bottom line for student-centered education may be that it's more profitable to teach students than to help them learn how to learn.

NOTES

1. This paragraph draws on the essay "Area of Concentration," in the *UWW Handbook, 1979–80.*

2. Now numbering five, officially: at University of Massachusetts–Amherst, Chicago State University, Northern Illinois University, Hofstra University and, as of this writing, still at Skidmore College.

3. UWW's director, Ed Harris, encouraged staff to use the term "learners" in place of "students" to signal the respect owed the adults who came to us, who were often experts in their own right, and who were joining our "community of learners" not as receptacles for our knowledge but as active agents of their own educations. Along these same lines, we were encouraged to think of ourselves as facilitators rather than teachers.

4. Embodied in the slogan Lombardi coined upon coming to UMass in 2002: "Money Matters, Persistence Counts, Time is the Enemy" (Cambo 2007).

5. A list of these can be found on the UWW website: *http://www.umass.edu/uww/forms/PS-concentrations.pdf*

REFERENCES

Cambo, Carol. 2007. A fond farewell. *UMass Amherst,* Summer.

Eldridge, J. 1984. *A historical study of the relationship between the philosophy of John Dewey and the Early Progressive Colleges: An investigation of the role of science.* Amherst, Mass: University of Massachusetts.

Harris, Edward. 1985. The creation of UWW. *UWW Update,* 10 (9) (Nov.): 7.

Hendra, Rick F., and Edward Harris. 2002. "Unpublished results: The University Without Walls experiment." http://www-unix.oit.umass.edu/~hendra/Unpublished%20 Results.html (accessed 10/21/08).

UWW Handbook, 1979–80.

UWW Handbook, 1983–84.

Union for Experimenting Colleges and Universities. 1972. *UWW: A first year report* (May). Yellow Springs, OH.

CHAPTER 3

To Educate the People: The Department of Interdisciplinary Studies at Wayne State University

Andre Furtado, Linda Lora Hulbert, Julie Thompson Klein, Lisa Maruca, Caroline Maun, Daphne W. Ntiri and Roslyn Abt Schindler

By September 6, 2007, the faculty, administrators, and students of the Department of Interdisciplinary Studies (IS) who gathered in the McGregor Memorial Conference Center at Wayne State University (WSU) in Detroit, Michigan, already knew the outcome, the end of a brief but catastrophic struggle. That foreknowledge didn't stop them from gathering outside the building that morning. The Board of Governors was meeting to approve a recommendation of its Budget and Finance Subcommittee that included a number of measures to cut costs across the university in response to a projected budget shortfall. The members of the audience who crowded the room were there to witness the dismantling of the only academic department required to close. Although the matter would not come to a final vote until September 26, 2007, this was the last stage of a process that had actually been ongoing for many years. A foregone conclusion, however, did not stop key alumni and the chair of the department from delivering impassioned pleas to the Board.

The vast majority of spectators in the room, who were supporters of the department, were accustomed to being called on to defend the program. Just two years earlier, the department had survived closing of the College of Urban,

Labor and Metropolitan Affairs (CULMA) and prior to that its previous home the College of Lifelong Learning (CLL) had also been closed. Stakeholders were assured multiple times that this department was a "jewel in the university's crown," that it addressed in a singular and indispensable way the urban mission of the university, and that it would be protected in spite of reorganization. The provost herself had offered to house the department as a program in her unit. Considering it wiser to have a degree program housed in an academic college, the department entered the College of Liberal Arts and Sciences in 2005. The final assault took place with draconian speed and intensity, all the more startling given the department's national visibility, productivity, and high revenue production.

Members of the thirty-four-year-old Department of Interdisciplinary Studies received their first inkling of probable demise only three weeks prior on August 15, 2007. The University's Finance and Budget Subcommittee had met several times during the summer in order to review cost-cutting measures, which included the elimination of IS. Perhaps most surprising — and telling: with 800 active majors and 19 full-time dedicated faculty, this was by no means a failing program. Several of the characteristics that made the department distinctive were delineated in its recent reviews, both internal and external. These affirmed its national status as an exemplar of an integrated and interdisciplinary curriculum that catered with imagination and care to returning adult students. They also applauded its keenly designed and rigorous curriculum for students who would otherwise not qualify to attend Wayne State due to admissions requirements in place for the traditional population of recent high school graduates.

The university president assured the audience how cuts were taking place across the University and that no program was sacred. However, in an article printed in the student newspaper, *The South End*, an assistant professor in the department observed what others were thinking: targeting Interdisciplinary Studies for extinction while other departments of the College of Liberal Arts and Sciences (CLAS) remained untouched was political: "How else can you justify closing the second largest department in [the college] which generates $7 million a year in tuition revenue?" (quoted in Nargis and Bublitz 2007). Nonetheless, the claim that Wayne State would actually lose money over the long run by disbanding the program fell on deaf ears. So did a statement also delivered on this day by the faculty representative to the board's Finance Subcommittee, who argued that the budget woes dictating the cuts were themselves based on faulty assumptions about revenue. Indeed, in just a month, by October 2007, he was proven right: the State of Michigan reinstated previously withdrawn funds — millions of dollars — to Wayne State for the last quarter of the budget year. Unfortunately, there was never any consideration of how a cancelled degree program might or could be reinstated if the financial scenario predicted did not come to pass.

Four alumni approached the podium to address the board. Each testified in turn about how the opportunity to attend Wayne State in a program that treated mostly part-time adult students with respect had changed the course of their lives. One alumna, who was 43 when she completed her degree, credited the department with her success as a management executive supervising the YMCA in the Midwest region. Another queried, "Do you believe in no adult student left behind?" A current student added that the Department offered educational opportunity to the people who are most deeply affected by the economic desolation that permeates Detroit. The last alumna to speak was a judge with a twenty-five year career in the Michigan Civil Rights Commission and Courts system, who came back to complete a Master's degree in Interdisciplinary Studies. She refuted the administration's claim that Interdisciplinary Studies was duplicative of other classes offered at the university. She extolled its challenging and integrated program of learning offered to all students, undergraduate and graduate level alike. And she ended by reminding board members that they were elected representatives of a constituency who would be deeply affected by the closing of the department.

Finally, the department chair took her turn at the podium. She represented not only the leadership of the department, but also the many faculty who had invested their careers to create a program that would encompass the intertwined interests of adult learning and interdisciplinary studies (Ntiri, Henry and Schindler, 2004). She spoke about the proud history of the department and argued that the department could find ways to produce the projected savings of $220,000 without the irrevocable measure of destroying it.

All of the speakers received thunderous applause from supporters of the program. The board, however, with the exception of only one member, was unmoved. The final vote was seven to one in favor of closing the program.

To understand the outcome of that September 6 vote, one must turn back to the origins of the Department of Interdisciplinary Studies. It was born the University Studies/Weekend College Program (US/WCP) in May 1973. Its history is filled with highs and lows, innovations and adaptations in a relentless mission to deliver an education that was different in kind but not in quality from that delivered to traditionally-aged students at the university. And, the department was successful ... perhaps too successful.

Interdisciplinary Education in National Context

The department traced its roots back to Monteith College, founded in 1959 as an alternative, interdisciplinary, humanistic curriculum-centered undergraduate degree program for traditional college-age students. Monteith was not an honors program per se, but like counterpart experimental colleges founded in the 1960s and early 1970s, included a self-selected group of students ideally suited to a challenging interdisciplinary curriculum that focused on historical to contemporary issues, problems, and topics. Monteith and the Department of Interdisciplinary Studies are both linked to a larger history of interdisciplinary developments in higher education in the United States that needs to be understood as the backcloth for the local developments.

The history of interdisciplinary studies (IDS) in the United States dates to the opening decades of the 20th century, in the rise of integrated models of general education, new interdisciplinary fields of American studies and area studies, and experimental colleges inspired by the progressive reform movement. During the 1960s and 1970s, a new wave of reform and innovation led to the founding of new institutions, as well as new interdisciplinary fields such as Black, women's, ethnic, environmental, urban, science, technology, and cultural studies. A number of cluster or stand-alone programs also arose within traditional universities, including Monteith College and the US/WCP. Rick Harris and Ed Hendra situated Monteith within a larger movement known as the "University Without Walls," including the earlier models of Antioch, Bard, and Sarah Lawrence. "These colleges," they explain, "developed in conscious opposition to the growing hegemony of the comprehensive research university" (Hendra and Harris 2002). They differed in founding dates and degree of experimentation, but all of them placed the undergraduate student at the center of education. They also emphasized individualized or interdisciplinary programs inclusive of fine arts, independent study and greater student responsibility for learning, development of a community of learners, experiential learning based in work or service, small seminars, and a mentoring relationship with faculty (Hendra and Harris, 2002).

More broadly, the University Studies/Weekend College Program was a "telic" institution, in the sense that Gerald Grant and David Reisman (1958) used the term to classify "purposive" reforms centered on four different conceptions of undergraduate education. The University Studies/Weekend College Program was not a "neo-classical" model along the lines of St. John's or Tussman College at Berkeley. Neither was it one of the "aesthetic expressives," akin to Bennington, Sarah Lawrence, and Black Mountain. However, it did share communal-expressive goals of "human community" with Kresge College in Santa Cruz and Bensalem at Fordham University. Many of its faculty also embraced values of "social change and the activist profession" promoted by activist-radical institutions such as Antioch College, Old Westbury, and the College for Human Services in New York.

Recalling the history of telic institutions, Martin Trow (1984/85) highlighted a number of additional traits also evident in the University Studies/ Weekend College Program. In refiguring the relationship of teacher and student in a student-centered model of education, the faculty emphasized active pedagogies, collaborative course design, and multicultural learning. In promoting "anti-institutional" values within their discipline-dominated host universities, they introduced a more open, flexible administrative structure. Their value system also prioritized a commitment to teaching and service over research and the curriculum centered on a sequence moving from broad thematic clusters to advanced seminars and thesis. Many counterpart institutions catered to a more selective student body in small colleges, in contrast to the open-enrollment policy of the University Studies/Weekend College Program. Yet, the early faculty of the program were, likewise, "enthusiasts" and "true believers" who shared what Trow deems "the romantic, evangelical and utopian ideologies" of its founders (Trow 1984/5, 6–7). In the early institution-building phase, as well, the program was not perceived as a threat to existing disciplinary-based departments.

The transition from birth to maturity brought problems for telic institutions. "For every Eden," Trow reflected, "there is a world, and for young innovative institutions the agents of the world come not in the form of a serpent and an apple, but of growth" (Trow 1984/5, 8). Work overload, a common challenge in these institutions, resulted in widespread subordination of curricular activities in favor of research activities needed to secure tenure. Several of the program's pioneers were lost when reviewed by higher-level tenure and promotion committees, and tension developed between faculty who published and those non-publishers who were primarily dedicated teachers.

The early faculty also underwent change of another kind observed in counterpart programs. Some were trained in interdisciplinary fields, such as American studies or women's studies. Most, however, were not. Over time, they evolved from predominately disciplinary modes of thinking to multidisciplinary outlooks and eventually to interdisciplinary integrations anchored in common themes, problems, and ideas with attendant methodological and conceptual approaches framed for many by cultural and historical analysis. In counterpart programs, this kind of learning-on-the job is typical. As interdisciplinarity became more widely accepted and expanded nationally, the University Studies Weekend College was able to hire new faculty schooled in interdisciplinary fields and trends in the disciplines across the social sciences, humanities, and science and technology.

Even so, as Trow's model also predicts, faculty and staff had to search for ways of managing overload at the same time pressure for accountability within the University at large mounted. Routinization, conflict, and privatization were typical responses in telic institutions, resulting in diminished levels of spontaneity, creativity, community, commitment, and involvement. Some University Studies Weekend College faculty retreated into withdrawal and privatization, manifested in lowered participation in the numerous meetings essential to the day-to-day business of developing and continually enhancing the curriculum. The Golden Age of these institutions, Trow concluded, usually lies in the institution-building years. Some persist, but others die. Even when innovations die, though, they may live on in other ways. The programs that survive the longest typically moved from experimentation to regularization (a move Repko refers to in this volume as sustainability), though the recent demise of a number of long-standing cluster colleges indicates that even normalization is not a guarantee. The persistence of a strong core committed to the original ideals of the program and inculcating those ideals in new hires proved to be crucial to longer-term vitality and viability. The high percentage of tenured and tenure-track faculty within the program was an added factor, in contrast to the more common pattern of borrowing faculty from traditional departments. It was in this developing context then, that WSU's experimental program was born, took shape, was transformed, and eventually terminated. To comprehend the local factors that shaped its unique history it is necessary to place it in Detroit's changing socio-political climate and the charismatic vision of its founders.

Interdisciplinarity for Adults: A Detroit History

The University Studies/Weekend College Program arose from the ashes of Monteith College when it was eliminated in 1974, ostensibly for budget reasons. However, many of the faculty believed that discomfort on the part of disciplinary units in the College of Liberal Arts and Sciences was the real reason, expressing fear that the college would draw majors from their departments. The US/WCP would later be named the Interdisciplinary Studies Program (1992) and much later yet, the Department of Interdisciplinary Studies (2002). The US/WCP was founded by Dr. Otto Feinstein and a group of academics who had taught in Monteith. In the early 1970s, they began a movement called "To Educate the People." The people to whom they referred were the working adults of Detroit; nontraditional students and workers who would respond to, be engaged by, or come to Marton and Saljo's (1976) "deep learning stage" when taught in the teacher-centered mode so common in classrooms of the day. They refused to be silos for others' poured-in content. Instead, they sought relevance by making connections between and among new information and their background knowledge. If they could not connect to it, they did not want to understand it. If they could not make use of it, they would just as soon not discuss it. In other words, contextual learning is a key pedagogical component of successful outcomes in adult and lifelong learning and interdisciplinary studies (Schindler 2006). To the founders' way of thinking, the adult learner and interdisciplinarity were a natural fit. And, according to Wayne State University's mission statement, these students were the very target population that it set out to serve.

The typical adult student learner the founders envisioned had lived typically three decades before deciding — or being in a position to decide — that higher education might be valuable. That learner often had a full-time job, a family, community obligations and from 1973–76, was quite often a male veteran who had endured at least one tour of duty in Vietnam and worked on the line at one of metro Detroit's automobile factories. Because Feinstein was committed to andragogy, the method of teaching of adults, he took a comprehensive education to these workers, using a connected course format of once-weekly workshops, faculty-produced telecourses, and weekend conference courses. Each set of three was either thematically- or issue-linked. Most weekly workshops were taught in the community or the workplace through a then unique structure: the module.

The module was an instructional unit/curricular year (each year spanning humanities, science and technology, social science, theory and method, or advanced studies) that served from 180 to 360 full-time students from a regional or occupational grouping. This structure allowed the program to maintain close links with many institutions — labor unions, public libraries, private corporations, government agencies, community service organizations, even the State Prison of Southern Michigan in Jackson 76 miles from the main Detroit campus (Furtado and Johnson, 1980). During the program's period of greatest enrollment (about 3,600 students by spring 1976), it offered classes throughout an eight-county area. Approximately 2,000 students met in UAW local halls; 800 met on or near the main campus, at facilities run by corporations (e.g., Blue Cross/Blue Shield) or local government agencies (e.g., City of Detroit); 600 met in public libraries, public schools (after-hours), and parochial schools (also, after-hours); 200 met in community organization facilities; and 75 inmates met in Jackson Prison (Feinstein and Angelo 1977, 8). In other words, the program educated the people where they lived and worked.

In the beginning, the modular structure worked well to serve thousands of students who spent their undergraduate years pursuing the core interdisciplinary curriculum. By the late 1970s, however, that structure became more of a liability than an asset. First, enrollments began to shrink due to U. S. Congressional cut-off of veterans' educational benefits. By 1980, enrollments were down to about 900 students, and numbers continued on a downward slide until enrollment reached 450 in 1984. Second, an increasing number of enrollees came to the program with previous college credits. These transfer students came less often from the blue-collar ranks and more from white-collar, lower- to mid-management positions within the automobile companies, Michigan Bell, Blue Cross/Blue Shield, and the public sector. Further, they were slightly older than their predecessors: the average age had risen from 32 in the mid–1970s to 37 by the early 1980s. These students had plans for their futures, which entailed not only making prudent use of their previous college credits and experience, but also securing or advancing their employment future through attaining at least a bachelor's degree and, quite possibly, a graduate or professional degree.

These factors undermined the founding assumption that students would remain together for four years of study in regional or occupational cohorts. Thus the original modular structure evolved into a master divisional structure consisting of Humanities, Science and Technology, Social Sciences, and Upper Divisions. Shifting from a regional/occupational focus to a focus on broad interdisciplinary "subject areas" allowed the program to address the educational needs of its new, yet smaller, student constituency. The program also added several skills-building courses at this time, which assisted many students not only in honing rusty composition and mathematics skills but also in passing Wayne State's required university-wide English and Math Proficiency Examinations.

It soon became apparent, however, that a more dramatic change was in order. By this time, the University Studies Weekend College Program was no longer the "only game in town"; several other Michigan colleges and universities had recognized the fruitfulness of offering degree programs suited to the area's growing adult student population. Colleges and universities that had never had a presence near, let alone in, Detroit began offering similar programs. Therefore, in 1983 the program sought approval of a new degree option, the Bachelor of General Studies–Capstone (BGS); approval came from the WSU Board of Governors in July 1984. This "reverse 2 + 2" degree option allowed holders of Associate of Applied Science (AAS) degrees from accredited community colleges to transfer up to 64 credits, a bold accomplishment for the only open admissions program at WSU. Students who had already earned specialized technology AAS degrees could now come to the university for two years of general (interdisciplinary) studies, earning a BGS–Capstone degree through our open admissions program. Subsequently, in 1985, the Board of Governors approved a new degree title: Bachelor of Technical and General Studies (BTGS), designed for graduates of two-year technical, vocational, or professional associate of applied science programs.

Students worked with resident academic advisers to develop an individual-ized plan of work consisting of a coherent sequence of broad, cognate, or spe-cialized courses in a technical, vocational, or professional field, or in an applied area that enhanced prior training.

These new options helped to stabilize enrollment at about 650 from 1986 to 1990. Then, just when faculty and academic staff thought that they could get back to their primary mission of providing an interdisciplinary edu-cation for adult students, the university announced plans for implementation of a new comprehensive General Education Requirements (GERs), in keep-ing with new national trends. These GERs included six competency and eight group requirements. From 1986 to 1987, IS faculty and administration worked aggressively to ensure that the program had at least one course approved in each requirement (initially, sixteen courses were approved). Over the next eight years, several more course proposals withstood rigorous scrutiny of the university's Gen Ed Implementation Committee. By 1995, 25 courses had been approved to satisfy GERs. Again, this was a student-centered mandate: failure to have obtained general education approval for these courses would have added several semesters to our students' time-to-graduation.

In the meantime, the program had survived yet another major transi-tion. In 1992, the University Studies/Weekend Program became the Interdis-ciplinary Studies Program (ISP). For some years, faculty and staff believed that the program should have a name commensurate with its academic content — interdisciplinary studies. This new name, along with a change in degree titles (Bachelor of Interdisciplinary Studies and Bachelor of Tech-nical and Interdisciplinary Studies), gave the program appropriate profes-sional status in the field nationally and internationally. It was also the occa-sion to include a graduate component sought by faculty and students, the Mas-ter of Interdisciplinary Studies, approved in 1994 after five years of develop-ment.

In the years from 1995 to its demise in 2007, the program continued to provide an education in an integrated, student-centered, collaborative learn-ing community (Schindler 2006). To facilitate the self-actualization of adult learners necessitated going beyond the boundaries of regular university courses to develop significant offerings in the public service domain. The program enhanced its Service Agency Administration minor (begun as an American Humanics Program under a Kellogg grant in 1989) to the Nonprofit Sector Studies (NPSS) program in 1999, offering, in addition to the minor, a post-baccalaureate certificate in NPSS as of 2000, and a Master's concentration in NPSS as of 2004. This program attracted students who needed leadership and management training and offered them knowledge and hands-on skills from faculty with practical experience in the field of nonprofit organizations, community-based and public agencies. ISP's faculty were also among the first at WSU to offer online courses in the late 1990s.

The new millennium brought another host of changes — which can now be seen in retrospect as the beginning of the end. In 2002, the College of Lifelong Learning was dismantled following the retirement of its dean, and ISP was relocated in another nontraditional college, the College of Urban, Labor and Metropolitan Affairs, or CULMA. The program became the Department of Interdisciplinary Studies (IS) with all the benefits of departmental status, including stability, retaining tenure in the department, and greater academic recognition. While some within IS worried about the fate of the humanities courses within a predominantly social science curriculum in CULMA, and some inside CULMA worried that IS teaching priorities would "water down" their research-oriented mission, the young shot-gun "marriage," as many termed it, was by most considered a success. IS offered the college undergraduate numbers; CULMA offered IS academic respectability. Faculty within both began forging connections and constructing relationships that enhanced a variety of units and programs across the college. The college was committed to the urban mission, to the City of Detroit, and to the State of Michigan, including regional, national, and global perspectives as these interfaced with local and state problems and issues. IS mirrored these concerns. One initiative, for example, promoted adult literacy in a city challenged by staggering illiteracy rates. Students received training to serve in the community in housing projects and shelters, working with populations that included recovering addicts, seniors, and domestic abuse victims. Thus the Department of Interdisciplinary Studies, with its open structures of governance and community-orientation, was able dexterously to meet the needs of its urban, adult students in its new home. Unfortunately, in 2004, after a rushed self-study, following the sudden death of the CULMA dean, and against the wishes of protesting faculty and students, the entire college was dismantled. After negotiation between the IS leadership and the administration, the department, along with a number of other units, was placed into the recently merged College of Liberal Arts and Sciences (CLAS), which at the time was seen as a better option than demotion from the status of department to program under the provost's office. As a program, IS would be perceived primarily as a unit serving the University's remedial mission and would have no promise of future security.

Shortly after the Fall 2005 transfer to CLAS, the then chair learned that the college's Curriculum Committee — consisting of faculty volunteers rather than elected members — would be investigating the department's general education requirements for "duplication." This prospect immediately alarmed the faculty since they were not sure what "duplication" meant. To recall, IS, like other units on campus, offered a wide array of general education courses, which had all been vetted and approved, originally and through biannual review, by the university's General Education Oversight Committee. Would IS's interdisciplinary foreign culture course now be considered "duplicative" of offerings by one or another of the language department on a different topic and with a different methodology? Would IS's first-year writing class, which fulfilled the basic composition requirement, be seen as redundant since the English Department also taught one? The administration neither supplied criteria by which IS courses would be judged nor provided a rationale for why the program was being singled out. Even a quick glance at the list of Wayne State's Gen Ed courses revealed that, typical of most colleges and universities, a number of courses were offered fulfilling each requirement. Students could thus choose from courses that best suited their interests or fields. It only seemed equitable that Interdisciplinary Studies students be offered the same opportunity and through an accessible delivery system that met their unique needs through nightly and weekend classes. IS faculty believed, moreover, that the Gen Ed program offered more than just extra courses on a menu of choices. Thus, IS's Curriculum Committee voluntarily mounted a defense in the form of a letter designed "to acquaint our colleagues with our student-centered program of interdisciplinary general education" (see Appendix 1).

This letter, penned by the chair of the committee and accompanied by a cover memorandum from the department chair, once more justified IS as a unique program. It illustrated in detail what the department had become by the early 2000s. It explained that the department prided itself on being an integrative learning community for working adults. As such, its general education offerings did not stand merely as distinct courses, but were fully and consistently integrated into the program's undergraduate curriculum and, in fact, constituted the interdisciplinary studies "major." The letter described the first-year seminar, divisional offerings, and course linkages. It rehearsed the department's interdisciplinary methodology, cross-curricular integration, and ongoing dedication to andragogy. Finally, it showcased IS faculty's campus leadership in curricular assessment. Despite its detail, however, the letter fell on deaf ears. Although the IS Curriculum Committee suggested meeting with the CLAS Curriculum Committee, neither the committee nor the dean's office ever responded.

The next time supporters heard the term "duplication," the provost was explaining to the Board of Governors on September 6, 2007, why IS was such an obvious target for downsizing. What the provost did not say was this: if IS had continued to exist in CLAS, its general education courses would have had to be accepted by other CLAS departments according to CLAS rules. With over 25 such course offerings, IS was perceived as a threat by other CLAS departments since the attractive, rigorous IS courses could then also have been selected by non–IS students to fulfill their Gen Ed requirements.

Interdisciplinary Studies had always been unique in its accomplishments and progress. It served underserved populations of students through interdisciplinary education. It provided distance and extension education long before doing so became trendy — offering almost a third of its courses as telecourses in the 1970s and early 1980s, and taking the weekly workshop courses to the students — even if faculty had to travel more than 75 miles one-way to do so. Through it all, faculty and staff never lost sight of Otto Feinstein's vision of educating the people.

Open Access and Diversity

Besides the program's commitment to an interdisciplinary curriculum that met the needs of adult students, another characteristic set it apart from both other peer programs across the country and other degree programs within Wayne State: its insistence on open admissions. The Department of Interdisciplinary Studies was a major contributor to the university's urban mission and its Strategic Plan of 2004, which underscored, as one of its four core principles, ready access to the programs and services of the university for a diverse body of students who work, have family responsibilities, and commute to campus. The Core Principles are: Urban Mission, Global Presence, Commitment to Innovative Technology, and Commitment to Diversity. The department produced a rich history of offering traditionally disadvantaged groups — first generation, racial minorities (predominantly African Americans), female and low-income students — with access and a unique opportunity for university education through its open admissions policy.

Women and underrepresented groups, particularly African Americans, constituted the majority of the IS student population, at a peak of over 70 percent in 2007. As nontraditional learners, they have not always been able to benefit from a tradition of access to higher education. In fact, women's enrollment in higher education in Michigan and around the nation trailed that of men until the 1970s, when the Women's Movement helped to change societal attitudes, and *gender convergence*, a parallelism in educational goals and career aspirations between men and women, became more apparent (Ntiri 2001). African Americans locally and nationally have historically been faced with inequitable access to higher education due to both internal and external factors that include residential segregation, lack of availability of family resources, institutional barriers, and other cultural factors. At Wayne State, however, located in downtown Detroit, social and public forces applied continuous pressure over the last three decades. As a result, the number of women and underrepresented groups, particularly African Americans, pursuing a higher education, increased measurably. The Interdisciplinary Studies Program's enrollment reflected these advances. Enrollment patterns in the program also mirrored another trend: the most significant gains in higher education in the U.S.A. have occurred among nontraditional learners, adults between 25 and 34 years of age. In 1970, about 16 percent of this age group had completed four or more years of college; by 1990, the proportion who had attended college (to some extent) jumped to 70 percent, with 24 percent of this group having completed at least four years of college. Among African Americans of the same age group, women surpassed men in college attendance, with 33 percent men and 35 percent women having participated in higher education (*American Universities and Colleges* 1997).

The decision to close the Department of Interdisciplinary Studies, with its predominance of African American students and females, may be indirectly linked to the political consequences of "Proposal 2." Passed in November 2006, the Michigan legislation banned affirmative action throughout the state. It put an end to admission preferences for minorities and also to state funding policies for support in higher education. As a premier urban university, WSU has not had an impressive record of retention and graduation of African Americans even when the community was responsive to affirmative action. For example, out of 16 institutions of higher education in the state, Wayne State consistently ranked the lowest or in the lowest five in retention and graduation of African Americans from 2001 to 2005 (Education Trust 2008). In 2004, its graduation rate for undergraduates for African Americans was 12.8 percent compared to 42.5 percent for whites, while the University of Michigan showed a marked advantage with 67 percent graduation for African Americans and 88.5 percent for whites (Education Trust 2008). Indeed, nationwide, among 25 comparable institutions, WSU's graduation rates for African Americans was ranked the second lowest.

Another related, if unstated issue in the reorganization that resulted in dissolution of the Department of Interdisciplinary Studies, is retention of students to graduation. Increasing concern about low retention rates at WSU, including coverage of these rates in the local media, resulted in WSU's president organizing a retention committee in 2007 to address retention campus-wide. It was rumored that IS's open admissions policy was partly to blame. The factors working against IS included the fact that most students were working adults with families, so less than 56 percent typically attended full-time in any given semester. Therefore, six- and eight-year graduation rates are more meaningful measures of student success than the four- or six-year graduation rates, which are typically used for program evaluation. The information analyzed in Appendix 2 shows that the WSU White six-year graduation rate is better (43.6 percent) than the equivalent White IS graduation rate (37.5 percent), but the IS Black six-year graduation rate (12.5 percent) is better than the equivalent WSU Black graduation rate (10.0 percent). While only 19 percent of WSU graduates are African-American, IS had the highest percent of African-American graduates (45.1 percent) of any major over the time period from Fall 1998 to Spring/Summer 2007. Over this same period, IS produced over 2.6 percent of all WSU graduates. Thus the data presented in Appendix 2 indicates that IS had a sensitivity and receptiveness to the urban mission of Wayne State University and specifically to the African-American community that surrounds it.

Whither the African American population now that IS has gone? Based on statistical evidence presented and our more than three decades of experience in IS, there is reason to believe that the elimination of affirmative action will further foster the stagnation of enrollment and graduation success of African Americans and deepen the social divide. A study by Theodore Cross and Robert Bruce Slater (1997) on African American participation in higher education, particularly in prestigious universities, proves that contrary to popular belief, affirmative action has not outlived its usefulness. As metro Detroit witnesses rapid changes in all sectors of today's global economy — restructuring in the automobile industry, increasing automation to take advantage of rapid technological innovations in response to overseas competition, shifting demographics, and an economy that is restructuring itself dramatically — its residents (many of whom have been forced to pursue new careers or mid-career changes) cannot escape the push for renewal through continuous learning to meet the needs and challenges of the 21st century workplace and society. These nontraditional adult learners who came to Detroit's only urban research university now have to contend with a higher education system that is explicitly market driven and marked by increasing elitism in its academic orientation.

The Final Blow: Justice Denied

As the history of the program indicates, Interdisciplinary Studies was no stranger to political struggle. Ever since its creation in 1973, the program had struggled. It struggled for its very birth and for its continuation, recognition, and support within the university for more than three decades. Its journey — from the experimental University Studies/Weekend College Program in 1973, to an established program in the late 1970s, to its new identity as the Interdisciplinary Studies Program in 1992, to its conversion into the Department of Interdisciplinary Studies in 2002 — was a constant battle. As William Newell concludes earlier in this book, in his personal account of the fate of Western College at Miami University, interdisciplinary programs are *"always at political risk."* The ongoing battle at Wayne State was aimed at preserving IS's unique integration of the urban mission, open admissions policy, interdisciplinary curriculum, critical thinking and writing/intensive instruction, and dedication to working, commuting, mostly part-time adult learners, including mostly African-American and women students. Acknowledged by the Association for Integrative Studies (AIS) and by numerous external North Central Association of Colleges and Schools accreditation reviews through the years as one of the best programs of its kind in the nation, IS was an interactive, student-centered, teaching-learning community delivering its curriculum in a variety of creative and innovative teaching modes.

When both of its host colleges were eliminated by the WSU administration and Board of Governors, and IS accepted the lesser of two evils to move to the College of Liberal Arts and Sciences (CLAS), the historical disregard and lack of recognition for the department and its students, alumni, faculty, and staff turned into an aggressive effort to discredit the department with allegations of course duplication, an attack on the quality of open access/open admissions, denigration of its faculty and students, and a charge of budgetary inefficiency. In addition, it was charged with not being needed, based on the premise that interdisciplinarity is "the air we breathe," evident in all academic programs at WSU and at other institutions nationwide. This erroneous declaration only reinforces the gap between the rhetoric of endorsement and the reality of programs that lack resources and work that is discounted in the reward system. That reality was a driving force behind recent formation of a national Consortium on Fostering Interdisciplinary Inquiry (Consortium 2007). The ten prestigious universities in the consortium are at the forefront of interdisciplinary research and education, but they also recognize that obstacles continue to mark the limits of institutional support and sustainability (Consortium 2007). Scant attention was paid to compelling testimony from students and alumni as well as community and legislative supporters. The exceptional records and contributions of faculty who enhanced the teaching, research, scholarly, urban, and service missions of the university were discounted. The uniqueness of the department's nontraditional, often first-generation student population was minimized, and its innovative interdisciplinary curriculum and the nature of its pedagogy were denied appropriate recognition. In addition, IS's impressive record of growing enrollment and high evaluative revenues, all while serving the university's urban mission through a sustained commitment to the program's primarily African American and women adult students, was simply ignored.

And then, with the stroke of a pen, in a swift, unprecedented action, the department was eliminated. There was no due process, no study, no discussion of alternatives. The justification was the "perfect storm" of state- and university-wide financial shortfalls — budget troubles that turned out not to be so troubling, after all. The state shortfall was reinstated within a month. Flush with funds, the university went on to grant new lines to some traditional departments. Thus the alleged savings and charge of being "duplicative" were smokescreens for what influential powerful voices from disciplinary departments had wanted to see happen for years. A clear shift in priorities at WSU was made clear when it was revealed in 2008 that the defunct CULMA (disbanded for supposedly budgetary reasons, among others) would be replaced with an Honors College. Scholarship money is flowing to students aggressively recruited for this new college. Now, the university's urban mission, so integral to both CULMA and IS, will ostensibly be served by the newly funded ($2.1 million) Chair of Community Engagement, to be held by the same president, since resigned, who oversaw their dismantling. But it was not just an ideological turn-about for the university: there were smaller politics as well. In essence, IS had become so successful that it was already, during its brief, two-year tenure in CLAS, attracting an ever larger number of students into its general education courses. The department attracted a student population and revenues otherwise lost to the university, in addition to traditional students from other majors.

Moreover, while the department's overall undergraduate retention and graduation rates were similar to those of the university-at-large, the retention and graduation rates for African American students stood out positively. Unfortunately, the part-time, non-residential, commuting adult student population that IS served did not bring in the same kinds of revenues traditional undergraduate students do, especially students from outside of Detroit, particularly from the suburbs, who live in the dormitories established at WSU over the last several years and who attend full-time to complete their degrees in a shorter period of time. Thus the department's commitment to access for working class students, whose academic accomplishment might be less than that of middle class students, was perhaps its greatest vulnerability.

Could anything have been done differently to preserve the department's programs? The faculty and staff employed many of the strategies delineated in numerous publications and documents on interdisciplinary studies, research, and their cross-secting prospects. (See, for instance, Consortium on Fostering Interdisciplinary Inquiry; *Facilitating Interdisciplinary Research* 2004; Henry 2005; Klein 1996; Klein 2005; Klein, forthcoming). These strategies spanned the critical mass factors for programmatic strength and sustainability and, when pressed for survival, internal and external political activism. Unfortunately, the complex political, ideological, academic, and economic climate which produced the final crushing result overwhelmed even the most reasoned of arguments, the most tested of strategies, and a demonstrated track record of success. In the end, the demise of the program reflected a final irony, for interdisciplinarity has become a new mantra across the entire country, including Wayne State University, where scientific and medical examples of integrative collaboration have become the privileged models.

On September 6, 2007, powerful people at the highest levels of the university prevailed in destroying one of WSU's major assets while spouting misleading and erroneous arguments. The faculty and staff who had come together over the 34-year history of the Department of Interdisciplinary Studies, and who worked with ingenuity and diligence to create an interdisciplinary and integrative curriculum serving a crucial population of students in the Detroit metropolitan area, have been dispersed in almost every case to departments that correspond to the disciplines in which they received their Ph.Ds (even, in some cases, if they have not taught disciplinary content in over thirty years). In the end, a faculty that evolved to think across disciplinary lines and to integrate knowledge and deliver it in ways that were truly student-centered and collaborative now find themselves re-tooling to continue their careers in the very departments where some opponents labored to eliminate the program.

And what about students still in the former department's program "pipeline"? An ISP Infrastructure, composed of a director, two academic advisors, and a support staff member, is set up to advise and otherwise assist students still seeking their degree. In addition, even as ISP faculty integrate into their new CLAS departments, they also continue to be involved in helping students through their programs. After the 2008–2009 academic year when IS courses will no longer be offered, students will still be permitted to earn their BIS and MIS degrees, but only until the end of the 2010–2011 academic year, taking courses elsewhere at the university to fulfill remaining requirements, even if those courses are inconsistent with the mission of the degree program.

The outrage and disappointment of IS faculty and staff are fueled by the same principles of efficacy, transparency, and community that were part of the founding imperatives of the program. The population of students they primarily served is asked now to follow a route through community colleges to the university. While this option may serve many students well, the reductive equation of that path with an intricate and integrated curriculum is a betrayal of the urban mission of the university and the mature interdisciplinary design of the degree program. Moreover, the closure of IS does not only have local implications. It is part of a larger marginalization of alternative and open access programs that is occurring at a time when claims of universal interdisciplinarity are belied by inadequate institutional support for and informed understanding of what it truly entails. Moreover, at a time when many universities are investing millions of dollars in creating on-campus, residential learning communities, heightening their interdisciplinary institutional profiles, and aligning the concept with problem solving, collaborative skills, contextual and holistic thinking, and the ability to integrate multiple sources of knowledge and information, eliminating a nationally recognized model of integrative curriculum, teaching, and learning shortchanges the future for all students in interdisciplinary programs, including the working adult students of Detroit.

REFERENCES

American Universities and Colleges (15th ed.). 1997. New York: Walter de Gruyter.

Consortium on Fostering Interdisciplinary Inquiry. 2007. Minneapolis: Office of Interdisciplinary Initiatives, University of Minnesota. *http://academic.umn.edu/provost/inter disc/inquiry* (accessed August 25, 2008).

Cross, Theodore, and Robert Bruce Slater. 1997. Vital signs: The statistics that describe the present and suggest the future of African Americans in higher education. *Journal of Blacks in Higher Education*, 18: 81–86.

Education Trust. 2008. *Michigan 16 grad rates by race. http://www.collegeresults.org* (accessed August 25, 2008).

Facilitating Interdisciplinary Research. 2004. Washington, D.C.: National Academies Press.

Feinstein, Otto, and Frank Angelo. 1977. *To educate the people: An experimental model for urban adult higher education for the working adult.* Detroit: Center for Urban Studies at Wayne State University.

Furtado, Andre W., and Don Johnson. 1980. Education and rehabilitation in a prison setting. *Journal of Offender Counseling, Services and Rehabilitation* 4 (3): 247–274.

Grant, Gerald, and David Reisman. 1958. *The perpetual dream: Reform and experiment in the American college.* Chicago: University of Chicago Press.

Hendra, Rick, and Edward Harris. 2002. Unpublished results: The University without Walls experiment. *http://www-unix.oit.umass.edu/~hendra/Unpublished%20Results.html* (accessed May 12, 2008).

Henry, Stuart. 2005. Disciplinary hegemony meets interdisciplinary ascendancy: Can interdisciplinary/integrative studies survive, and if so, how? *Issues in Integrative Studies* 2: 1–37.

Klein, Julie Thompson. 1996. *Crossing boundaries: Knowledge, disciplinarities, and interdisciplinarities.* Charlottesville, VA: University Press of Virginia.

_____. 2005. *Humanities, culture, and interdisciplinarity: The changing American academy.* Albany: SUNY Press.

_____. Forthcoming. *Creating interdisciplinary campus cultures.* Hoboken, NJ: Jossey Bass Wiley.

Marton, Ference, and Roger Saljo. 1976. On qualitative differences in learning. *British Journal of Educational Psychology* 46: 4–11, 115–127.

Maruca, Lisa. 2006. Re: Review of IS general education courses. Memo to Roslyn Schindler, Acting Chair, Department of Interdisciplinary Studies. March 29.

Nargis, Hakim, and Peter Bublitz. 2007. BOG approves $9.1 million in cuts. *The South End.* September 12. <*http://media.www.thesouthendnews.com*>.

Ntiri, Daphne W. 2001. Access to higher education for nontraditional students and minorities in a technology-focused society. *Urban Education* 36(1): 129–144.

Ntiri, Daphne W., Stuart Henry, and Roslyn Abt Schindler. 2004. Enhancing adult learning through interdisciplinary studies." In *Degrees of change: Developing and delivering adult degree programs*, ed., Jerry Jerman and James P. Pappas, 41–50. San Francisco: Jossey-Bass.

Schindler, Roslyn Abt. 2006. 'Forming a circle': Creating a learning community for urban commuting adult students in an interdisciplinary studies program. In *The Praeger handbook of urban education* eds., Joe L. Kincheloe, Kecia Hayes, Karel Rose, and Philip M. Anderson, 241–50. Westport, CT: Greenwood Press.

_____. 2002. Interdisciplinarity and the adult/lifelong learning connection: Lessons from the classroom. In *Innovations in interdisciplinary teaching*, ed., Carolyn Haynes, 221–235. Washington D.C.: American Council on Education/Oryx Press.

Trow, Martin. 1984/85. Interdisciplinary studies as a counterculture: Problems of birth, growth, and survival. *Issues in Integrative Studies* 3: 1–15.

CHAPTER 4

Phoenix: From Ashes to Reincarnation at Appalachian State University

Jay Wentworth and Richard M. Carp

After thirty-seven years at Appalachian State University, eighteen as a department, Interdisciplinary Studies has again been re-organized. It is now one of five equally supported interdisciplinary degree-granting programs that had been part of the former Department of Interdisciplinary Studies. The five programs are joined with a residential learning community called Watauga College, a new interdisciplinary general education program, Honors, and academic advising in a new university college under a vice-provost for undergraduate education. All tenure-line faculty members have been located in disciplinary departments and reassigned wholly or partly to interdisciplinary programs. In this chapter we wrestle with "why" and "why now."

The Interdisciplinary Studies programs at Appalachian State have a complex past that requires some general discussion. The history of politics regarding Interdisciplinary Studies can be understood, apart from the not insignificant matter of personalities in four broad categories: (1) issues of periphery and core regarding the institution, including academic encroachment issues; (2) tension that developed because Interdisciplinary Studies originated as, and still includes, the Watauga College living/learning program, and because of this, Interdisciplinary Studies has always had to serve and satisfy the academic vice-chancellor/provost[1] and, in a less obvious way, the student affairs vice chancellor; (3) our "image" on campus; and 4) core/periphery issues within the department.

In addition, we must consider the odd paradox of interdisciplinary studies within the disciplinary academy. From the standpoint of institutions, this situation expresses itself as an illogic of institutional form, while for Interdisciplinary Studies units it expresses itself as a tension between the need for normalization and a mission for insurgency. By "normalization" we mean processes through which Interdisciplinary Studies becomes one among other practices enmeshed in the academy and gains institutional support, gathering control over resources such as space, tenure lines, operating budgets, and status, i.e., joins the core. By "insurgency" we mean processes by which Interdisciplinary Studies unsettles and destabilizes those practices and also, therefore, the resources deployed by the institution for the production of knowledge — such things as space, tenure lines, operating budgets, and status and the means, structures, and processes by which they are acquired and distributed. As we'll argue, this destabilization has to do with a fundamental incongruity between the constitution of interdisciplinarity and the current organizational structures designed to deliver academic programs.

We take it for granted that the content and form of knowledge is affected by the institutional forms in which it is produced, distributed, maintained, and transmitted and that these forms include practices — flexible but routinized — and shared patterns of instrumental behavior that are important components of institutions of knowledge production. That is one reason Interdisciplinary Studies faculty at Appalachian State have been so concerned about their own institutional structures. Based on developments here and at Miami University of Ohio and Wayne State University in Detroit, as well as others discussed in this volume, we now think that stable institutional forms capable of sustaining open-ended, disciplined, interdisciplinary inquiry are to some extent incompatible with those that currently sustain disciplinarity, and that interdisciplinary units are for that reason inherently unstable in the academy. We should say at once that "institutional forms capable of sustaining open-ended, disciplined, interdisciplinary inquiry" have never been fully imagined or completely realized.

At Appalachian, "upper administration" (a useful euphemism in a collegial setting) wanted a change and effected it. Much the same can be said, we believe, about Miami of Ohio and Wayne State. This is not, perhaps, simply because interdisciplinarians have not yet won the battle of normalization. In fact, we agree that our provost is right in noticing the anomaly of a Department of Interdisciplinary Studies inside a College of Arts and Sciences since we used his arguments in 1990! However, given time, he may be similarly uncomfortable about a college run by his office and devoted to interdisciplinarity. It's just a conundrum; interdisciplinarity does not fit into the department and college structure that organizes knowledge production on campus. It requires either a hybrid form (our University College) or a logical absurdity (the old department in a college) or a different logical absurdity, a separate college whose mission includes integrating the work of the other colleges. The dilemma is that being inside the structure toward the core undermines integrity and renders one vulnerable to inside forces such as personalities and departmental politics, while being outside on the periphery is unprotected and tangential to the university's core goals, rendering interdisciplinary studies vulnerable to university-level forces such as budget cuts, regime changes, and new operating models.

As Stan Bailis used to remind us at AIS Board and Annual meetings, interdisciplinarity is as old as disciplinarity. Just when knowledge production divided into disciplines, a critique developed insisting on the interconnection of knowledge and the unity or integration of the world. Yet despite its co-existence with disciplinarity, interdisciplinarity has been persistently institutionally ephemeral. The reason lies, at least in part, in that interdisciplinarity *per se* has no object. The conceit of disciplines is that they are the study of some *thing*: matter in its chemical interactions (chemistry); people insofar as they are mental (psychology); how to present products so people will buy them (marketing). "Interdisciplinarity" is not the study of anything in particular, although each interdisciplinarian or interdisciplinary team studies something. Interdisciplinarity is a method or approach to studying anything rather than something. As Richard has written:

> Interdisciplinarity involves an always developing ensemble of practices for marshalling and integrating knowledge from multiple sources on behalf of a complex and evolving understanding of the world. It insists on the transdisciplinarity of the world, which, as we live in it, requires that we marshal and integrate knowledge from multiple sources on behalf of a complex and evolving understanding [Carp 2008, 6].

This may well be why our provost can't imagine a Department of Interdisciplinary Studies or tenure in interdisciplinarity.

We were never comfortable being a department and cannot be a discipline with a particular object of study, but that we have no subject matter is not true; our subject is whatever makes the world whole. And, although we may also study whatever fragments the world, as in the interdisciplinary study of conflict or terrorism, we are looking for how conflict or terrorism fit because until we understand the connections to the world as it is, we cannot understand how to create a better fit. We uncover the connectedness that makes the world a complex whole rather than just a patchwork of religions, political systems, and so on. We are akin to mathematicians and theoretical physicists who look for elegant expressions of wholeness, but our subject is not numbers or motion; we are akin to poets, whose business it is to take something from here and something from there and demonstrate the startling similarity which emerges when they are juxtaposed just so, but our subject is not words. Our subject, again, is all the ways the world is made whole.

If anything, we are a transdiscipline in that we have a worldview, and frankly, that is what we teach — a view of the world as a complex but inextricably interrelated whole. Our assumption of interrelatedness allows us to be more horizontal, more networking than hierarchical, both linear and nonlinear. In our individual work, we study a particular interstice of knowledges, but we remain a bit Baroque in leaving loose ends. However, we trust those will attach to other research, and we study the ways the parts attach. Though we make maps, we recognize, with Alford Korzybski, that "the map is not the territory"; as we continue to look at larger configurations that make sense of the detail, we are convinced we must not lose the detail. Our underlying belief is that the disciplines cannot see the world fully enough as it is, but can provide gritty detail that interdisciplinarians can fit into broader patterns. We recognize that we cannot know the truth about the whole either, but we continue to elucidate the ways in which it *is* whole.

Historical Development

Overall, Interdisciplinary Studies at Appalachian State has followed, to a point, the historical path predicted by Carroll Quigley (1961 chapter 5), viz., moving from periphery to core and from instrumentality to institution and, until recently, from insurgency to normalization. That we have never fully left periphery, instrumentality, or insurgency, is our glory and our problem.

There have been six major steps in the dance of Interdisciplinary Studies toward and away from the core of the university. Steps one and two were simultaneous. Appalachian State authorized an individually designed, interdisciplinary BA in 1971–72 that still exists in Interdisciplinary Studies. At the same time, three faculty members were given grant money that resulted in a fall 1972 opening of Watauga College — an interdisciplinary, experimental, residential, coed alternative for social science and humanities general education requirements. This program was instrumental and insurgent in that it was a response to rising criticism of American education during the sixties and to the artificial fragmentation of knowledge in the academy; it was seen as a return to the world, where problems and themes do not recognize disciplinary boundaries and education is reconnected with individual learners. Watauga College was firmly in the liberal education tradition (Foxx 1985) yet at the periphery of the institution.

The third step, taken in 1974, was to create tenure track faculty lines in Interdisciplinary Studies; this assured program continuity and promoted longevity, a step toward normalization (though Interdisciplinary Studies was not at the time a department) and the core.

After the gradual addition of faculty positions and interdisciplinary programs, the fourth step was to make Interdisciplinary Studies a department in Arts and Sciences in 1990, concurrent with the dissolution of the General College in which Interdisciplinary Studies was born. The Department included Watauga College, Women's Studies and several interdisciplinary minors — a big step toward normalization and the core.

The fifth step (taken 2007; official July 1, 2008) was to disband the department — a move out to the periphery. As we will explain, this was a top-down decision made with little consultation by a new administration. The sixth step (Spring 2008), was establishing the University College. All Interdisciplinary Studies Department faculty were retained and nominally assigned to disciplinary departments, but most were reassigned 100 percent to one or more interdisciplinary program(s). On August 7, 2008, we discovered that there are a few faculty lines in University College (tenurable, but the person filling the position would be placed in a department and reassigned), yet, for now, all University College programs "borrow" most faculty from departments.

Our Student Constituency

Watauga College students have always been risk-takers; they seem to be generally bright and willing to work, somewhat rebellious or distrustful of authority, more "left" than "right"; they tend to see themselves as "different," and while we get a percentage of "slackers," they tend to last a semester or two or reform. We do recruit, so we advertise for creative, adventuresome students and tend to get them, and we use scholarship lists, so we often get a percentage of very good students.

The Interdisciplinary Studies major always attracted some Watauga College students, who generally do well because of their interdisciplinary preparation. Others represent the range of Appalachian State students — some are seeking a way out of requirements (we weed them out); some are highly motivated, with clear purposes; and between these are many who are not sure what they are seeking but are pretty clear that they don't want the usual disciplinary approach.

Our students are a factor in some of the criticism we have received. While some teachers outside Interdisciplinary Studies like their tendency to ask questions and offer alternatives, some don't; some say our students are "just like other Appalachian State students"; others say they are bright and creative (Foxx 1985, Ch 4). However, most faculty don't know which students are from Watauga/Interdisciplinary Studies, and that's largely our fault.[2] Unfair images — "hippie," "granola," "druggie," "partiers"— stuck to our students. On the Meyers-Briggs Type Indicator, the majority of students in every class Jay tested from the 70s till the present are either INFP or ENFP, but usually every type is represented or only a few of the SJ types are missing. The student body tends to be liberal politically and religiously, but again, we usually have exceptions. We are largely white and middle class. We attempt to help every student understand the value and importance of exceptions of all kinds.

Interdisciplinary Curriculum

The curriculum in Watauga College has been driven, on one hand, by the desire to experiment with: 1) themes and problems, 2) pedagogies (with a bias against straight lecture) that were more active and interactive, and 3) the potential for team teaching. Together this approach made the curriculum responsive to student needs, requests, and ideas. Rubric numbers originally supported these aspects of our curriculum: approved blocks of ten, six, three, and one hour(s). This arrangement allowed enormous freedom and flexibility but also invited constant attention to curricular modification. On the other hand, our curriculum has also been driven by general education requirements for the whole institution. We had to translate our courses into general education equivalencies. As part of a department, Watauga College lost flexibility by having courses listed separately; having a single person do the advising rather than all of us being involved; and during the break-up of Interdisciplinary Studies, losing four of our first-year hours (Wentworth 1985).[3]

The initial Interdisciplinary Studies major curriculum (1990) has been described in detail in two articles in the *AIS Newsletter* (Wentworth 1991a; 1991b). Briefly, we designed a core of 13 hours and a concentration of 24 hours. The core involved a one-hour professional course, an introduction to interdisciplinarity (current topics), and courses on interdisciplinary social science, either interdisciplinary arts or interdisciplinary thinkers and thinking, and a senior seminar. The Individually Designed concentration remained, but we worked with people all over campus to generate new concentrations in environmental policy and planning, women's studies, American studies, liberal studies, urban studies, and a series of "area" concentrations. This provided us with a pool of more or less committed people to be advisors and to promote each concentration. It also created a pool of people committed to the subject matter of the concentration rather than the interdisciplinary context of the concentration.

In 2000, we established a curriculum committee composed of sympathetic faculty members from outside as well as inside the department, ultimately creating a course that looks at knowledge formation, one on ID praxis (including establishment of a portfolio), a seminar on transdisciplinarity, one on method, and a senior seminar. This curriculum works well, and the "Knowledges" course is exceptional. However, the core had always been contentious because of the concentration faculties' commitment to their topic rather than to interdisciplinarity, so the 15-hour core in a now 39-hour major was strategically poor, even though it strengthened the interdisciplinary elements in a way appropriate to a department. This is a key problem in interdisciplinary design; we give a concentration and a minor to specialties without enough students to have a major, but because we add courses that make the students interdisciplinary, we are resented along with, or instead of, being appreciated. That is, we were never a "real" department in the eyes of many; our offerings were seen as irrelevant, and we never made the case that they were relevant to enough people to be able to defend our status as a department.

Disciplinary Threats

From the first year, Watauga College has been doubted, criticized, and threatened. A marijuana incident during that first year gave Watauga a reputation as having druggies, hippies, and other undesirables. Many seem to have resented our freedom with regard to curriculum and resented the fact that we encroached on disciplinary turf without having PhDs in those disciplines.

The latter was emphasized in an article written by two Appalachian State anthropologists. It germinated when Jay said to one of them, excitedly but jokingly, "I think I'm becoming an anthropologist." Of course, at no time did he pass himself off as an anthropologist to faculty or students. However, these "professionals" were incensed that anyone but a "qualified" anthropologist should use their materials (Reck and Keefe 1989).[4] Two attempts to eliminate the department seemed influenced by this view, in spite of discussions we had with the authors after the article appeared.

The most egregious threat was the successful attack mounted on the earth studies program, which Interdisciplinary Studies faculty conceived between 1973–1977. The faculty had a biologist, a chemist/social ecologist, a savvy farmer/counselor, a gardener, an interdisciplinarian and others. According to the director, the program offered 70+ courses and had over $250,000 in grants (private conversation) before the program was ended, largely due to complaints from faculty in the sciences. These ranged from distrust of our holistic health course to complaints that our earth studies mail was coming to the Geology Department. Genuine concerns were not brought to our faculty for discussion; they just festered. After five years, the program was simply eliminated by the administration, though two courses went to the Department of Technology.

Leadership and Faculty

Institutional leadership for Watauga College/Interdisciplinary Studies began with an innovative chancellor, a conservative provost, and a collegial, innovative, supportive, experienced, and respected dean of the General College. The General College housed general education, student advising and orientation, and special programs such as Honors and Watauga that fell outside the other colleges. It had no "departments" and it could not confer degrees, so the Individually Designed BA was conferred by the College of Arts and Sciences, though it was administered through the General College. In 1979, a new provost took over and saw us through our long, mostly successful period from then until his retirement in 2003. He said recently that he "supported undergraduate education primarily," not research. He accepted the idea that departments look at knowledge in ways different than how the "real world" works, and he liked Interdisciplinary Studies because we worked in ways that were more in line with the real world.[5] Thus, the presence of supportive or at least neutral chancellors, a supportive provost for thirty-four years, and, for the first eighteen years, a very supportive dean, was the key to our existence and astonishingly good fortune.

As a living/learning program, Watauga College also had a "shadow" vice-chancellor of student affairs, which involved often heated issues of control over the residence hall and its staff, as well as politics between the provost and the vice-chancellor for student affairs. These issues plagued Watauga College and thus Interdisciplinary Studies, but now they are separate programs, so Interdisciplinary Studies is no longer residential.

Internally, leadership in Watauga College/Interdisciplinary Studies goes hand-in-hand with faculty because all but two leaders have come from the program faculty. Furthermore, we have always had student-centered, hard-working, creative, collegial, and highly qualified faculty with degrees from such schools as Duke, UNC–Chapel Hill, Emory, Cambridge, Stanford, and Northwestern. Three were interdisciplinary; one was interdisciplinary, though given in a discipline; and the others were disciplinary. The founders were three faculty from English, art, and philosophy. Only one was a director, our first, a charismatic man but a poor administrator who lasted one year. Then came four directors in four years, which was both a problem of continuity and a blessing since we may have avoided the cult of personality so often associated with alternative programs. The turnover also gave faculty and students more responsibility for and stake in the program.

The fourth director stayed for five years (1975–1980) and set the tone for all directors thereafter. He was learning on the job, a listener and facilitator who respected the faculty and students and was intent on protecting and serving them. He was also made responsible for General Honors and for faculty lines in Interdisciplinary Studies and for the Individually Designed Major in Interdisciplinary Studies. His successor stayed for ten years and functioned in a similar way. He presided over the move to department status in the College of Arts and Sciences, which happened in 1990 when the General College dean stepped down and the provost eliminated the General College. We did not want to be a department in Arts and Sciences on the grounds that we would move closer to cooptive institutionalization (normalization), but with the General College gone, no other option was offered; we would become a department or be disbanded. Both the dean and the provost thought that we would be safer as a department in any case, and we would be able to grant degrees. To move Interdisciplinary Studies, the provost overcame determined resistance from science chairs, who did not see Interdisciplinary Studies as legitimate or rigorous, and the resource worries of others.[6] As a result of this move, Watauga College became a kind of general education wing of the Department of Interdisciplinary Studies.

Dr. Kay Smith[7] succeeded as chair in 1990 and continued to be collegial and supportive, but as chair of a department, many duties/decisions fell to her that had not been part of the purview of previous leaders. She had directors of Watauga College and women's studies under her, as well as a personal tendency to take on projects and decisions in deference to the busy faculty, so there were more top-down processes than previously, yet because Kay was loved and respected and was obviously working for us, objections tended to be constructive.

Other top-down effects came as the result of becoming a department. For example, the provost stopped our habit of doing everything (curriculum, student management, personnel decisions, etc.) as a committee of the whole. The huge advantage of a committee of the whole is the transparency that diminishes communication issues. Committee structures invite cliquishness and poor communication, so this loss was a factor in the breakdown of collegiality within the department. A huge disadvantage of committees of the whole is a tendency toward overwork for faculty members and a sense that no smaller group can be trusted to act on behalf of the whole. This was a factor in our difficulty integrating new junior faculty members into the department. It was also a factor in Kay's tendency "to take on projects and decisions in deference to the busy faculty," which might have benefited from collegial participation, and it contributed to estrangement on the periphery, for Kay was in the core and when she acted alone, it was seen as core-driven action.

During Kay's tenure, we arrived at a time when everyone was a full professor and new faculty were hired or assigned to us. This situation was partly generational and partly, and ironically, a core/periphery issue within our department. There were six faculty who had been in Watauga College for a long time, and these faculty continued as though the Watauga assumptions were shared, and as though Watauga College was the *raison d'être* of the department. It also reflects the residual resentment about being made a department on the part of some of the Watauga College faculty. Any new member was likely to feel left out, the more so if they imagined they had been hired into the Department of Interdisciplinary Studies, which included Watauga as one among several programs. Richard must be included among this group.

Furthermore, the Watauga College core's experience in a protected program did not suit them for the new demands made by being a department. The situation was uncomfortable for all and threatening to new faculty who did not feel accepted yet needed to get tenure and promotion. Someone needed to create procedures that allowed the core and periphery within the department to communicate. Kay, as a person who had quickly accommodated to the core and been a director of Watauga, wasn't in a good position to create those processes or even to recognize the problem.

Kay stepped down in 1999, at least in part in response to tensions between the department and the larger university, along with very complex politics between the vice chancellors of academic affairs and student development. Only one older (but peripheral) member was left willing to become chair; new faculty were not yet ready; and our department was still chaffing against some of the demands of being a department. We needed new leadership.

Richard Carp was hired as the first leader of Interdisciplinary Studies from outside the program and the university and was the first with experience as a chair. He brought a more sophisticated but also more institutional approach to the job, which was required by the dean and provost, so he also presided over an even more complete development of our journey to the core of the university. Since he came from outside, it was easier for him to recognize problems and make changes, and the more alienated faculty could voice complaints they did not express to Kay. Whether newer faculty fears of alienation and not being heard were justified or not, the core/periphery situation had to be exposed and ameliorated because feelings could have easily gotten worse. In response, Richard worked with the faculty to establish written criteria for personnel practices and decisions that were fair and equitably applied, along with reducing the teaching load from 4/4 to 3/3 and establishing a research expectation. Still, part of the issue was that the core group began to feel less respected under some of the rules for faculty meetings, for example, and resisted the loss of free-wheeling discussions (previously dominated, unintentionally, by core faculty), the focus on "business" rather than curriculum (as in Watauga College), and so on, while some of the peripheral group were relieved by these same developments. We see these changes as the costs of institutionalization rather than, as Richard's methods *per se,* but we also see them as the costs of opening the Department core to its periphery. The core did in fact lose some control to the periphery. In spite of the fact that Richard's leadership was privately facilitative and respectful of the faculty and staff in the best possible way, publicly, he was Chair, and some of the old Watauga faculty never did trust him, leaving him feeling a part of the periphery rather than joined to the core.

Disbanding the Department

There are at least seven contributing factors and a probability that bear on both "Why have major reorganization?" and "Why now?" First, we had a turnover in administration that included, in July 2004, a new chancellor, who is an accountant, and a new interim provost, who became permanent in December of that year. He is an experimental psychologist and a reductionist. According to a reliable source, the new dean of Arts and Sciences arrived from the University of Alabama in the fall of 2005, willing, for reasons unknown to us, to dissolve Interdisciplinary Studies. All three are decent men trying to do a good job, and in fact are doing a good job in many ways, but these changes eliminated all our support above the level of department chair. Everyone who had any history of supporting our department had moved on. That's bad luck, but also at least partly the result of larger factors.

Second, and a key larger factor, more in Jay's mind more than Richard's, is the general trend toward a business/corporate model for higher education that was put firmly in place at Appalachian. For Jay, the business model seems to explain the kind of people chosen for leadership positions, and it came to us with a top-down view of management. The decision to dissolve Interdisciplinary Studies clearly came from the provost.

A third factor was the department's failure to develop leadership within itself or among supportive faculty members in the larger university. In the first three years after Richard was appointed chair, three important leadership positions became open — the directors of Watauga College, women's studies, and sustainable development. In each case, no qualified tenure-line faculty members applied for the position. This led to a director of Watauga

College from student development, rather than the faculty, and part-time, temporary faculty members directing sustainable development, women's studies, and, later, Watauga College. The stature of the department in the university was further diminished, which lessened the effectiveness of program leadership, and which contributed to the loyalty problems alluded to below.

The fourth factor was in the department itself. A department that had been among the most collegial departments on campus for nearly thirty years became contentious for the first time. As we know from experience, departments have cycles; we picked a poor time for a downturn. We've mentioned the aging of faculty and the core/periphery split in the department. Additionally, there were outside directors of interdisciplinary programs with allegiance to those programs but not Interdisciplinary Studies. Simultaneously, the provost's office announced that we were going on a matrix system and that each department would be held to higher FTE (full time equivalent) numbers, and our department was low and thus, expensive.[8] Richard, as chair, saw we were in serious trouble and suggested dramatic changes, which were widely resisted, which in turn, raised his anxiety level and fueled the contention. He then pushed, necessarily but not always in the best way, and people got testy, and resisted more, not in the best way either, and another personnel issue with Watauga College leadership festered.

The fifth factor, having to do with personalities, was that Jay (the senior core member) was gone the spring semester of '05 and the spring semester of '06 and Richard was on leave for '05–'06. With both gone, Richard was easily scapegoated by some in the department, to the point of a petition for his dismissal that split the department. The Department Personnel Committee refused to recommend one of two junior faculty members for early tenure, dividing along a line similar to that regarding the petition, further dividing the department. We were in bad shape and looked worse.

Sixth, we had been privileged for a long time and we had stopped most of our publicizing and proselytizing. We had become insular as a way of protecting ourselves and because we were so busy with recruiting, designing curriculum, learning new subjects, working with students, etc. We tended to be arrogant in our view of our own accomplishments and as ignorant of others' work as they were of ours. These factors made it hard for the department to get a clear sense of how it looked from outside and to adapt to a changing institution. Critically, over its first ten years as a department, Interdisciplinary Studies did not establish either a publication requirement for faculty, or a scholarly profile visible from the outside.[9] This contributed to the appearance that Interdisciplinary Studies is a field that "studies nothing."

Finally, we didn't really make the case for our department and its curriculum in ways that were sufficient to create a large, loyal faculty following who would support us, though we thought we had one, and surely had supporters, but their voice was silent or ignored. While Jay suspects that we could have mounted a letter-writing campaign from alums (Richard has different intuitions),[10] neither of us thought it would do any good because the decision seemed irrevocably made.

On the other hand, we did several things to meet objections. The department voted to let sustainable development, the largest interdisciplinary program, become independent. We sent letters outlining reasons to maintain the department. By stepping up individual class enrollment and teaching a large class in Watauga College and another in Interdisciplinary Studies, we dramatically increased our FTE/faculty member (one of Richard's change goals) in one year — thus answering the charge of being expensive (which had been true) and inflexible (which had not).[11] We introduced a new research agenda in Watauga College and started an Edible Schoolyard (a student-run garden on the grounds of the Living Learning Center) while initiating innovative processes in the residence hall — all to no avail. Money and productivity were not the real issues, and the department was all but officially scuttled while Richard was on leave.

We must also consider the possibility that "why now" has as much to do with cyclical factors outside our control, including the aging out of most of the tenured faculty members. Establishing a second generation of tenured faculty members is a key step in normalization, one not completed at Appalachian State, Miami of Ohio, or Wayne State. Of course, all of these programs had added new faculty members over the years, due to growth and retirement replacements. However, at the time of disbanding, stalwart original or near original members of the department remained and exerted substantial leadership in the departments (e.g., Ron Aronson, Roz Schindler and Julie Thompson Klein at Wayne State; Bill Newell, William Green and Gene Metcalf at Miami of Ohio; and Jay Wentworth and Leslie [Bud] Gerber at Appalachian). A full new generation of faculty, with renewed senior leadership from a second generation, was not fully established. This was not, we believe, primarily the result of any of the factors considered above in the history of our department. On the other hand, concerns such as insularity, self-satisfaction, and institutional naïveté may be occupational hazards for Interdisciplinary Studies departments. If so, they are pitfalls, and should be guarded against.

Conclusion

There were probably no strategies we could have employed to save our department once the provost took office, especially with our ducks scattered all over the pond. When Jay talked with the provost he said, "All departments are disciplines; Interdisciplinary Studies is by definition not a discipline; therefore, Interdisciplinary Studies cannot be a department" (private conversation). Whatever way one interprets this statement we are left with the fact that the administration had the power and exercised it for inexplicit reasons and without consultation with us of any substantive kind. However, we didn't make it nearly difficult enough. Part of the problem was our preoccupation with planning the new facilities built expressly for us by the vice chancellor for student affairs and by the provost who retired in 2003, the actual move over two semesters, and the design and implementation of a new Watauga College curriculum for our new circumstances. We now see the new facility as a "sunset" effect that gave the maximum sense of acceptance and security at the exact moment when we became least secure; it was like building a house before a divorce. A result was that we did not have a lot of current assessment data. We had some older material for Watauga College but almost none for Interdisciplinary Studies, though we had begun formative assessment of our program by assessing Senior Seminar presentations. Our Watauga College data had always returned with the same positive result, so we weren't worried about that. We also had never looked for large donations from alums, and we had not done anything visible for the university recently, except provide excellent education for our students.

For now, interdisciplinary practices that are institutionally, culturally, and individually transforming and can survive over time are *ad hoc* and have practical and time-limited work to do. These practices survive over time by being repeatedly, though perhaps sporadically, practiced, rather than by creating enduring entities. The work persists, but the groups do not. However they create a network of intellectually productive relationships with little regard for disciplinary and departmental definitions. In this way they subtly but persistently develop practices outside disciplines. We believe over time such networks of faculty relationships may also give rise to novel interdisciplinary activities, and we speculate that our rich history of such groups is connected with the contemporary resilience of interdisciplinarity at Appalachian State, though clearly other factors are at work, as well.

We conclude:

- Support from administration above the department level is crucial; more is better.
- Do excellent assessment regularly and keep it in front of your chief academic officer.
- Keep your bottom line as in-line as possible.
- Avoid isolation by regularly providing useful, visible service to the university.

- Gather sustained alumnae support and raise money. Programs with endowments, grants, gifts, and sustained giving are more solid in this business environment.
- Most important, we will never fit comfortably in a discipline-driven culture as a department or any other administrative unit. Of course, if "fits" are offered, take them if you wish, being aware that neither choice makes the program necessarily more secure.
- Anticipate periodic disruptions; anticipating disruption, remember the virtues of dispersed (or guerilla) organizational models, despite their weaknesses.
- Value insurgency as well as normalization.
- Use whatever resources can be obtained, without becoming attached to them.
- Stay lucky, but don't ever expect to stay safe!

All this said, we at Appalachian State are left with considerable opportunity. Again, while the department officially ended on July 1 of 2008, our programs are all intact and housed in a new, degree-granting University College so, in a sense we traded a department for a college — not a bad deal. The junior faculty members in the department received tenure, albeit in disciplinary departments, and all faculty members are in secure, full-time employment. In addition, Interdisciplinary Studies has retained its degree and several of our former concentrations have been awarded degrees: sustainable development, women's studies, global studies (housing all international area concentrations), and Appalachian Studies. Indeed, we'd be elated if it were not for two facts. The first is that there is reassigned time (sometimes 100 percent) but *no designated faculty* for any of the programs in UC.[12]

The second fact is that while the provost's distaste is for a *Department* of Interdisciplinary Studies, not for interdisciplinarity, the kind of interdisciplinarity that he supports might be defined differently than we would like. We applaud his vision in creating the University College, which followed a model initially suggested by Richard. However, since the provost believes that the Department of Psychology is interdisciplinary because it includes experimental, industrial, clinical, and school psychology (private conversation with Jay), it is unlikely that his views square with our own worldview regarding our integrative function. We have no way of knowing how restrictive such a view might be, but as part of the politics in interdisciplinarity, definitions can be important.

We are certainly fortunate that our provost has allowed and supported so much interdisciplinarity and that he chose a vice provost of undergraduate education who seems eager and able to provide the upper administration mediating function so long provided by two former deans and a provost and without which our form of insurgency doesn't seem to be possible. Thus, in our new incarnation we have an exciting opportunity to improve, clarify, and even expand interdisciplinarity at Appalachian State, so we'll set a path to rectify former errors without becoming too attached to our current place in the University.

NOTES

1. His title changed, but we will refer to that position as Provost for simplicity.

2. Note the continued need for the /. This represents the extent to which, eighteen years later, the marriage between the degree granting department and the general education program is incomplete.

3. Those interested in our curriculum can see an example of our experimentation in Wentworth (1985).

4. This article was poorly researched and biased, but it presented real issues that would have been better resolved if they had come up before such an article was written. Emotions were too high to solve them afterward, when all trust was gone.

5. Harvey Durham, interview by Jay Wentworth. Boone, NC, 22 July 2008.

6. Durham interview.

7. For this audience, names are not so important. However, we'll use her name and our names to simplify discussion of our roles/perspectives in some detail.

8. In 2003/2004, our FTE/faculty member was 274.8, whereas our target, established by the provost, was 486.2.

9. Faculty members engaged in a lot of scholarship as they mastered new bodies of material in order to teach new classes. The classes themselves and some conference publications were often the only outcomes.

10. From Richard's point of view, the long time insularity and tendency to arrogance are probably more important than the failure to make a case. Both the provost and the chancellor developed their ideas about departments of Interdisciplinary Studies from their outsider's view of the one at Appalachian State. Since it was insular, they were never able to get a realistic sense of what was really going on or enter into substantive dialogue about interdisciplinarity. To the extent it was arrogant, they may have felt disrespected and dismissed, rather than valued and invited to participate. Of course, they also made little attempt to communicate and thereby showed their disrespect.

11. In 2003/2004, our FTE/faculty member was 274.8 compared to a target of 486.2; in 2004/2005, FTE/faculty member rose to 340 compared to a target of 428.9, in 2004/2005 it rose again to 423.2 compared to a target of 421.7. Despite the fact that we had met our target, and raised FTE/faculty member by 53.5 percent, we were informed in 2004/2005 that the department would be disbanded.

12. This threatens Watauga College the most because of the time and commitment required to sustain it, so will it die a slow death? What about women's studies with its small classes? Who will put in the untold hours needed to design experimental programs, to make living-learning programs work when all but a few faculty are in departments subject to departmental personnel committees? We know where depending "on the kindness of strangers" got Blanche Dubois.

REFERENCES

Bateson, Gregory. 1979. *Mind and nature: A necessary unity.* New York: Bantam Books.

Carp, Richard. 2008. Relying on the kindness of strangers: CEDD's report on hiring, tenure, promotion in interdisciplinary studies. *Association for Integrative Studies Newsletter* 30 (2): 1–7.

Durham, Harvey. 2008. Interview by Jay Wentworth in Boone, NC, 22 July.

Foxx, Virginia. 1985. *Watauga College: The residential college at Appalachian State University,* PhD diss. University of North Carolina at Greensboro.

Hubbard, Glenda T. 1961. *The effects of a residential college upon the level of interpersonal communication, academic achievement, environmental perceptions, and attrition of college freshmen.* PhD diss., University of Miami.

Messer-Davidow, Ellen. 2002. *Disciplining feminism: From social activism to academic discourse.* Durham, NC: Duke University Press.

Quigley, Carroll. 1961. *The evolution of civilizations: An introduction to historical analysis.* New York: Macmillan.

Reck, Gregory G., and Susan E. Keefe. 1989. Nonanthropologists teaching anthropology: Anthropology as intellectual hobby," *Urban Anthropology and Studies of Cultural Systems and World Economic Development* 18(1): 67–75.

Wentworth, Jay. 1985. The Watauga College United Nations core curriculum. *Association for Integrative Studies Newsletter* 7(2): 1ff.

_____. 1991a. Creating an interdisciplinary studies major: Interdisciplinary process in the state university setting. *Association for Integrative Studies Newsletter* 13(1) 1ff.

_____. 1991b. Creating an interdisciplinary studies major: Interdisciplinary content in the state university setting." *Association for Integrative Studies Newsletter* 13(2): 1ff.

CHAPTER 5

From Cutting Edge to Cutting Board: The Inter-Arts Center at San Francisco State University

James W. Davis

The Inter-Arts Center (IAC) programs at San Francisco State University represented a level of accomplishment and innovation that could easily be compared with the legendary programs at Black Mountain College during an earlier part of the twentieth century. Founded in 1954, the IAC programs focused upon experimental and interdisciplinary expression in the arts. At a new Creative Arts building dedication ceremony in fall 1994 NEA Director Jane Alexander stated, "Of all the programs in the arts at SFSU, there are two that people frequently speak of on the East Coast, and one of these is the Inter-Arts Center" (with the other being the recently developed multimedia program at the Downtown Center of SFSU). Similarly, the fall 1994 issue of *Art Journal* (an official scholarly publication of the College Art Association) carried a major article on new and experimental directions in the arts on the West Coast. Over 50 percent of the extensive number of artists, critics, and arts teachers mentioned as representing the "cutting edge" were IAC graduates and current or former IAC faculty. In the same article many of the arts presentation sites on the West Coast mentioned as those most representative of significant new directions were founded or directed by IAC graduates (Weiffenbach 1994).

On a more local level, the IAC offered distinct alternatives from the more conventional discipline-based programs in the other departments in the College of Creative Arts at San Francisco State University and elsewhere. While students in single-discipline programs pursued studies leading to a traditional goal (musician, dancer, broadcast specialist, visual artist, art historian, etc.), studies in IAC allowed one to investigate new, emerging fields of study that combined and synthesized these separate areas, and, for the more adventurous and imaginative student, it was possible to even forge entirely new forms of expression.

"Interdisciplinary arts" at San Francisco State thus came to be defined as original, creative works that synthesized theory and practice (ideas and applications), and that also integrated two or more elements of expression (choosing from sound, image, movement, text, and spatial/temporal modes of expression). Such works were also perceived as bridges between life and art, as well as ones that could not ordinarily be pursued in courses in the more conventional arts disciplines. Examples of the kinds of creative works that had been commonly produced by students in both the undergraduate and masters level IAC degree programs included video art, acoustic and digital sound art and sound installations, installation art, computer art, interactive media and multimedia installations, non-traditional performance art, and book arts.

The IAC's cutting edge approaches to interdisciplinary arts education and its national status did not prevent it from eventually being permanently "cut" from the university, after years of inadequate funding that left it extremely vulnerable during a period of financial downsizing. This essay will briefly review its history, emphasizing the structural and financial vulnerabilities that ultimately precipitated its gradual but inevitable downfall.

History

Founded in 1954, the IAC programs focused upon experimental and interdisciplinary expression in the arts. More specifically, the first interdisciplinary arts program at San Francisco State began as a concentration in creative arts education. Historical program internal review and academic program proposal documents indicate that this program was instituted due to a need perceived by faculty and students for a "broad based cross-divisional major" for candidates with at least "one year teaching experience," and that could be used for the "improvement of teaching the arts in the public schools." This goal, no doubt, reflects the primary stress upon teacher education on the San Francisco State campus, which has had a long tradition of teacher training. The interest in interdisciplinary studies in this new program also may be perceived as an early example of the interest in cross-disciplinary and experimental studies that would appear on many campuses during the coming two decades of the 1960s and 70s.

In 1962 the concentration in creative arts education was supplemented with the establishment of an additional, complementary interdisciplinary major in "Interdisciplinary Studies: Concentration in Creative Arts." A "CAI" prefix (Creative Arts Interdisciplinary) was instituted to identify the courses in both of these programs (the older arts education one and newer interdisciplinary studies one). Both programs were viewed as college-wide programs within creative arts, but with a stated purpose to inquire into "connections between arts and society." Unlike the arts education program, the newer concentration was devised for development of interdisciplinary artists through the pursuit of disciplinary courses in the various departments (separate disciplines) in the arts.

A BA in Interdisciplinary Studies: Creative Arts first appeared in 1964–65 — a full decade after the concentration in creative arts education began. The structure of this undergraduate degree program involved 20 credit hours in a variety of creative arts departments, plus 20 additional credits in a single department. As such, this program was more multidisciplinary than interdisciplinary for there were no "synthesis" courses specifically designed to develop integrative ideas, understanding, or creative methodologies in the arts.

An effort was made in 1969–70 to address the fragmented and multidisciplinary nature of the programs that had continued up to this point through development and requirement of synthesis courses. In the BA, for example, 10 credits of such courses were instituted, with the remaining 30 credits being required to be in at least five of the creative arts departments. The number of declared undergraduate majors had reached 175 in 1968.

Creative Arts Interdisciplinary was then merged with the Film Department in 1974, and, according to program documents of that time, was stated to stress "new" and "experimental" areas of study. A 1974 program review written by faculty supervising and teaching in the program stressed a societal need for "integrative" rather than "compartmentalized" studies, and a need for "innovative" programs. The review documents from that time did not clearly state what "integrative" or "innovative" programs were intended to imply. Also, the programs were revised to be even more integrative in nature, and to encompass studies throughout the entire campus, drawing from knowledge and experiences outside the arts. Some of the concerns expressed at that time by the faculty with oversight over the program as well as students enrolled within it included an over-stress upon theoretical studies over creative applications. Students, especially, wanted more interdisciplinary studio practice courses. Documents from that time indicate that the emphasis upon theory over practice may have been largely rooted in a lack of funding. As we all probably know, studio courses are more costly due to their equipment and space needs, as well as their time-intensive nature, when compared with lecture and discussion courses.

In 1979 the CAI program was established as an "Auxiliary Academic Unit," apart from the Film Department, and the name for the unit was changed to the Center for Experimental and Interdisciplinary Arts (CEIA). Reasons cited for the change were that the programs were not inherently film programs per se and the new name was required to establish a clearer identity. The choice of a "center" rather than a "department" was reflective of a desire that the program have more "flexible relationships" involving active instructional and administrative participation by faulty from the various departments in creative arts.

The name of the center was changed to the Inter-Arts Center (IAC) in fall 1986. Additionally, the dean of the School (now College) of Creative Arts assigned a group of non-degree functions between 1986–89, which considerably expanded the roles of IAC from its academic degrees to general College-wide support functions. These new roles were called "Special Programs," and included: (1) an AudioVision Institute and program, which devised an Emmy Award–winning program using a method of doing audio transcriptions of the visual imagery appearing in films for the visually impaired; (2) an Arts Bridge to College Program, which offered courses each term for disadvantaged but talented high school students to encourage them to continue on to college studies in the arts; (3) College of Creative Arts Computer Lab supervision, which involved two labs, with one being used as a site where computer arts courses could be offered by the various creative arts departments, and the other being an Advanced Computer Imaging Center where advanced computer animation courses were offered using the IAC prefix; (4) the offering of introductory and advanced computer animation courses using the IAC prefix, and which were applicable to most departmental majors in the college; (5) liberal studies major coordination, advisement, and core course offerings (see Goldsmith in this volume); and (6) coordination of the Creative Arts Symposia, a major annual panel and lecture series bringing together major figures with expertise in contemporary social, creative, and educational issues in the arts. All of these "Special Programs" were to be fulfilled within the limited resources assigned to IAC in addition to its three academic programs.

By 1992, the bachelor's and two master's programs had evolved further from their origins as multidisciplinary studies that stressed studies within the disciplines in the departments of the College of Creative Arts. As this time, it had become apparent that the degree titles and required courses needed to reflect the increased interdisciplinarity desired by the students and faculty who were directly involved in the program, and that could not be meaningfully fulfilled only by taking disciplinary courses. As a consequence, the titles for these degree programs were both changed to have a common title of Creative Arts: Concentration in Interdisciplinary Arts. Consistent with this, many of the courses required within both of these programs were re-titled and redefined to emphasize their actual emphasis upon a synthesis of knowledge and expressive elements.

Concurrent with the above changes in the Interdisciplinary Arts programs it became obvious that the originating master's level program in creative arts education was in drastic need of updating. This program had received very little attention during the preceding fifteen to twenty years, and had become outdated. An in-depth study of this program along with the needs of constituencies that it had served was conducted by the faculty teaching in the program, along with an advisory committee comprised of faculty from the Art and Broadcast departments. It was clear that the clientele that this program served extended well beyond the usual learning sites served by traditional arts education programs in art, music, theatre, or dance, as these are found on most campuses. Many of the program's graduates had become among the major leaders in the arts organizations (in art, music, theatre, dance, and interdisciplinary arts) throughout the San Francisco Bay Area, and it was clear that its thrust was broadly facilitative in nature. The first stage in the changes was to change the program title to be a master's Concentration in Creativity and Arts Education. The term "creativity" was chosen to go with that of "arts education" due to the vast range of public roles the graduates of the program had come to serve over the years, including curators and learning facilitators in museums, gallery directors, facilitators in non-traditional arts presentation organizations (which by then had come to proliferate in the Bay Area), and other, related professional roles. As a consequence, the program became a two-track opportunity to meet the needs of those wishing to teach in the arts and those wishing to found, direct, or otherwise facilitate within arts organizations. At this point, the master's degree in creativity and arts education encompassed several goals: (1) stimulate creativity; (2) explore ways in which creativity can build bridges between differing groups; (3) develop skills in ways that new media and technologies were changing the creative process in contemporary society; (4) learn ways to initiate and oversee/develop programs in the arts outside of traditional classrooms; and (5) investigate of ways in which creativity varies according to ethnic, gender, and other differences between individuals and groups.

During the final years of its existence from 1992–2003, IAC programs explored several additional opportunities that were perceived by the faculty and students to be of significance. These included: (1) collaborations between teams of artists with expertise from varying media and creative methodologies (unlike traditional disciplinary programs in the arts, IAC students came from backgrounds in all of the arts, rather than a single discipline); (2) integration of issues between the arts and life/society (in courses with potent titles such as "Arts and Social Change" or "Thought and Image"); (3) study of methods for employing creative expressions as catalysts for constructive social change (this possibility emerged within almost all IAC courses); (4) creation of new art forms combining visual, audio, spatial/temporal, textual, and kinesthetic elements that were not available within traditional disciplines in the arts; (5) synthesis of theory and practice in all courses (also very uncommon in most traditional disciplines where they are rigidly separated, and taught, respectively, only by "theorists/historians" or "practitioners"); (6) a merging of knowledge and methodologies in the arts with knowledge and methodologies in non-arts fields of inquiry and pursuit, including the sciences, social sciences, and humanities; and (7) community outreach efforts related to all three programs to assure that studies were rooted in conditions found in the real world, as opposed to the more detached nature dominant within traditional academic departments.

Faculty Issues

Between 1970 and 1985 the CEIA/IAC academic center hired both lecturers and five tenure-track faculty members. The periodic self-review and program proposal documents from this period indicate that the hiring of the tenure track faculty was accomplished to provide stability, continuity, and academic legitimacy for the program. An "associates" program was also developed during this same period. The associates were faculty from the various departments in the College, and were intended to provide input from the other programs in the College. The term "associates" was later changed in the 1980s to "mentors," reflecting what was perceived as an advisory role, as opposed to a central faculty role in the conventional sense. The purpose of the associates/mentors was to provide input to students in the CEIA/IAC program, with the expectation that student projects (and especially the culminating ones in the two graduate programs) would develop at an advanced, graduate level. The culminating projects were also perceived as developing under the tutelage of the sponsoring mentor's department taken as a whole. One goal of this approach was the hope that the experimental and interdisciplinary nature of the project would inspire students majoring in that discipline to think and work in a more interdisciplinary manner. However, two significant problems arose from this system: (1) the faculty mentors were generally not interdisciplinary artists/theorists and (2) it was extremely difficult to convince instructors whom a student barely knew to consent to spend the considerable extra time with someone who wasn't in their own department. These problems occurred despite the College of Creative Arts having a policy requiring the departments to "sponsor an agreed upon number of students" in the CEIA/IAC programs. It seems clear that, while a significant number of Creative Arts faculty idealized a collaborative venture in support of interdisciplinary pursuits of the CEIA/IAC students, they were simply overwhelmed with other duties in their own departments. Another issue was equally problematic: it is close to impossible to imagine a graduate student "culminating" an entire "program" in the form of a final, interdisciplinary project when the very faculty members who were supervising them had only a minimal involvement in the student's overall program.

The five tenure and tenure-track positions that had accumulated between 1970 and 1985 were gradually eliminated between 1985 and 1989. The resignations of these faculty appear to be the result of various forms of pressure from the dean of the College of Creative Arts, who had come to perceive the primary function of the CEIA/IAC as a service organization for the School that was at as least as important as its academic, degree granting purpose. As of fall 1989, the only faculty member who was tenure/tenure track and who was specifically assigned to the degree programs and their students was the director of IAC and Special Programs who was hired in 1989. At this point in time, the remaining five full-time equivalent faculty members in IAC (other than the director) were all part-time and temporary lecturers. The assumption was that the new director would somehow inspire a substantive, reliable, and on-going allegiance on the part of the faculty in the departments in the School for the IAC, and that there would be an adequate number of truly interdisciplinary arts faculty regularly available from these departments to lend stability and continuity to the programs as mentors. This expectation was assumed despite evidence that the use of "associates" and "mentors" borrowed from the departments applied in previous years didn't work, lowered program performance standards, fragmented the program, and contributed to an unstable and rather depressing environment for both the students and faculty.

Between 1990 and 1994, several waves of economic hardships struck California. This, in turn, resulted in a loss of 40 percent of the IAC faculty, far in excess of the reductions experienced in the departments representing the traditional arts disciplines. As one finds on other campuses, it is far easier to eliminate temporary faculty than those who are on tenure track or have tenure. Between 1992 and 1995 almost all of the earlier mentioned "Special Programs" assigned to IAC were eliminated, including the AudioVision Institute, Arts Bridge to College, the annual Creative Arts Symposia, and the college-wide computer lab.

When a new dean (Dean Morrison) was hired in fall 1995, one of the first things he decided was that the BA program in IAC must be suspended (no new applications accepted). Although it is true that this program discontinuance represented a sad testimony to the status of interdisciplinary studies in the arts at San Francisco State, there was also some logic to the decision in the prevailing context of dramatically reduced faculty, space, and equipment resources that resulted from the economic collapse in California. It was simply impossible to meaningfully sustain an undergraduate major along with two master's degree programs with two classrooms devoted to the program (one lecture room and one studio), what had become the equivalent of three full-time lecturers, and practically no program support funds. After four years with no increase in program resources allocated by the dean, the BA was entirely discontinued in 1997.

Four years later, in October 2001, the two Inter-Arts Center MA programs were also discontinued at the conclusion of a painful and lengthy campus-wide proposal process. This decision was reached despite the many significant accomplishments of faculty, students, and graduates summarized in this commentary. The proposal for discontinuance was initiated by the dean of creative arts, who stated that he did not foresee adequate funds forthcoming, which would have been necessary to provide the support that was necessary to meaningfully continue the programs. Reluctantly, the IAC director concurred with the dean that significantly more resources would be required to continue the program, and that there were no known sources for such funds. The IAC director had to acknowledge that the IAC program was possibly the only graduate program in the country with two self-contained, complex, interdisciplinary programs covering the arts as a whole, yet that had only one tenured faculty member. Most IAC faculty and students disagreed with this view, and strongly believed that the programs should continue based upon their belief in its inherent quality, service to the community, and accomplishments, even without the funds needed to fulfill these goals. Many IAC faculty and students throughout the campus discussions presented fervent arguments, but the lack of funds ultimately led to the last IAC class being offered in 2003.

Conclusion

There are many conclusions that this author could draw from his experiences while sustaining and developing the above interdisciplinary programs at San Francisco State, but five should be acknowledged here. The first of these is that the necessity for a dean's understanding, appreciation, and support of an interdisciplinary program cannot be overestimated. Deans have enormous power over the allocation of resources for programs, and can "starve" a program out of existence, even when its faculty (and, hopefully, others) avidly support it. While most deans are screened and hired for their broad understanding of the disciplines within their college or school, their insights and appreciation of true interdisciplinary pursuits are typically confused with "multidisciplinary" efforts. Understanding the emerging and significant role of synthesis between what have historically been distinct fields of study is still relatively un-evolved in American higher education, even though it clearly will shape the future more than the insular and compartmentalized form of education that shaped the past. Interviewing and hiring deans must include clear discussion, and assurance must be made that there is this kind of understanding.

A second, but very similar concern, relates to the general lack of understanding and appreciation for authentic forms of interdisciplinary expression among many of our colleagues in the traditional disciplines. This author found that he has had to relentlessly explain and re-explain the fundamental differences between interdisciplinary and multidisciplinary pursuits to colleagues in all academic departments. At the same time, it is imperative for those teaching within interdisciplinary programs to pursue frequent dialogue, and even pursue collaborative efforts, with faculty in related fields outside their academic unit in order to nourish the kinds of understanding that this can enhance.

A third issue pertains to what should be the actual relationship between an academic interdisciplinary program and its affiliated departments/programs. This is probably a topic worthy of an entire chapter in itself due to its complexity and varied possibilities. But, as a minimum, it is clear to this observer that there must be meeting points between the events and interest within an interdisciplinary program and those occurring within traditional departments. These could be in the form of shared visiting artists and lecturers, shared symposia, cross-listed courses that overlap the concerns of both the interdisciplinary program and those in one or more departments, and related possibilities.

A fourth matter is the saddling of a program with an insurmountable number of responsibilities well beyond its primary academic mission, merely for the sake of justifying its existence to those who question its validity in other departments. An academic unit cannot become mired in the demands of being a service organization in order to justify its existence. The pressure is enormous, and can deflect attention, not to mention energy and resources, from the true purpose of the program. The merits of a program must be clear in themselves, and no peripheral concerns should deflect attention from this primary purpose. If such ancillary responsibilities are expected, additional resources must be made available to accomplish them. One cannot squeeze an ocean out of a teacup.

The final conclusion to be drawn from the above discussion is that it would probably be wisest to place interdisciplinary programs within an academic unit that is the equivalent to that of a department, and preferably independent of a traditional discipline. The downside of this, of course, is that, with its departmental status, the program might come to see itself in the same insular manner that is commonly found within traditional disciplinary departments. However, this writer's experience suggests that there is little wisdom in placing an interdisciplinary program within a disciplinary-based department, especially when this will most likely overwhelm the fulfillment of the purpose of the interdisciplinary program. It may be tempting to do this to save a few administrative dollars, especially in smaller colleges and universities, but the possible endangerment to the interdisciplinary program should be obvious from the above discussion.

REFERENCE

Weiffenbach, Jean-Edith. 1994. "What Bay Area?" *Art Journal* 53 (Autumn): 46–58.

CHAPTER 6

Interdisciplinary Studies at San Francisco State University: A Personal Perspective[*]

Raymond C. Miller

Introduction

This chapter discusses aspects of the history of interdisciplinary studies at San Francisco State University, where the author spent 43 years of his professional career. It provides his personal perspective on several topics: general education, the rise and sometimes fall of specific interdisciplinary programs, the President's Task Force on Interdisciplinary Studies, and the factors involved in the relative viability of interdisciplinary programs. Finally, the author contends that the endangered species is not "weak" interdisciplinary programs but "strong" interdisciplinarity.

Weak interdisciplinary approaches involve the act of juxtaposing parts or all of conventional disciplines without any serious effort to integrate substance or personnel. Consequently, there are no challenges to conventional knowledge or departmental structures. Strong interdisciplinary approaches seek to combine, synthesize and/or integrate across or beyond existing disciplinary boundaries. They challenge the "conventional wisdom." They self-consciously interrogate the efficacy of the existing way of pursuing knowledge. In practice there is a continuum from the weakest to the strongest interdisciplinary approaches. The weakest approaches actually reinforce the existing knowledge structure whereas the strongest approaches facilitate the reorgan-

*My thanks to Tanya Augsburg, Stan Bailis, Stuart Henry and Anja Miller for their comments and suggestions.

ization of the knowledge strategies in research, teaching and institutional practice.

History

San Francisco State University traces its origin to the establishment of a state-funded teacher training or "normal" school in 1899. That was just seven years before the great 1906 earthquake and fire that destroyed its first building. The first director of the school was Frederick Burk who served for 25 years (1899–1924). Under his leadership the school became famous for its individualized instruction method. The school's classic logo featured the Latin motto, *Experientia docet* (experience teaches). In 1921 the Normal School became San Francisco State Teachers College. Then in 1935, as more liberal arts offerings had begun to appear in the curriculum, the "Teachers" was dropped. However, despite the increase in status, the campus continued to suffer from poor facilities. Conditions were so miserable, including rats in the cafeteria, that there were student protests in the 1930s. Finally in 1939 the state legislature purchased 65 acres of land in southwestern San Francisco for the construction of a real college campus. But before construction could begin, World War II broke out. After the war, local real estate developers, in cahoots with the mayor, tried to rescind the whole deal. Fortunately, after a major political battle, a compromise was reached, though only about half of the land originally targeted for the campus was retained. The northern part of the land that was originally planned for San Francisco State became the Stonestown shopping center and apartments. The first San Francisco State building, the gymnasium, was completed in 1949, and the new campus was officially opened in 1954 with eight buildings (Chandler 1986; Eliassen 2007).

General Education

In the 1920s and 30s several departments in the sciences, humanities and social sciences were founded. One of my home departments, International Relations, was founded by Olive Thompson Cowell in 1933. However, in 1945, when J. Paul Leonard became president, he reorganized the somewhat fragmented and ad hoc departmental system into a seven-division system, which reduced the independence of departments. Leonard's division structure was connected to his vision for a core-curriculum general education system. Working with the president, the faculty in several of the divisions created interdisciplinary general education courses that were required of all students.

Some of the most enthusiastic backers of President Leonard's core-curriculum vision had experience with a similar General Education Program at the University of Chicago. In the San Francisco State General Education Program there was one interdisciplinary course in creative arts, one in physical science, two in humanities, and four in social science. The four-course sequence in social science was probably the most noteworthy, especially since it did not include psychology. Psychology not only had two courses of its own in the General Education Program, but also its own division, a legacy of its central role in the teacher education program. The four social science courses were Social Science 10: Culture and Society, Social Science 20: The Development of American Institutions and Ideals, Social Science 30: Contemporary Economic Society, and Social Science 40: International and Intercultural Relations (Lewenstein 1960). All of these courses were structured so that they integrated parts of more than one discipline. The culture and society course included parts of anthropology, geography, history and sociology. The American institutions and ideals course combined history and political science. Contemporary economic society was really political economy as it focused on public policy. The international and intercultural relations course integrated parts of anthropology, geography, history, and political science. Some observers believed that President Leonard's General Education Program gave San Francisco State national distinction. However, a 1959–60 study by sociologists Christopher Jencks and David Reisman found that most San Francisco State students just wanted to get through the first two general education years so that they could get to the vocational preparation presumably provided by their majors, their real reason for being in college (1962, 187).

President Leonard left San Francisco State in 1957. After his departure, his integrated vision for the College General Education Program began to unravel. At the time of my arrival in 1962, his General Education (GE) Program was formally still in place. By the end of the decade it was gone. The first erosion of his GE program came from the reconstituted disciplinary departments who wanted their introductory courses to count as alternatives to the interdisciplinary courses. As the divisions were replaced by schools with disciplinary departments, one problem was what to do with the faculty who were hired specifically to teach the interdisciplinary GE courses. Because of their interdisciplinary orientations, they did not fit easily into the disciplinary departments. So the division heads decided to create departments of interdisciplinary studies specifically for them. Thus interdisciplinary departments were established in the Schools of Creative Arts, Humanities, Science and Social Science. The latter was my main home for my first 30 years at San Francisco State.

The reincarnation of the disciplinary departments at San Francisco State in the 1960s was in tune with developments across the country in higher education at the time. The explosion in college enrollments, associated initially with returning veterans on the GI Bill and secondarily with the baby boomers, meant great increases in the numbers of faculty and associated bureaucrats. The departmental system provided a ready structural means for handling this massive transformation of higher education. The chief proponent of this institutional strategy was situated on the other side of San Francisco Bay, Clark Kerr, president of the University of California. The influence of his "multiversity" departmental structure approach to higher education was pervasive (Kerr 1963).

Ironically, the other force that was undermining the commitment to a required integrated core interdisciplinary general-education curriculum was the rising counter-culture movement of the 1960s. So far as movement participants were concerned, all requirements were anathema to "authentic" education. Education had to be based on relevance and individual choice. At San Francisco State this movement was manifest in the Experimental College, a program that started in the early 1960s. Anyone who had an idea could propose a course and see if any students would show up. Courses ranged from Black Identity Formation to Psychedelic Experimentation to Eastern Meditation. At its height over 2,000 students were enrolled in the Experimental College. The culmination of the counter-culture movement was the faculty decision in 1968 to eliminate all specific general-education course requirements. All that was left were the state-wide distribution requirements in general education, that is, students had to take a minimum number of units in broad areas of knowledge such as natural science, arts and humanities, and the social sciences. With no specific course requirements, any disciplinary or interdisciplinary course in the broad areas could count toward meeting the general-education minimums. With student options now wide open, the offerings of the originally required interdisciplinary GE courses dropped from 30 sections per semester to three. My course load, which initially consisted only of SS 30 and SS 40, had to shift to other courses.

In a few years both students and faculty recognized that they had created an educational and administrative disaster. Thus, yet another General Education Program design process was set in place. Efforts were made to recreate interdisciplinary sequences, especially by Dean DeVere Pentony of the School of Behavioral and Social Sciences; but the mood of the faculty across the campus and the upper administration of the university was resistant to cross-departmental cooperation. (By 1972 San Francisco State had become a university.) Instead of integrated interdisciplinary general education courses taught by faculty members from several departments, categories with lists of mostly disciplinary courses were agreed upon, based on the fiction that the listed courses were comparable experiences. The driving force of this fragmented approach, of course, was "FTE." FTE is the full-time equivalent enrollment numbers generated by the course offerings of academic programs. Since all departments' budgetary allocations are based on the numbers of students enrolled in their courses, the competition for students is fierce. The upper administration could have softened this resource struggle by establishing budgetary parameters, but they preferred a free-for-all competition among departments in which they would serve as arbiters. Thus general education became a political battlefield in which all parties sought to maximize their enrollment situations. After several years of negotiations, the best that the faculty could do was to reduce the choices in the General Education Program from thousands of courses to about 900 (Pentony 1982).

However, after the 1981 revision there still was an ostensibly interdisciplinary part of the GE program. It was the new upper division part, called the Relationships of Knowledge, in which students pick a 9-unit cluster (three courses from at least two different disciplines) with a coherent theme. Many of the clusters consisted of the core courses of existing interdisciplinary minors. A special committee (Segment III) was established to oversee this part of the program, but unfortunately, the committee has never developed an effective method for determining whether the three separate courses in a student's cluster actually produce a coherent experience and that the hoped for multi-perspective experience actually happens. Because of the lack of persuasive data that the interdisciplinary segment is working as intended, in combination with some undercurrent of hostility to the whole idea, the continuation of this upper division Segment as explicitly interdisciplinary is currently in jeopardy. In 2008–9 the General Education Program is undergoing yet another full review. Everyone recognizes, including supporters of Segment III, that there have been some implementation problems with the upper division interdisciplinary component, but the solution of some faculty is to scuttle the whole thing and create yet another cafeteria set of choices. The disciplinary reductionists have a strong argument on their side. The cafeteria approach is simpler. It requires less advising time with students and less time spent coordinating with colleagues, which is desirable to many faculty because their major concern is finding enough time to do the research and writing that earns them tenure and promotion and recognition in their respective fields. The students are usually not aware of how their education could be improved with a well-implemented interdisciplinary component, and the disciplinary faculty can easily rationalize that their "in-depth" major curricula are the real essence of quality education anyway. Supporters of retaining the interdisciplinary quality of Segment III have proposed an all-university schema that privileges breadth and highly abstract themes. Each cluster would have to include one science course, one humanities course, and one social science course. Since all of these clusters would be freshly created, the likelihood of a coherent educational experience seems even less likely than under the current system. It is a classic multi-disciplinary or weak interdisciplinary solution.

Activism of the Late 1960s

Fads in higher education seem to be cyclical. Students of the 1950s were characterized as the "silent generation." In the 1960s students were at the forefront of a number of activist social movements: anti-war, pro-civil rights, feminism, environmentalism, pro–Third World, freer expression, etc. In all of these movements, San Francisco State was at the epicenter. In 1968–69 San Francisco State experienced the longest student and faculty strike in the history of American higher education. For months the campus was essentially a war zone. Despite seemingly irreconcilable positions, a resolution of the conflict was finally reached. Probably the most notable outcome was the establishment of the first and still the only School of Ethnic Studies in a mainstream, publicly funded university in the United States. The School included the first Department of Black Studies (subsequently renamed as Africana Studies) as well as departments of Asian-American Studies, La Raza Studies and Native American Studies. The curricula of all the Ethnic Studies Programs were interdisciplinary in format, but the phrase "interdisciplinary" was not on the banners demanding this major innovation. Phrases that were used included "Black pride, Black identity, Black power, Black consciousness," etc. The argument was strongly enunciated that not only did all the conventional departments ignore the needs and accomplishments of people of color, but they also denigrated them through the insidious practices of "institutional racism" (Orrick 1969). A very similar argument was made by feminists on behalf of women. Instead of being housed in a separate school, the Women Studies Program was initially set up as an all-university interdisciplinary program, but eventually it too became a department in the School, now College, of Humanities. Both ethnic studies and women and gender studies started with strong activist ties to the community. However, over time they have moved in the conservative direction, becoming more like other departments in the university. This transformation Ellen Messer-Davidow has characterized as "disciplining" (2002).

The Innovative 1970s

While the 1960s witnessed the overthrow of the interdisciplinarily structured general education requirements, the 1970s were the period of innovating new interdisciplinary programs. The School (later College) of Behavioral and Social Sciences (the combination of the old Divisions of Psychology and Social Science) established a Division of Cross-Disciplinary Programs. It encompassed the already existing programs in international relations and social science plus a variety of newly created programs: criminal justice, critical social thought, employment studies, gerontology, human sexuality studies, information science, labor studies, liberal studies (social science emphasis), public administration, and urban studies. The multiple school programs of area studies and American studies were also associated with the division when the faculty coordinator was based in the School of Behavioral and Social Sciences. The interdisciplinary programs attracted faculty from many different departments, who voluntarily contributed their time and energy for curriculum development, advising and teaching. When faculty members used some of their position-time to teach courses in one of the interdisciplinary programs, their home departments would accrue the FTE. The division was a school within a school, and its meetings had as many attendees as the College Council, which was composed of the disciplinary department chairs and the head of the division. Ironically, and not surprisingly, the division came under critical scrutiny both from within and beyond the school, probably because it had become too successful. By success I mean the number of new interdisciplinary programs that were developed and approved by the university. Some of the participating programs, especially those with permanent faculty positions, such as urban studies, did not like being one-step removed from the dean. They wanted a seat on the Dean's Council. On the other hand, the conventional disciplinary departments saw the division as threatening — threatening to their power, threatening to their resources, and threatening to their status. As agreed at the division's formation, a five-year fully participatory review was conducted. In 1980 at the conclusion of the review, the decision was taken by the dean in consultation with the academic vice president to dismember the division. Some of its constituent programs were scattered throughout the school, some on their own and others attached to disciplinary departments. A few remained in a Center for Interdisciplinary Programs, which did not have any centralized administrative structure. Eventually the center was also abolished. Despite the Division's demise, the dean of another school liked the concept and set up her own Center for Humanistic Studies. Possibly because it only contains a few very small interdisciplinary programs, such as religious studies, it still exists.

The President and the Division
of Cross-Disciplinary Programs

In his Fall 1977 opening address to the faculty President Paul Romberg raised questions about the quality of the proliferating interdisciplinary programs. His criticism was surprising because his own 1976 Long Range Planning Commission Report took a quite opposite stance:

> Without assuming that an interdisciplinary curriculum can solve all curricular difficulties, the Commission nevertheless is strongly convinced that interdisciplinary approaches provide cohesion within a differentiated academic environment and offer a necessary curricular option to the students and faculty of San Francisco State University. The Commission therefore strongly believes that future and present circumstances of knowledge require the University to place a priority on curriculum developments which are interdisciplinary in scope, i.e. a curriculum which calls for combination, synthesis, and integration of concepts and information [1976, 32].

Why did a president who had just endorsed in the previous year such a strong pro-interdisciplinary statement turn around and make this criticism? The attacks on interdisciplinary programs, in my opinion, come from three sources: national trends, institutional culture, and idiosyncratic campus-specific personal politics. In the 1970s the national trend was definitely pro-interdisciplinary. It was the period when interdisciplinary programs such as ethnic studies and women's studies were sweeping the country (Miller 2009). Furthermore, San Francisco State had an institutional culture that was generally supportive of interdisciplinary education. Therefore, the third source, campus-specific personal politics, is the most likely explanation for his switch in position.

Since the Division of Cross-Disciplinary Programs in the Behavioral and Social Sciences was the major generator of new interdisciplinary programs at SF State in the 1970s, the president's criticism was most likely directed against it. The likely source, which was subsequently confirmed, was the president's chief of staff. He was also critical of the division in comments he made later to the external accreditation team. This individual had recently been removed by the dean as associate dean of the School of Behavioral and Social Sciences after numerous complaints from department chairs. If he had stayed on, he would very likely have been the head of the division. Paradoxically, this same individual was probably responsible for writing the very pro-interdisciplinary statement in the President's Long Range Planning Report. Consequently, it seems reasonable to infer that the criticism of the division and its "proliferating" interdisciplinary programs was not due to animosity toward interdisciplinary studies in general but due to personal hostility against the dean who removed him from office and the head of the division who took his "right-ful" place. Though the personal/political was pre-eminent in producing the criticisms from the president's office, it reinforced the other factors that were undoubtedly more responsible for the dissolution of the division. Those other factors, as mentioned above, were the power objectives of some of the con-stituent interdisciplinary programs and resource complaints from the disci-plinary departments. Only a few of the disciplinary departments openly expressed anti-interdisciplinary sentiments.

Because I felt that the president's remarks were directed primarily against the Division of Cross-Disciplinary Programs, I responded with a memo in my capacity as head of the division. In the memo I pointed out that most of the interdisciplinary programs with which I was familiar were very high qual-ity. In fact, their reputations for excellence in teaching and research were bet-ter than some of the disciplinary departments. The interdisciplinary programs of the 1970s did not suffer from the erratic and uneven qualities that pre-vailed in the Experimental College of the 1960s. The president's response was to establish the President's Task Force on Interdisciplinary Studies to inves-tigate all of these issues, and he named me as its chair. More on the task force appears below. As a final observation on this topic, it should be noted that many of the interdisciplinary programs that were part of the division are still thriving in 2008, especially criminal justice, international relations, human sexuality studies, public administration, and urban studies. However, some are gone, the most notable being social science. That loss will also be dis-cussed below.

NEXA

Another interesting and innovative interdisciplinary program that was founded in the mid 1970s was NEXA. NEXA was an effort to respond to the gap between the sciences and the humanities that was brought to the center of public attention by C. P. Snow in his best selling book, *The Two Cultures* (1959). Michael Gregory, professor of anthropology and English, was the leader of a group that successfully applied to the National Endowment for the Humanities for a nearly half million-dollar grant. Part of the proposal was the development of new topical courses that bridged the gap between the two areas not only by content but also by having each course team-taught by a scientist and humanist. The teachers would all convene on Friday afternoon for the famous NEXA seminars that were the center of intellectual excitement on campus for the first few years of their existence. As long as grant money was available, NEXA was a thriving program. Unfortunately, the team-teaching method utilized by the NEXA program was more expensive than the normal amounts allocated to classes. When the grants ran out, team teaching was mostly abandoned. The other weakness of NEXA was its intellectual and organizational dependence on its founder and director. A few years after his death, the program was discontinued.

During NEXA's heyday in the 1970s, the program issued a list of approximately 50 "new" course ideas for which they were soliciting faculty teaching proposals. In my role as head of the Division of Cross-Disciplinary Programs in the School of Behavioral and Social Sciences and the person in the dean's office responsible for curriculum, I wrote a memo to NEXA noting that of the 50-odd courses in their list, half were already being offered by BSS programs, and the other half were really social science topics: "It seemed as if a NEXA committee composed of scientists and humanists had just reinvented Social Science." Needless to say, my observation was not well received by NEXA. It was interesting, therefore, that when President Romberg picked the members for his 1977 Presidential Task Force on Interdisciplinary Studies, he included both the director of NEXA and the head of the BSS Division of Cross-Disciplinary Programs. Despite trepidation in some circles, the task force actually functioned quite effectively as a group. Its findings and recommendations are discussed next.

Presidential Task Force on Interdisciplinary Studies

The President gave the task force six charges. They included reviewing, evaluating, identifying new options and goals, and making recommendations on the university's interdisciplinary programs (Final Report, 1). Besides the director of NEXA and the head of the BSS Division of Cross-Disciplinary Programs, the task force included two professors of biology, one of whom was director of the Center for Interdisciplinary Science, a professor of interdisciplinary education, a professor of comparative literature, and two academic administrators. The first step of the task force was to establish what it meant by interdisciplinary studies. The definition it adopted was an adaptation of the definition provided by President Romberg's Long Range Planning Commission's Report, namely, "any academic program which juxtaposes, applies, combines, synthesizes, or integrates material from two or more disciplines" (Final Report, 2). This was a very pragmatic definition, which I continue to use. Its inclusive nature incorporates the full continuum of interdisciplinary approaches discussed above from the weakest to the strongest. The building blocks are the conventional disciplines that were professionally established at the beginning of the twentieth century. The second step was to invite testimony.

Twenty-three groups came forward. They ranged from the General Education Council to the Clinical Science Program. The newly created programs in ethnic studies and women studies were eager to testify and share their frustrations with the rigidity of the university bureaucracy. Professional programs testifying who considered themselves interdisciplinary included social work, nursing, and health education. At the time the School of Business had a very strong dean, a former corporate executive, who did not believe that interdisciplinary studies had anything to do with business, even though the definition of the task force certainly fit most of the programs in his school. He believed that admitting to being interdisciplinary meant accepting a lower status. Furthermore, he felt that an interdisciplinary curriculum was necessarily "boundary-crossing," that is, composed of courses from different departments, whereas the task force believed that an interdisciplinary curriculum could also be "self-contained," that is, integrating material from several disciplines relevant to that field within its own courses. These curricular characterizations (boundary-crossing vs. self-contained) were a part of a set of typologies presented in the findings of the task force, the third step in the report. The typologies included: 1) types of administrative arrangements, 2) types of faculty appointments, 3) types of curricula, 4) types of program organizations, and 5) types of conceptual orientations (Final Report 1980, 2–8).

The fourth step of the task force was making recommendations (11–17). A big emphasis was placed on developing interdisciplinary minors. It was hoped that all students would be required to take a minor, and all those majoring in conventional disciplines would have to take an interdisciplinary minor. Though many interdisciplinary minors were developed, it was politically impossible to get a required minor policy adopted by the Academic Senate. Thus, most minors have never attracted many students, with a few exceptions such as human sexuality studies.

Probably the most successful recommendation of the task force was the establishment of a University Interdisciplinary Council. All eight of the university's schools (colleges), as well as the deans of undergraduate and graduate studies, are represented on the council. I represented the College of Behavioral and Social Sciences on the council from its inception in 1981 until my retirement in 2006; and during most of that time I served as chair. The council is charged with facilitating and reviewing existing and proposed interdisciplinary programs. It has allowed programs to self-identify as to whether they are interdisciplinary, and the reviewing process has always been consultative, not judgmental. Probably the member of the council most responsible for these approaches was George Araki, professor of biology. He was a member of the original task force and served on the council for about 15 years while also serving as director of the Center for Interdisciplinary Science. The council is still alive and well and represents the commitment that the university has to provide opportunities for interdisciplinary education.

Originally, the task force had hoped that the university administration would add a new academic affairs position to be titled the University Coordinator of Interdisciplinary Studies. However, because the provost did not want to incur the additional expense, he assigned the responsibility and title to one of his existing positions, the dean of undergraduate studies. Fortuitously, the person occupying that position at the time had come to San Francisco State from the deanship of the School of Interdisciplinary Studies at Miami University. The final report of the task force, he said, was one of the reasons he decided to apply for the position at San Francisco State. An earlier chapter in this book describes the subsequent demise of his school at Miami University.

Other Interdisciplinary Programs

In the late 1990s the University Interdisciplinary Council conducted a university-wide survey in which the directors of all curricular programs were asked whether or not they wished to identify as interdisciplinary. The programs declaring themselves as interdisciplinary included 18 free-standing interdisciplinary minors, 33 baccalaureate majors, 23 minors associated with majors, 23 Master's majors, and 3 certificates. Half of the free-standing interdisciplinary minors are based in the College of Behavioral and Social Science; four of them are area studies. As mentioned above, human sexuality studies is the only one with substantial enrollments. Hospitality management is the only program based in the College of Business. In the College of Science only the Center for Interdisciplinary Science identified itself as interdisciplinary. No programs in engineering identified themselves, nor did any of the hybrids in science, such as biochemistry. On the other hand, somewhat surprisingly, two of the conventional disciplines in the Behavioral and Social Sciences considered themselves interdisciplinary: anthropology and geography (UIC 1997).

The complete formal name of the latter discipline is Geography and Human Environmental Studies, a compromise forged out of a turf battle between geography and geosciences. In the 1960s, in response to the fledgling environmental movement, the president of the university requested that these departments from two different schools create an interdisciplinary environmental studies program. However, due to a combination of territorial imperatives and interpersonal conflicts, the effort failed. More than 20 years passed before a new effort was initiated, and this time the leadership came from students. The committee crafting the proposed program was co-chaired by two female faculty members, one from geography and one from geosciences. They had the help of supportive deans and the University Interdisciplinary Council. But even then, in order to get approval from the political gauntlet known as the curriculum review process, they had to come up with one of the most complicated curricular structures ever invented on campus. The resulting program has a core and five concentrations: 1) environmental sustainability and social justice, 2) urban environment, 3) humanities and the environment, 4) earth system science, and 5) natural resource management and conservation. Students in one of the first three concentrations would earn a B.A., whereas students in the latter two would earn a B.S. Tentative efforts have been made to simplify the program, but progress has been slow. Despite its complexity, the program is actually popular with students. There are some students and faculty who recognize that not only does humanity have serious ecological problems facing it, but also that contributions from many disciplines and interdisciplines are required in order to make realistic progress in dealing with these problems.

Another complex and interesting all-university interdisciplinary program is liberal studies. It has been one of the largest majors on campus because it was designated as the most appropriate major to take if one wanted to obtain an elementary school teaching credential. Many decades ago the California legislature decided that prospective teachers should have undergraduate majors in substantive academic fields, not education. When the liberal studies major was first offered it was a category grab bag, just like the General Education Program of the 1970s. Of course, it was an advising nightmare. Consequently, a serious effort was made in the early 1980s to construct a more coherent curriculum. For this purpose a Liberal Studies Council was created, and I served as its chair during this formative period. The major has four areas: 1) communication, languages and literature, 2) life science, physical science, and mathematics, 3) behavoral and social sciences, and 4) creative arts and humanities. Several of the council members argued that each of the areas should have integrated core courses. The strongest proponent was an associate dean of the College of Education. Social science already had two integrated courses that could serve this purpose, but they had to be modified in order to obtain political approval. The previous integrated structure of these courses had to be scuttled for courses, which amounted to mini-introductions to all the major disciplines of the social sciences. This was the only structure that a BSS College Council composed mostly of disciplinary department chairs would approve. At the request of the Liberal Studies Council, Creative Arts and Humanities actually managed to create two integrated core courses, probably because they had interdisciplinary units with experience in teaching such courses. Several efforts were made in science to create an integrated sequence, and though the participating faculty came close, they did not succeed. The faculty in the English and Communications departments would not even try. Because the full liberal studies story is told in another chapter, I would like to move on to a related story, namely, what happened to the interdisciplinary departments created out of President Leonard's divisions of the 1950s.

The Generic Interdisciplinary Departments

As discussed in the section on general education above, four generic interdisciplinary departments were created for the faculty who came to SF State primarily to teach the interdisciplinary general education courses (Creative Arts, Humanities, Science and Social Science). These departments were also given specific responsibilities for dealing with the academic preparation of prospective elementary and secondary teachers. At the elementary level that meant teaching liberal studies courses and serving as advisers. At the secondary level that responsibility meant staffing the curriculum and instruction courses that were part of the post-baccalaureate education credential program. The Interdisciplinary Creative Arts Program focused on arts education. In fact, one of the program's early directors was also editor of the national *Journal of Arts Education.* The Interdisciplinary Social Science Program was also nationally recognized. Personally, I served as the first editor of the journal of the Association for Integrative Studies and the Association's national president in 1985–86. Another social science faculty member, Stan Bailis, was the longest serving editor of that journal, *Issues in Integrative Studies.*

All four of the departments developed their own interdisciplinary majors at the undergraduate and graduate levels. However, in 2008 only one of the four is still in existence: the program in humanities. In thinking about reasons for survival, it is very instructive that the Humanities Department is the only one of the four programs to follow a self-contained curriculum strategy for its majors. The other three followed a core/satellite model, which meant that most of the courses that students in their respective majors took were likely to be in other departments, following the boundary-crossing approach. Naturally, these courses were chosen, in consultation with an adviser, to contribute to a coherent theme. In contrast, students in the humanities program take most of the courses required for their majors within the department. Since the self-contained approach requires a larger cadre of faculty, it gave the department more political protection. However, that only works as long as the university policy is not to lay off tenure-track faculty.

What led to the disappearance of the other three generic interdisciplinary departments/centers? The first to go was science. The Center for Interdisciplinary Science did not have liberal studies core courses to replace the bread-and-butter interdisciplinary general education courses. Furthermore, the center's director was more interested in holistic health and Chinese medicine than a more generic interdisciplinarity. He received program approval for the former but not the latter. When he felt that his popular program in holistic health was not being properly funded by the dean of the College of Science, he took his program to the College of Health and Human Services. Thus the center was left with no faculty or viable program, so it was discontinued. Next to close was the Center for Interdisciplinary Creative Arts. Ironically, the proposal for discontinuance came initially from the center's director himself, who felt that he was unfairly burdened by the many tasks of the center. There was a small student protest, but the discontinuance proposal was ultimately approved.

The last to go was my program, social science (interdisciplinary studies). During the recession of 2000–2001, budgetary cutbacks motivated the university's president to suggest that instead of across-the-board cuts, the university should discontinue entire programs. However, he also proclaimed a seemingly contradictory policy that no tenure-track faculty would be laid off. His first trial balloon was the School of Engineering. A firestorm of protest ensued, making the front page of the *San Francisco Chronicle*, so that proposal was dropped. Then he asked the Deans for suggestions. Of the 11 programs that they proposed for discontinuance, 10 were interdisciplinary; one of them was social science (interdisciplinary studies). The dean of the College of Behavioral and Social Sciences (BSS), along with a committee of his chairs, made three arguments for discontinuance: 1) that the program was expensive, 2) that it was out-of-date, and 3) that its interdisciplinary mission was being fulfilled in other programs. The proposal for discontinuance states, "Currently, interdisciplinarity is a widely-accepted value throughout the College of BSS where several programs can be so characterized, thus the role of the Social Science's distinguishing characteristic and *raison d'etre* no longer applies in the BSS College of the 21st century" (College of BSS 2004, 1).

In my view all three of these arguments are totally false. 1) The lecturer expense was not connected to the offering of the Social Science Program but to the offering of the multiple sections of the core courses for the liberal studies major. Their teaching was a service provided by the Social Science Program, not an expense of the Social Science Program itself. Those resources have now been returned to the central administration, and the faculty members teaching these courses are working directly for the Liberal Studies Council. So nothing has been saved. 2) The core/satellite curricular model used by social science is present all over the country. In fact, the San Francisco State model was copied by many other institutions. The core consisted of two courses which taught disciplinary and interdisciplinary approaches to knowledge and two courses which focused on interdisciplinary research methodology and a culminating paper based on the student's individual theme. It is not out-of-date, nor is it expensive! Boundary-crossing programs are not expensive in dedicated faculty time as students are taking most of their major courses in other departments, which would have been offered in any case. 3) Finally, the most troubling argument of all was, namely, that other interdisciplinary programs were now performing its mission, making it redundant. This argument demonstrates a "weak" understanding of interdisciplinarity.

Unfortunately, such limiting of the understanding of interdisciplinarity to its weakest form is shared by most faculty members, including those located in ostensibly interdisciplinary programs. For many faculty members interdisciplinary approaches really mean just multidisciplinary approaches, that is, the mere juxtaposition of several disciplines for some teaching or research purpose. There is no substantial reflection on the implications of the different perspectives provided by the different disciplines or on how parts of those disciplines could be merged in some kind of integrative strategy. Interdisciplinary methodology of a cross-disciplinary or transdisciplinary nature involves this type of understanding and its implications. It is an academic specialization of its own. Faculty members who focus on topics such as urban studies or human sexuality studies probably seldom even think about these issues. Faculty members in conventional disciplines may never reflect on the philosophical and normative assumptions of their respective disciplines' worldviews. One of the reasons that many faculty members in conventional disciplines find students, faculty and programs in strong interdisciplinarity annoying is the questions and challenges they present to their mostly unexamined beliefs. These kinds of questions flow naturally from faculty members and students in generic (strong) interdisciplinary programs because they methodologically specialize in the nature of multiple perspectives and their implications for knowledge production and transmission. The loss of generic interdisciplinary studies programs means that the university most likely loses this important intellectual perspective (Miller 2009, 198).

The argument made by the dean of the College of Behavioral and Social Sciences and several of his chairs for the discontinuance of social science demonstrates no recognition of the strong interdisciplinarity contributions of generic interdisciplinary programs. The irony is that the dean considers himself a strong proponent of interdisciplinary education. Evidently that advocacy does not include a programmatic location for specialization in strong interdisciplinarity within his college. Besides this lack of commitment to strong interdisciplinarity and possible lack of understanding, what else accounts for his proposal to discontinue social science? In my opinion the explanation goes back to the third of the three variables that affect the viability of interdisciplinary programs, the personal/political. A few years before, the top administrators of the University had arbitrarily usurped the personnel processes of the Social Science Department. As a consequence, disgusted senior members of the department accepted positions or administrative relocations in other departments. In my case, the refuge was international relations. Essentially, the only faculty members left in social science were those few who could not find positions elsewhere and lecturers. Therefore, in my view, the dean's discontinuance proposal was primarily a personnel strategy, though, of course, one is never supposed to mention that in public. This strategy was facilitated by a few chairs who were happy to see the demise of the generic interdisciplinary unit, especially the chair of sociology who was frustrated by continuously being asked to explain, including to the late President Romberg, the difference between sociology and social science.

In the 1983 edition of *Issues in Integrative Studies* I had a brief commentary in which I argued that embedding the generic interdisciplinary programs within their respective areas of knowledge provides a better protection against their dissolution than having one comprehensive school or department of interdisciplinary studies. The latter is a more visible and singular target. In a multiple college-based system, such as the one at San Francisco State, there is always the chance that one or more deans will protect their generic interdisciplinary units. Well, three of the four generic units are now gone. Most of the deans do not seem to understand why that is a problem. On the other hand, most faculty members seem delighted with interdisciplinary programs, as long as they are multidisciplinary and do not threaten the resources and institutional security of the disciplinary departments. Weak interdisciplinarity prevails while strong interdisciplinarity withers away.

REFERENCES

Chandler, Arthur. 1986. *The biography of San Francisco State University.* San Francisco: Lexikos Press.

College of Behavioral and Social Sciences. 2004. Proposal for the discontinuance of the B.A. Degree in Social Science: Concentration in interdisciplinary studies, Fall.

Eliassen, Meredith. 2007. *The campus history series: San Francisco State University.* San Francisco: Arcadia Publishing.

Kerr, Clark. 1963. *The uses of the university.* Cambridge: Harvard University Press.

Lewenstein, Morris. 1960. Final report and recommendations: General Education Study Committee Social Science Division, February 1 (ditto).

Messer-Davidow, Ellen. 2002. *Disciplining feminism: From social activism to academic discourse.* Durham, North Carolina: Duke University Press.

Miller, Raymond C. 1980. Final report of the President's Task Force on Interdisciplinary Studies: A proposal for faculty and curricular development," revised, April (mimeo).

_____. 1982. Varieties of interdisciplinary approaches in the social sciences. *Issues in Integrative Studies* 1: 1–37.

_____. 1983. What do you say to a devil's advocate? *Issues in Integrative Studies*, 2: 25–30.

_____. In Press. Interdisciplinary fields with special reference to the social sciences. In the *Oxford handbook of interdisciplinarity*, eds. Robert Frodeman, Julie Thompson Klein, and Carl Mitcham, Oxford, UK: Oxford University Press.

Orrick, William H., Jr. 1969. *Shut it down! A college in crisis: San Francisco State College October, 1968 — April, 1969* (A Report to the National Commission on the Causes and Prevention of Violence). Washington, D.C.: U.S. Government Printing Office.

Pentony, DeVere. 1982. "New General Education Program," January 12 (Xerox).

Reisman, David, and Christopher Jencks. 1962. The viability of the American college. In *The American college: A psychological and social interpretation of the higher learning*, ed. Nevitt Sanford. New York: Wiley.

Romberg, Paul. 1976. *Action today: Agenda for tomorrow* (Final Report Presidential Commission on Long Range Planning: San Francisco State University), January.

Snow, C.P. 1959. *The two cultures.* Cambridge: Cambridge University Press.

University Interdisciplinary Council. 1997. Interdisciplinary programs at San Francisco State University (brochure).

PART II. NEW DIRECTIONS

CHAPTER 7

Interdisciplinarity and Teacher Preparation at San Francisco State University

Helen Goldsmith[1]

History

San Francisco State University (SFSU) created its liberal studies major in 1972 in response to California's preparation standards for future elementary school teachers. From the beginning, the major served multiple purposes and audiences. In particular it: (1) provided future teachers with pre-professional subject matter competency and (2) provided students with a broad liberal arts background in focused liberal arts education. Because of San Francisco State's institutional values and the faculty members who created and led this program, it has always attracted an almost equal number of students who choose it for the pre-professional training or for an interest in the multidisciplinary curriculum and even some who choose it for both reasons. This choice of a non-career oriented major in interdisciplinary studies through liberal arts is unusual in the California State University (CSU) system where, on most campuses, well over 90 percent of the students majoring in Liberal Studies intend to become teachers.

Throughout the CSU system, the liberal studies major is housed in a variety of locations — colleges of education, colleges of arts and sciences, and less frequently, undergraduate studies. At San Francisco State the major has always been housed in the Division of Undergraduate Studies. This made sense since the program was an all-university endeavor that relied on existing courses across campus. San Francisco State has tried, with varying degrees of success, to embrace the concept that training future teachers should be a university-wide responsibility, not be relegated only to the College of Education.

When the program began in 1972 university life was simpler: the student body was much smaller (in 1972 there were approximately 21,000 undergraduate and graduate students on campus; in Fall 2007, more than 30,000 students attended San Francisco State, over 24,000 of whom were undergraduates); the expectations for faculty allowed more time for students, even for students outside the faculty member's home department; and interdisciplinary programs were evolving and growing in all areas of campus. As discussed in other chapters in this book, over the past decade, interdisciplinary majors in the sciences, creative arts, and social sciences have been discontinued and most of the faculty who led these programs have retired. The liberal studies program relied heavily on many of these faculty members to serve as: instructors of key courses, student advisors, and as program leadership on the Liberal Studies Council (LSC), which is the curricular governing board for the program. In contrast to earlier periods, recently hired San Francisco State faculty members have different and increased pressures and expectations from their home departments, particularly as they work towards tenure. Such institutional changes have made it difficult to attract interested and involved faculty to serve as advisors and in leadership roles (or often, even as members) on the Liberal Studies Council. At the same time, faculty members in all majors were required to assess their programs. The campus assessment coordinator (a variety of people with different titles over the years) would meet with the Liberal Studies Council, offer suggestions, and when presented with our efforts, would agree with us that we were attempting the impossible. We could not accomplish authentic and useful assessment without dedicated courses and resident faculty, particularly in a major as large as ours.

Structure of the Major

For many years San Francisco State program leaders grappled with whether the liberal studies program was "interdisciplinary" or "multidisciplinary," and until recently we have opted for the latter term. This decision reflected the lack of opportunity, absence of a curriculum requirement or any significant student experience that made the necessary connections that would make it a truly interdisciplinary program.

Historically, the liberal studies major consisted of 46 semester units structured around four discipline-based areas: Area I — communication, language, and literature; Area II — life science, physical science, and mathematics; Area III — behavioral and social sciences; and Area IV — creative arts and humanities. When originally created in 1972 the liberal studies major was self-designed, envisioned as an opportunity for students to identify an over-arching theme and choose courses from the four areas that would address the theme. However, we found that students did not really understand the concept, spent very little time thinking about how their courses fit together, and often came to the theme after the fact, trying to tie together a disparate bunch of course so that they could graduate as soon as possible. This was particularly true for future teachers, who had chosen the major because they were told that it was the best pathway to teaching rather than because they liked the idea of an interdisciplinary major. Since the thematic statement was not required of majors in any course, and since the faculty advisors volunteered their time to assist students, there was little incentive on any faculty member's part to put in the time, effort, and thought necessary to make the theme a meaningful experience. In addition, students felt disconnected from each other and felt no identity in the major because they rarely took the same courses.

In the late 1980s, a common 25-unit core of eight courses, two in each subject area, was developed to give students a more cohesive educational experience. The original goal was that there would be specific courses in each of the areas, but that was only a reality in the behavioral and social sciences and in the creative arts and humanities. The areas covering literacy, math and science skills always had a menu of courses. In good budgetary times and when classes were not full to overflowing, this arrangement worked fine. However, during critical budgetary times, understandably colleges and departments put the needs of their own majors first.

In addition to the core courses of the major, students choose an area of emphasis. At first, the emphasis was six semester units or two courses, which when compared to the typical 18 units for a minor, is hardly an emphasis at all. However, a 1985 program review, the "Curricular Problem in Brief," captured some essential weaknesses that resonate with criticisms of interdisciplinary programs nationwide:

1. Insufficient upper-division depth.
2. Failure of thematic planning.
3. Many dubious majors approved with no discernible pattern other than the unit numbers in the four Areas.
4. Requirements in some Areas for many majors met entirely by lightweight and/or introductory courses.
5. Lack of common experiences.
6. Lack of a basis upon which to build a Liberal Studies faculty and associated advising commitment.

In response to this review, the emphasis requirement was increased to 12 units. The final 9 units of the major were electives on advisement. Changes to the curriculum during the mid–1980s helped alleviate some, but not all, of the problems with depth and strength of courses, thematic planning, and commonality of experience. Over the years, the LSC discussed the feasibility of portfolios and other types of experiences that might help students make sense of a seemingly unrelated set of courses but without our own courses and faculty, our vision remained but a fantasy. Since 1985, additional programmatic changes and institutional commitment improved advising and the general extra-curricular experience for students. However, the fundamental underlying structural problems remained that we believed could only by solved by having our own program faculty.

Growth and Change

In 1984, there were 400 students in the liberal studies major; at its peak in 1999, over 1,100 students were enrolled in the major, and it became one of the top three majors by enrollment on campus. More recently with public education facing many challenges, the number of future teachers in our program fell dramatically. In fall 2006, 675 students (2.6 percent of the undergraduate population) were enrolled in the major, making it one of the top 10 majors at San Francisco State, but no longer among the top three. However, in 2006–2007 the liberal studies major granted the fourth largest number of degrees (4.1 percent of all undergraduate degrees awarded at San Francisco State), following business, psychology, and radio and television. Currently, approximately 250 liberal studies majors graduate from San Francisco State each year.

In addition to campus-wide assessment efforts the university's current strategic plan states: "San Francisco State University makes writing central to education and ensures that its graduates write proficiently" (http://academic. sfsu.edu/apee/planning/goal_2.php). In order to achieve this goal, programs are to define performance expectations for writing and are encouraged to create capstone or portfolio projects in order to assess student work. We realized that the liberal studies program could not achieve these goals without faculty members with the time, expertise, and ability to implement them. We knew that, with regard to these objectives, other departments would be unable to provide enough seats in their classes for our students and that the goals and experiences that they would create for their own majors would not always be appropriate for our students.

Another pressing issue was program leadership. Without liberal studies faculty, the program leadership has been somewhat complicated and cumbersome. The dean of undergraduate studies serves as the principal administrative head of the program. The Liberal Studies Council, which includes faculty from all of the colleges that have courses or interest in the program, serves as the primary curricular review body. The chair of the council receives a course release each semester. Finally, a full-time student services professional serves as the liberal studies program advising coordinator, who is responsible for all student advising and operations of the program. Over the past twenty years, the Liberal Studies Council and the dean of undergraduate studies have discussed the need for a different form of leadership, with at least one faculty member whose first responsibility is to the liberal studies program. We considered "borrowing" a faculty member from another department on either a full- or part-time basis. However, the part-time faculty option was not acceptable, as the faculty member's primary commitment would be to his or her home department. Such a position was unlikely to attract faculty members who were still working toward tenure and promotion, as service to the liberal studies program would not likely count in any substantial way. Yet the alternative of borrowing faculty would mean the same rotating leadership and lack of institutional memory that is already a problem with the current model.

With increasing program expectations, the exodus of retiring faculty members, the demise of several long-standing interdisciplinary programs that had wonderful goals but few students, and an influx of new faculty in all disciplines, the leadership of liberal studies felt that the time was right to request its own faculty members. Such a request had never been made previously. To our delight, the Provost approved our request to hire tenure-track faculty members, and in fall 2007, we welcomed five new tenure-track assistant professors to liberal studies. We view these hires as providing the opportunity to strengthen our program, improve the student experience, and reinvigorate interdisciplinarity on our campus. We recognize that these new faculty members will help revise the curriculum and create liberal studies courses, but that they cannot serve all of our majors. Thus, we will continue to be dependent on course offerings and faculty involvement from across campus. Since their arrival the liberal studies faculty members have been making connections and building bridges across disciplinary departments to maintain and improve our relationships across campus.

Teacher Education and Liberal Studies in California

As mentioned earlier, liberal studies was created in response to state teacher preparation standards in the early 1970s. Over the years, the standards have changed and our program has evolved accordingly. In California, it is not possible to earn a bachelors degree in education. The goal is that students be well educated in the subject matter they will teach. Thus, students take the subject matter at the undergraduate level [usually majoring in the subject(s) they plan to teach] and then earn a credential at the post-baccalaureate level. Since future elementary school teachers must teach all subjects, they earn a multiple subject credential, and the best undergraduate preparation is one that introduces students to all of the subject matter areas they will teach, such as an interdisciplinary studies major. Although other majors offer such preparation, liberal studies is the most popular major to do this. At San Francisco State, all LS majors, whether they want to become teachers or not, take the same 46 unit major. In addition, those students desiring to become teachers are urged to take additional coursework specific for the preparation of future teachers: courses such as elementary school PE, math for elementary teachers, art for children, etc. Until 2003, if students completed this package of courses (the proved subject matter competency) they were not required to take a subject matter examination (currently the CSET Multiple Subject — the California Subject Examination for Teachers). However, in 2003, in response to "No Child Left Behind," the rules changed and now all future elementary school teachers in California must pass the CSET, regardless of the undergraduate preparation they completed (students pursuing a single subject credential to teach in the middle and high school grades must either major in the subject they want to teach or pass the CSET in that subject and then complete a single subject credential). This test requirement, as well as a surfeit of bad press about teaching, led to a dramatic decrease in the number of students who pursued the liberal studies major across the state. At San Francisco State, the courses specifically designed for future teachers were outside the major, which also led to a dramatic decrease in the number of students completing these valuable courses. Consequently, we have recently begun to revisit something we have always avoided — having a separate major "track" for future teachers, which would include subject matter areas such as math, which are currently unpopular with students. We have discussed and decided against this approach many times over the years for at least three reasons. First, we believe that primarily, a teacher should be a well-educated person, not just one who has taken a set of courses that introduces her to a specific body of knowledge. Second, we have always valued the cross-pollination of the two populations of students in the liberal studies major and the fact that sometimes they crossed over — for example, often a student who has chosen liberal studies because it was interesting will discover that so many of her classmates are future teachers that she decides to pursue that path as well. Third, we value the tension inherent in the dual nature of the program, which provides its distinct nature that makes it attractive to students who choose the major.

Recent and Future Changes to the Major and Program

Several changes were implemented in liberal studies during the first year it had its own faculty. The first two major changes were curriculum related. First, the faculty created gateway and capstone courses in the major, the first major courses on campus to have a liberal studies prefix. With the creation of the gateway and capstone courses, the program is shifting to become more explicitly interdisciplinary. Second, the faculty implemented program electronic portfolios. The launching of these portfolios coincided with the first time the gateway course was taught in Fall 2008. The portfolios serve two purposes: 1) to help students understand and articulate the interdisciplinary nature of their education and 2) to help provide the framework for program assessment.

The third major change was geared towards increased program visibility. Over the past year we have worked on marketing the program both on the campus-wide level and nationally. Taking advantage of a leap year, on February 29, 2008, we held a campus-wide meeting entitled "Leaping Into the Future with Liberal Studies," which brought together stakeholders in the program — interested faculty members and administrators across campus — for a discussion of where the program might be headed. We discussed questions that will occupy much of our time over the next few years: (1) Should we reconsider the area structure of the major? (2) Should the list of core courses be expanded or contracted? (3) Should the emphasis structure change (e.g., students might choose a minor, create an interdisciplinary emphasis, etc.)? Should we have a separate specific track for teachers? We were heartened by the enthusiasm and energy of all involved in the meeting. The challenge will be to maintain that level of energy and involvement in the years to come.

Challenges and Work to Be Done in the Future

The 2007–2008 academic year was an exciting and busy year for us at San Francisco State. The liberal studies program has been reinvigorated by our new faculty members and by the hope and vision that they bring. However, we face some real challenges ahead to ensure their future success. What follows are just a few of the challenges:

1. *Integrating the New Faculty into the Rest of the University.* For example, should liberal studies stay in the Division of Undergraduate Studies (DUS)? Currently, we believe that it makes sense to keep the faculty housed in DUS. However, we have found over the past year that there were unanticipated challenges and consequences. As the only major program in DUS with tenure-track faculty members, our LS faculty members are isolated from the rest of campus. Having never had faculty members of its own, DUS had no systems and structures in place that are taken for granted in traditional academic colleges and we are learning daily about what we don't know. We find that we must constantly remind the rest of campus that we have faculty members and need to be included in the communication structure. Additionally, we face the challenge of integrating the faculty into the campus governance structure. The Academic Senate and committee memberships are traditionally chosen from among the ranks of college faculty. We are working with the Academic Senate on trying to include our faculty. At present, the senate is reluctant to include our faculty because they would be disproportionately represented. So at present they are disproportionately *under*-represented. Here is the danger of burnout — with just five faculty members there is no way for them to be involved on every committee. As Trow (1984/1985) has pointed out, young new faculty are usually energetic, but as an interdisciplinary program ages, their energy tends to wane and/or is difficult to sustain. Finally, there is the challenge of leadership and potential burnout of that leadership: the director is currently the associate dean of undergraduate studies and the RTP committee consists of tenured faculty members from across campus. These faculty members have volunteered for the gargantuan task of shepherding five faculty members through the RTP maze, while having similar responsibilities in their home departments. The issue of program sustainability is one of which we are fully aware, and which plays a significant role in our concerns regarding program leadership and visibility.

2. *Keeping the program an all-university endeavor, even as we have our own faculty.* Before having liberal studies faculty, it was clear to the campus and individual departments that the program could not exist without university-wide support. However, even with five faculty members, it is extremely challenging to administer a major for almost 700 students! We need to work to find the balance of including programs and colleges in our discussions, planning, and revisions, while making sure our faculty members retain control of the curriculum.

3. *Reconsidering what it means to be a Subject Matter Preparation (SMP) program for elementary school teachers.* There seems to be general agreement that we do not want to totally segregate future teachers from other liberal studies majors, but SMP standards are so broad and detailed that it is difficult to

ensure that these students get the specific content while still receiving the broad interdisciplinary experience we think they should have. As mentioned above, we are considering a separate teacher "track" to ensure that future teachers study the necessary subject matter. We would then have to address how much overlap there should be between the teacher track and the traditional LS major.

4. *Redefining the role of the Liberal Studies Council (LSC).* This senate committee has served in the role of department curriculum committee and general overseer of the LS program since the late 1970s. The members of the LSC, in conjunction with the dean of undergraduate studies, made sure that LS remained a vital and viable program. With LS faculty, what should be the responsibility and membership of the LSC? Currently a number of LSC members are serving as members of the RTP committee.

5. *Re-examining our curriculum.* One of the unexpected outcomes of hiring five interdisciplinary faculty members is that each one crosses the disciplinary areas that have organized and categorized our program for so many years. Since their research and teaching experience crosses the disciplinary categorization we devised, we are now forced to re-examine our program structure and ask questions that we have never had to consider.

Conclusion

When describing the recent changes in the liberal studies program at San Francisco State, I often find myself at a loss to explain how we got to this place. What advice could I give to others hoping to accomplish what we have done? Was there some confluence of events, some circumstance or incident that led to the hiring of our faculty members? As I explained earlier in this chapter, there were several campus and national initiatives that made the need for LS faculty clear, but as anyone who has worked at a college or university knows, the fact that something makes sense and is needed is no guarantee of its success!

The best answer I can come up with is that the major has remained important in the eyes of campus administration thanks to those involved in the program. Each dean of undergraduate studies over the past 30 years saw the major as a priority — they recognized the value of a multidisciplinary major that prepares future teachers, but at the same time, they also had the vision of an interdisciplinary major that would serve teachers and non-teachers alike — one that would prepare students to be able to understand complex issues and problems from a variety of points of view and help make them responsible citizens and future leaders. I have known and worked with all of

the people who have served as dean of undergraduate studies since 1980—
each of them clearly valued the goals of the program and tried to keep it as
strong and viable as possible. Since the 1990s, each dean has considered
requesting faculty, but Dean Robert Cherny felt that we had come to a point
where it was impossible to offer a quality program without being able to hire
them. Fortunately, Provost and Vice President of Academic Affairs John
Gemello agreed and perhaps this was because both Drs. Cherny and Gemello
had been on campus for many years and had served as both tenured faculty
and department chairs in their disciplines. Perhaps their experiences gave
them an appreciation for the impossibility the liberal studies program faced
in trying to offer a quality program with no courses or faculty of our own.
In addition, the liberal studies leadership over the years kept the liberal studies program in the consciousness of the campus at large. The LSC was fortunate to have long-term membership and leadership of faculty members,
including Ray Miller and Jim Davis, both of whom have contributed chapters to this book. LSC members represented their colleges and departments
on the council, but also represented liberal studies to their home departments.
As former liberal studies program coordinator and current acting program
director, I have made every effort to communicate with department chairs
and college deans on a regular basis to make sure that they were aware of the
contribution their courses make to the success of the LS program.

Happily, our new faculty members also see the importance and value of
becoming involved outside of the program. In their first year on campus, they
taught courses in a variety of departments, based on their individual teaching backgrounds: English, environmental studies, humanities, mathematics,
science, social science. In addition, from the very beginning, they have looked
for ways to integrate themselves into the fabric of the campus community.
They have done so not just as something to go into their personnel file, but
because of a desire to become involved in the larger conversations happening
on campus. They have followed their interests to the appropriate areas: for
example, the University Interdisciplinary Council, the steering committee of
the Center for Science and Mathematics Education, the Committee on Written English Proficiency. Two of our faculty members were part of a team of
four San Francisco State faculty who attended the Intensive Session of the
Yale National Initiative in July 2008 to explore the feasibility of San Francisco State creating a Teachers Institute in our area.

As mentioned at the outset, over the years we have opted for the term
"multidisciplinary" in describing San Francisco State's liberal studies program. With the arrival of our new faculty members and with recent and antic-
ipated changes to the curriculum, we hope that we will soon be able to
honestly describe San Francisco State's liberal studies program as truly inter-

disciplinary. We also anticipate that the revised curriculum and enthusiasm and expertise of these faculty members will attract and inspire more students who choose to become teachers who will become lifelong learners and who will impart their curiosity and cross-disciplinary approach to learning to schoolchildren.

NOTE

1. Written with assistance from Robert Cherny, former acting dean of undergraduate studies, professor of history, San Francisco State University.

REFERENCE

Trow, Martin. 1984/85. Interdisciplinary studies as a counterculture. *Issues in Integrative Studies* 3: 1–16.

CHAPTER 8

Transforming an Experimental Innovation into a Sustainable Academic Program at the University of Texas–Arlington

Allen F. Repko

The thirty-year-old interdisciplinary studies (INTS) program at the University of Texas at Arlington (UT Arlington) is a case study of how an experimental innovation in undergraduate education is transforming itself into a sustainable academic program. The key to this transformation is a comprehensive strategic plan that is student-focused, cost-effective, data-driven, assessment-minded, research-oriented, carefully innovative, mindful of program history, and realistic about institutional context. Though "politics" is an ever-present reality and even a determining one in some contexts, "politics" does not always explain why some programs succeed and others fail. Sometimes "politics" has far less to do with a program's demise than, say, its inability to adapt to changes in the institution's mission or its failure to constructively engage misguided local perceptions of interdisciplinarity. The field of interdisciplinary studies needs to identify best practices of successful programs so that programs that are under development or under threat can effectively apply these to their local situation. Some of the features discussed in this chapter typically receive little or no attention in the literature on program administration and include such mundane matters as how to historically situate the program, the importance of databases, marketing strategies, and effective report writing. Increasingly, interdisciplinary programs are compelled to justify their existence on both academic and economic grounds. University administrations are as concerned about budgets, program costs, and student fees as they are about academic standards, class sizes, and student learning outcomes. At a time of intensifying competition for scarce institutional resources and persisting doubts about the value of interdisciplinary studies, it is prudent for program administrators and faculty to develop and execute strategic plans for sustainability.

The Program's Conception of Interdisciplinarity

Sustainability means *the capacity to function indefinitely*. Developing a sustainable interdisciplinary studies program begins with having a clear notion of the nature of interdisciplinarity. However, "interdisciplinarity" and "interdisciplinary studies" remain widely misunderstood concepts by academicians and administrators (Repko 2007, 130). At UT Arlington interdisciplinary studies involved transforming what was essentially a multidisciplinary degree building program into a genuinely interdisciplinary program with its own courses and tenure-line faculty. This began in fall 2004, over twenty years after the program's inception. Among the initial decisions that we made was to develop an integrated definition of interdisciplinary studies that was informed by the work of leading theorists and practitioners (Julie Klein, William Newell, and Veronica Boix Mansilla). Our integrated definition of interdisciplinary studies is

> a process of answering a question, solving a problem, or addressing a topic that is too broad or complex to be dealt with adequately by a single discipline and draws on disciplinary perspectives and integrates their insights to produce a more comprehensive understanding or cognitive advancement [Repko 2008a, 12].

Believing that the local conception of interdisciplinarity should inform every aspect of the program, a clear statement of the program's distinctive mission was developed:

> The mission of the interdisciplinary studies program at the University of Texas at Arlington is to enable students to develop personalized, coherent, and rigorous undergraduate and graduate degree plans on topics or themes that cannot be achieved by majoring in traditional disciplines. The program also introduces students to the academic field of interdisciplinary studies which is a proven way to learn, think, and produce knowledge. Thus, the program's curriculum equips students to evaluate critically, think integratively, work cooperatively, and produce interdisciplinary understandings of real world problems and meaningful questions that are purposeful, practical, performance-oriented, and comprehensive [*www.uta.edu/ints/*].

Embedded in our mission statement are five premises:

- Students need explicit training in interdisciplinarity in order to address complex social problems.
- Students should be empowered to design their academic programs to optimize the available relevant knowledge across a wide range of disciplines.
- INTS should be the local expression of the field of interdisciplinary studies to ensure that the problems and issues are contextually and situationally located.
- The curriculum should foster the development of students' higher order cognitive abilities so that they are prepared to effectively engage complex problems.
- Student learning outcomes should include outcomes that are more characteristic of interdisciplinary learning, thinking, and research in order to differentiate interdisciplinarity from disciplinarity and multidisciplinarity (Repko 2008b).

Program History

In 1980, the administration submitted a "Request for a New Academic Degree Program" to the Texas Coordinating Board who authorized the opening of an interdisciplinary studies program at the Arlington campus. The "Request" addressed three needs. The first was the administration's need to participate with other University of Texas system schools in the wave of innovation and experimentation then sweeping higher education. At that time, system schools were especially attracted to general studies programs because they were cost effective. Students were able to pursue theme-based programs of study without the university having to develop new curricula or add new faculty. By contrast, interdisciplinary studies programs typically involved the development of new courses that were often team-taught.

The administration steered a middle course between the popular general studies approach and the more innovative but expensive interdisciplinary studies approach, combining features of both approaches under the rubric of "interdisciplinary studies." This hybrid program allowed students to construct theme-based programs of study but without the university having to add new courses and faculty who were *explicitly* interdisciplinary.

The second need that the "Request" addressed was for a flexible degree plan. A new generation of students entering the university in the late 1970s and early 80s wanted to take charge of their education and pursue professional goals that could not be accommodated by traditional academic majors. The interdisciplinary studies program allowed students to develop "unique academic programs tailor-made to their career goals and intellectual concerns" (Request 1980, 2). The administration was concerned that INTS degree plans avoid "single-minded, narrow specializations" on the one hand, and "essentially duplicating existing departmental programs" on the other (p. 2). From its inception, the program had to steer a course between these extremes. It did this by limiting the number of credit hours that students were able to take in a particular discipline (outside of the general education requirements) to 18–20, well below the hours typically required for a major.

The third need that the "Request" addressed was "an alternative to the departmental major" and, by implication, disciplinary hegemony (Request 1980, 2). Drawing on models of established interdisciplinary studies programs to guide them, the program's architects also blended features of the honors college model with features of the general studies model. In practice, this called for developing degree plans patterned after the rigorous, coherent, and customized plans typical of honors programs. This strategy permitted students to take combinations of courses pertaining to a theme, but prohibited them from making "random" course selections. But, in contrast to the high GPA entrance requirements of honors programs, the INTS program was open to *any* student who was "highly motivated," "self-disciplined," "brilliant," and "imaginative" (Request 1980, 2). This open enrollment approach, it was hoped, would make the innovative program attractive to a broad spectrum of students. Unfortunately, this lofty vision for the program was not shared by subsequent university administrations who viewed it primarily as a way to retain marginally performing students. This resulted in the program being widely perceived as an academic dumping ground, a perception that has only recently begun to change. The program did achieve considerable success in helping the university retain students who would otherwise not have graduated.

Not addressed in the "Request" was where the INTS program should be housed. The administration believed that it needed a period of administrative oversight, which explains why the program was housed in the provost's office rather than in the College of Liberal Arts (COLA), its natural home, until 2005. This structure effectively insulated the program from the intense competition for resources within COLA and from the growing negativity towards the program by some departments in COLA who mistakenly believed that our growth was coming chiefly at their expense.

In the program's early years, degree plans were drawn up with the assistance of voluntary faculty advisors. By the late 1990s the program's growth necessitated hiring a full-time academic advisor. From 3 students in 1981, the program grew to 241 students by fall 1999 administered by a part-time director who reported to the provost/vice president for academic affairs, two full-time advisors, and an office assistant. One drawback of replacing voluntary faculty advisors with advisors who were administrative staff was that it further isolated the program from the faculty.

Administrative Context and Faculty Status

Three developments between fall 1999 and spring 2004 laid the groundwork for our later transformation from a multidisciplinary retention program into a rigorous and sustainable academic program. The first of these was the administration's approval of our proposal to develop a core curriculum consisting of an introductory course and a senior capstone course. These were the first *explicitly* interdisciplinary courses at UT Arlington and among the few such courses at any UT system school.[1] Offered initially as electives when introduced in 2000–2001, they became core requirements for all INTS majors in fall 2003.

The second development was the program's initiation of a series of articulation agreements with area community colleges begun in 2001. These agreements formed the basis of the UT Arlington/Community College Transfer, or "TWO-STEP Program," that was funded by the Carl D. Perkins Education Act of 1998 through the Texas Higher Education Coordinating Board.[2] The TWO-STEP Program enabled INTS to use technical hours from participating colleges in its B.A. and B.S. degree plans (INTS Program Review 2003–2004, 19). The results of this effort have been impressive: From 42 transfer students comprising 12.3 percent of active students in the INTS program in 2002 when the TWO-STEP Program began, the number of students matriculating into the INTS program with technical hours grew to 179 in spring 2008, constituting 88 percent of new students entering the program that semester (Budget Hearing Report, April 1, 2008, 4).

The third and most significant development was the Program Review of March 2004 whose principal contributors were two external reviewers from the Association for Integrative Studies (AIS). They praised the university's vision in supporting the development of interdisciplinary studies as consistent with the 1998 Boyer Report on Higher Education, which called for providing ways to create interdisciplinarity in undergraduate education. However, they identified several areas of concern that they characterized as "constraints" to the program's development. The most serious of these was its organizational structure, which placed it outside of a regular academic school or college, thus "hindering the program from making the critical shift from a multidisciplinary degree program to a genuinely interdisciplinary one." A second constraint was that the program did not have "its own tenure-line faculty" (Program Review, March 3–5, 2004, 1).

To move the program towards sustainability, the reviewers made five key recommendations: (1) add an additional INTS core course that focuses on the interdisciplinary research process, (2) hire immediately an "anchoring" academic faculty member, (3) relocate the program in a more conventional academic structure, (4) consolidate existing enrollment rather than continue to expand enrollment, and (5) close the graduate program (which INTS had absorbed in 2002) until the undergraduate program was adequately resourced (Program Review, March 3–5, 2004, 2).

The administration moved swiftly to address each of these concerns. It closed the graduate program to new applicants in May 2004, added an anchoring faculty member in the person of a full-time director (the present writer), and committed funds to hire two assistant professor tenure lines *in interdisciplinary studies* with the first hire scheduled for fall 2005. To meet the program's immediate need for faculty to teach its two core courses, the provost authorized hiring two full-time lecturers and moved the program into the multidisciplinary School of Urban and Public Affairs (SUPA), which all stakeholders agreed was the best "fit" for the program and its mission.

This arrangement brought mutual benefits to INTS and its host college SUPA. For SUPA, which offers three Masters and two Ph.D. programs with some 250 students enrolled, adding 300 undergraduates immediately doubled the size of the School. For INTS and its new director, this arrangement brought numerous benefits including an increased budget, two additional tenure track lines in interdisciplinary studies, a relatively free hand for the director to develop the program, and a dean who was not only philosophically committed to interdisciplinarity and to the program's growth but also saw the program as a major asset to SUPA and to the university.

Seminal Curricula Features

Five seminal curriculum features contribute to the program's sustainability as a rigorous and mainstream academic unit. These include (1) a core of three courses required of all majors that present interdisciplinary studies as an academic field in its own right, (2) an emphasis on integration as a defining characteristic of interdisciplinarity, (3) the assertion that the end product of the integrative process — an interdisciplinary understanding — must be practical, purposeful, and performance-oriented (and thus assessable), (4) the development of student learning outcomes that are more characteristic of interdisciplinary learning than they are of traditional approaches, and (5) the careful "turfing out" from the core in a way that complements rather than competes with other courses and programs.

The first seminal feature of the interdisciplinary studies curriculum is its core of three required courses that present interdisciplinary studies as an academic field in its own right. This claim is based on the following criteria:

- Interdisciplinary studies has a **burgeoning professional literature** of increasing sophistication, depth of analysis, and thus utility. This literature includes sub-specialties on interdisciplinary theory, program administration, curriculum design, research process, pedagogy, assessment, and student learning. Most importantly, a growing body of explicitly interdisciplinary research on real-world problems is emerging.
- It makes use of disciplinary methods but these are subsumed under a **research process of its own** that involves drawing on relevant disciplinary insights, concepts, theories, and methods to produce new knowledge.
- It **produces new knowledge**, more comprehensive understandings, new meanings, and cognitive advancements.
- It is beginning to form a **core of courses** designed to introduce students to the field.
- It is forming its own community of experts.
- It is **training future experts** in older fields such as American studies and in newer fields such as cultural studies through its masters and doctoral programs and undergraduate majors [Repko 2008a, 9].

Introducing interdisciplinary studies as an academic field to students in the introductory course produces two practical benefits. It fosters the development of students' self-identity as interdisciplinarians at the beginning of their major. And it clarifies how interdisciplinary studies is a proven way to learn, think, and research that is different from that of the disciplines, yet dependent upon them.

The second seminal feature of the curriculum is that it identifies integration as a defining characteristic of interdisciplinarity and challenges students at every level to integrate conflicting disciplinary insights into a problem with increasing sophistication. Interdisciplinary integration is "the process of creatively combining ideas and knowledge from disciplinary and other sources to produce a more comprehensive understanding or cognitive advancement" (Repko 2008a, 123). Integration, according to leading theorists, is the hallmark of interdisciplinarity and of the interdisciplinary research process (Boix Mansilla 2005, 16; Boix Mansilla, Miller, and Gardner 2000, 18; Haynes 2002, xii–xiii; Klein and Newell 1997, 393–394; National Academy 2005, 39; Newell 2007, 245; Rogers et al. 2005, 267; Vess and Linkon 2002, 89; Klein 1996, 224). Integrationists are especially concerned with the process and product of interdisciplinary research, arguing that process determines product (Rogers et al., 2005, 267; Boix Mansilla, Miller, and Gardner, 2000, 18). The objects of integration are the defining elements of disciplinary perspectives — i.e., theories, concepts, and assumptions — that are expressed in disciplinary insights pertaining to a particular problem or question (Repko 2008a, 117). The program's emphasis on integration produces three practical outcomes: (1) It removes (at least at the local level) much of the semantic evasiveness surrounding the term "interdisciplinarity" that characterizes some corners of the Academy;[3] (2) it clearly differentiates interdisciplinarity from multidisciplinarity; and (3) it presents integration as both a natural and an achievable cognitive activity for undergraduates. Students progress cognitively in their ability to integrate or rectify conflicting disciplinary insights (including insights from interdisciplines and schools of thought) into a particular problem in each of the three core courses.

The introductory course provides foundational understanding of key interdisciplinary concepts and theories, examines the role of the disciplines and introduces their defining elements (e.g., assumptions, epistemologies, concepts, theories, and methods) and their role in interdisciplinary work, discusses integration as a hallmark of interdisciplinarity, and introduces students to the rudiments of interdisciplinary research and problem solving by focusing on real world problems such as global warming or euthanasia. At the end of the course, students are challenged to integrate a handful of conflicting disciplinary insights into the course problem.

The intermediate course introduces students to the interdisciplinary research process and its underlying theory. Students are asked to identify a problem or question that pertains to their stated career or professional goal and that is suitable for interdisciplinary inquiry. This problem or question is also the subject of the follow-on capstone course. In the intermediate course students are asked to justify using an interdisciplinary approach, identify three disciplines that are "most relevant" to the problem, identify peer-reviewed sources from these disciplinary literatures, evaluate these using close reading techniques, and identify sources of conflict (i.e., their assumptions, theories, and concepts) between them. The course prepares students for the interdisciplinary capstone course by introducing them to techniques used to create common ground and perform integration.

A third seminal feature of the curriculum is its emphasis on "testing" the integrated product of the interdisciplinary research process which Boix Mansilla (2005), principal investigator of the Interdisciplinary Studies Project at Project Zero, Harvard Graduate School of Education, calls an "interdisciplinary understanding" of the problem (2005, 16). The cognitive abilities developed in the research process course are leveraged in the senior capstone course where students, continuing to research and write on the problem begun in the intermediate course, are challenged to "test" the new understanding by offering a solution to the problem that is practical, purposeful, performance-oriented, and demonstrably more comprehensive than what single disciplinary approaches offer (2005, 14, 16). The concept of the interdisciplinary understanding, central to the program's conception of interdisciplinarity, is addressed in all three core courses in progressively sophisticated ways. In the capstone course, students use the new understanding to propose a policy, a piece of legislation, a model, a rubric, or a product (2005, 16–17). For example, a student researching the causes of obesity in young children may use the new understanding to develop a rubric for evaluating a local school district's approach to the problem. Increasingly, graduating seniors are profitably using their capstone projects (or an executive summary of them) to demonstrate to prospective employers or graduate admissions committees their interest in and knowledge of their profession.

A fourth seminal feature of the curriculum is its development of student learning outcomes on the course and program level that are characteristic of interdisciplinary learning, thinking, and producing knowledge. Too often, interdisciplinary outcomes are fuzzy and, because they are uninformed by research in cognition and instruction, tend to mimic disciplinary outcomes. Consequently, assessing outcomes in interdisciplinary contexts is often difficult because there is so little that is distinctly interdisciplinary to assess.

A fifth seminal feature of the curriculum is the careful way it is "turfing out" from the core. Proposals for new courses must meet three criteria: (1) meet a student need that is supported by data, (2) offer content that is explicitly interdisciplinary and include "interdisciplinary" in the course title, and (3) support a curricular partnership between INTS and another academic unit. Interdisciplinary Internship is an example of a course that was added as an elective in response to a survey which showed that 76 percent of INTS majors would likely enroll in such a course. Interdisciplinary Perspectives of the City is a course that supports the partnership between INTS and SUPA. The INTS/SUPA 4-1 degree program enables qualified students to earn a BA in interdisciplinary studies and an MA in urban affairs in five years.

Student Profile

The INTS program continues to attract and retain a substantial number of students from groups traditionally underrepresented in higher education. Specifically, INTS has a slightly higher percentage of African American students (19 percent) than the overall UT Arlington population (14 percent), the same percentage of Asian students (5 percent) as the overall UT Arlington population, but far fewer international students (less than 1 percent) than the overall UT Arlington population. Spring 2008 enrollment shows no significant change in the number of African American students entering the program compared to Fall 2007, but shows a slight increase in Hispanic students entering the program to 14 percent compared to 13 percent in Fall 2007. The ethnicity of the transfer students entering the program shows a developing trend of more whites (64 percent), more Hispanics (22 percent), and fewer African Americans and other minorities (14 percent), a profile more reflective of the demographics of the Dallas–Forth Worth metroplex. This trend will likely continue since the program is drawing an increasing percentage of its students from area community colleges where the Hispanic student population continues to grow. Significantly, of the 635 students in the program in spring 2008, almost two-thirds are working 30 to 40 hours per week and commute to campus. Student work schedules, combined with higher transportation costs, are prompting the program to develop distance education versions of its core courses.

Perception of the Program within the Institution

The perception of the program within the university was determined by administering a Perceptions Questionnaire to all full-time faculty and administrators in February 2008. Of the 1040 persons who received the questionnaire, 42 faculty and administrators completed it (which is only a 4 percent response rate). The low response rate means that respondent views are likely unrepresentative of the larger population and that what the other 96 percent of faculty thinks about the program cannot be known with any certainty.

The questionnaire consisted of fifteen questions that addressed six issues, including the respondent's understanding of interdisciplinary studies, the purpose of the INTS program, its academic character, the sources of its students, their academic performance, and the future of the program at UT Arlington.

All respondents agreed that the defining characteristic of interdisciplinarity and of interdisciplinary work is integration. This finding was both surprising and encouraging given the indeterminacy of the term "interdisciplinarity" on many campuses and the different understandings of the role that integration should play in interdisciplinary work. Also encouraging was the finding that 63 percent of respondents agreed that the purpose of interdisciplinary research is to "produce a result that is practical, purposeful, performance-oriented," and more comprehensive than could be accomplished by using single disciplinary means (Boix Mansilla 2005, 17–18).

Perceptions of the purpose of the program were slightly less encouraging. Whereas 61 percent of respondents thought of the program as a designer major program, 50 percent of respondents still thought of the program as *primarily* a student retention program (which it no longer is). Fully two-thirds of respondents had accurate perceptions of the program's academic character with 68 percent of respondents believing that the program is the local expression of an emerging nationwide academic field and 66 percent believing that the program has its own core of required courses. However, 50 percent were unaware that the program has tenure-line faculty.

Most respondents were uninformed concerning the sources of INTS students. They mistakenly believed the following: Most students come from existing majors, a relatively small percentage of students come into the program from the pool of undeclared students, and few students come into the program from area community colleges. However, half of respondents correctly assumed that the average GPA of graduating INTS majors is the same as the average GPA of graduating UT Arlington seniors.

Two findings concerning the future of the program at UT Arlington were particularly encouraging. Only 31 percent of respondents believed that the program should be folded into existing programs whereas 69 percent *strongly agreed* that it should be allowed to continue developing as any other academic program. Respondents by the same percentage (69 percent) believed that the INTS program is a valuable component of the UT Arlington academic community.

The following conclusions can be drawn from these findings. Respondents were well informed about interdisciplinarity and viewed it as an emerging academic field. However, respondents were not aware of how the program has been transforming itself into a rigorous and sustainable academic unit. Even so, most respondents felt strongly that the program was an asset to the university and should be allowed to develop. Clearly, the program needs to do a better job of informing the university community of its accomplishments.

Assessment Results

The program is developing a rigorous and comprehensive approach to assessing its academic as well as its advising components. This is a response to the call by Rogers, Booth, and Eveline (2003) for interdisciplinary programs to develop their own criteria for methodological and theoretical rigor so as to "contest the structural determinations of [the] disciplines" (16). Their argument is similar to that of Karl Schilling (2001) and Repko (2008b, 345) who call for a distinctly interdisciplinary approach to assessment. Stuart Henry

(2005) is concerned about "the risk that interdisciplinarity will become a sub-ordinated dimension of disciplines" if it does not differentiate itself as a distinctive way to learn, think, and produce knowledge (2005, 27). Mindful of these concerns, the program at UT Arlington has developed a distinctive, comprehensive, and rigorous interdisciplinary approach to assessment.

This regime centers on course and program *student learning outcomes that are more characteristic of interdisciplinarity than they are of multidiscipli-narity or disciplinarity.* These outcomes, grounded in recent advances in learning theory, are the focal point of the program's assessment regime. They include the student's ability to

- develop a clear understanding of the differences between disciplines to distinguish the essential characteristics of disciplines (i.e., perspective-taking) including their assumptions, epistemologies, concepts, theories, and methods relevant to a problem
- perceive connections between seemingly unrelated or epistemologically distant knowledge domains
- develop a personalized process of organizing and constructing higher levels of structural knowledge when confronting a complex problem that requires crossing different knowledge domains
- integrate conflicting insights, assumptions, concepts, and theories
- produce a cognitive advancement or interdisciplinary understanding that would not be possible using single-subject approaches
- apply the new understanding in a way that is practical, purposeful, and performance-oriented.

The program is concerned to differentiate clearly between outcomes that are more characteristic of interdisciplinary learning than they are of traditional approaches and thus avoid using outcomes that can be just as easily claimed by disciplinary and multidisciplinary approaches. There are four compelling reasons for drawing this distinction. The first is to align the program's learning outcomes with recent advances in learning theory, which show that the intellectual and cognitive outcomes characteristic of each approach are different (Ivanitskaya et al. 2002, 96). The second is to sharpen the cognitive focus of the program, which will give it greater cohesion as the curriculum expands and as new faculty are added. The third is to establish a clear and defensible standard by which to evaluate possible claims by other academic units that they too are "doing interdisciplinarity." The fourth reason for drawing this distinction is to demonstrate quantitatively that students are achieving the program's stated learning outcomes. Given the persisting misunderstanding of interdisciplinarity, local programs are well advised to engage in the hard work of building a comprehensive and quantifiable assessment regime to justify their existence.

Strategies for Sustainability

The program has a multi-faceted strategy for "sustainability" that is informed by Stuart Henry's (2005) helpful list of twenty "responsibilities" that an interdisciplinary program should assume (2005, 29–30). As mentioned previously, *a program is sustainable when it has the capacity to function indefinitely.* Sustainability is achieved when students, faculty, and the administration perceive the program as an academic and financial asset that is necessary to help the university achieve its mission. By "financial asset" is meant that the program attracts tuition dollars that might not otherwise flow to the university, retains tuition dollars that might otherwise leave the university, and secures grants and scholarship funds from sources that are supportive of interdisciplinary work. Thus far, the program has met the first two criteria and is beginning to lay the groundwork for achieving the third.

Few programs, including UT Arlington's, have the resources to take on all of the twenty "responsibilities" that Henry recommends. A program should assume only those responsibilities that are most likely to contribute to its success and sustainability within the local context. The UT Arlington program has chosen to focus its efforts on six primary areas, the first three of which are from Henry's list: (1) the development of "bridges and links" to other academic units, (2) the development of articulation agreements with area community colleges, (3) collaboration with external professional associations for interdisciplinarity, (4) the refinement of the program's "diamond in the rough" program, (5) the development of the program's student database, and (6) the program's marketing strategy.

Building "bridges and links" to other academic units, particularly to UT Arlington's graduate programs, is a vital component of the INTS program's strategy for sustainability. The first such "bridge" program is the INTS/SUPA Fast Track (4-1) Masters degree program in urban affairs. As of this writing, INTS is discussing a second program with SUPA involving its Masters degree in public policy, and is developing a Fast Track Degree Program with the School of Architecture involving the Masters in landscape architecture. INTS has a "link" program with the Honors College that gives qualified INTS majors Honors College credit for both the INTS intermediate research process course and the capstone course. One goal of these "bridge" and "link" programs is to thoroughly integrate INTS into the academic life of the university and avoid the pitfall that some programs have fallen into of becoming another academic silo. This goal is consistent with the administration's emphasis on building connections across academic units.

The second component of the program's strategy for sustainability is its promotion of articulation agreements with area community colleges, an effort that began in 2001. These agreements permit students pursuing so-called "technical" majors (such as forensic science) to seamlessly transfer their technical hours to UT Arlington and use up to twenty-four of these hours on a student's interdisciplinary studies degree plan, provided that they are relevant to the student's professional goal. The effectiveness of the program's aggressive pursuit of these "technical" college students is impressive: Of the 203 new students entering the INTS program in spring 2008, 179 or 88 percent matriculated from area community colleges. These transfer students graduate with a GPA that is equivalent to the average undergraduate GPA. The program's pursuit of these students — and the new tuition dollars they represent — is consistent with the administration's emphasis on strengthening ties with area community colleges.

Another component of the program's strategy for sustainability is its collaboration with external professional associations for interdisciplinarity and its seeking out leadership roles in these organizations. The program's director actively serves on the Board of the Association for Integrative Studies (AIS). As the program gains national attention, officials from other universities interested in developing or upgrading their interdisciplinarity studies programs are visiting the UT Arlington campus to examine the program firsthand. This development complements the university's strategic plan, which calls for promoting the university locally, nationally, and internationally (2006–2010 Strategic Plan, 6).

A fourth component of the program's strategy for sustainability is its "diamond in the rough" (DIR) program for students who have fallen below the university's minimum GPA of 2.0 and who do not meet the program's entrance requirement of 2.25. Each applicant meets with a program advisor who develops a holistic understanding of the student's academic situation, assesses the program's ability to help the student achieve academic success, and evaluates the likelihood of the student achieving the program's minimum GPA within a reasonable amount of time. Acceptance into the DIR program is based on three criteria: (1) The student must have a compelling story to explain his/her academic underperformance; (2) the student must be highly motivated; and (3) the student must be able to benefit from the program. With "close advising" and careful course selection, most DIR students succeed in raising their GPAs to qualify for unconditional admittance into the INTS program. In spring 2008, 88 former DIR students were in the program. The DIR program is consistent with the founding purpose of the INTS program that calls for it to admit "*any* student" who is "highly motivated" and can benefit from the program. It is also supportive of the administration's emphasis on retaining students and the tuition dollars they represent.

A fifth component of the program's strategy for sustainability is its student database. This database, administered by one of the academic advisors, serves two critical functions. First, it enables the program to generate the biannual "INTS Program Status Report" that is presented to the SUPA faculty each semester. This report details the scholarly activities of INTS faculty, highlights significant program developments, and presents student data on a wide range of topics including program growth, sources of new students, ethnicity of students, the DIR program, course enrollment totals, the number of students successfully completing each of the core courses, average student GPA, graduating student GPA, length of time in the program, grade distribution, retention rates, the number of students accepted in graduate programs, and advising loads. Each semester's data is compared to data from preceding semesters.

The second critical function of the database is to provide quantitative support for funding requests that the director submits to the dean, provost, and vice-president for financial affairs at the annual budget hearing. This "Budget Hearing Report" consists of a brief executive summary of how the program is helping to advance the university's mission, the program's two-year strategic plan, and the resources needed to accomplish the plan and advance the university's mission. Bullet points under each category are keyed to supporting data in the appendix in the form of tables, graphs, and charts. The program's success in meeting most of its funding goals is due not only to the program's steady growth but also to the reliable data that the director presents in support of these requests. For example, from the number of students completing the introductory course in an academic year, the data manager is able to project accurately student enrollment in the research process and capstone courses in the coming year which enables the director to make a compelling case for additional instructional funds.

Each budget hearing provides the university administration the opportunity to either fund growth by keeping funding at current levels or restrict program growth by reducing funding. For example, rather than argue for additional advising resources, the director simply presents the administration with two options, each supported by data. For example, the funding request for an additional half-time advisor in January 2008 was presented as two options: Option A was to fund the position which would enable the program to grow by another 100–150 students over the next year; Option B was not to fund the position which meant that it would be difficult for the program to grow much beyond the 620 students already in it. Fortunately, the administration provided temporary supplemental funding for this position, enabling the program to grow to over 750 students by September 2008.

Future Directions

The program receives strong political support from SUPA's dean and faculty, and from the administration. The latter frankly acknowledges that the INTS program has been resource-starved for a very long time, that it is an important and growing program, and that it clearly needs additional resources. Indeed, the administration has worked very hard in recent years to "right size" the program's budget. The level of the program's political and budgetary support is exemplary and cause for great optimism. That said, the program, its new tenure-track faculty, and its director face four major near-term challenges. These challenges relate to the underlying premises of the program noted earlier.

The first challenge is to accommodate growing enrollment in core courses while maintaining academic rigor with limited full-time faculty and instructional funds. In spring 2008, the program began experimenting with a new model for teaching its introductory level course that features large lecture sessions in combination with small "break out" discussion labs. Graduate teaching assistants, who assist the faculty with grading, lead the labs.

In fall 2008, a surge in enrollment in the program and in its core courses is necessitating that we adopt a new model for teaching the intermediate and capstone courses. Multiple sections of these two courses capped at 25–30 students are bring replaced by fewer but much larger sections taught by program faculty and assisted either by graduate teaching assistants or student assistants. The faculty is developing strategies to teach these courses so that they achieve the learning outcomes that are characteristic of interdisciplinary learning, thinking, and problem-solving, and maintain academic rigor.[4]

A second challenge is to attract high school students to the new fast track programs. Though INTS is drawing more students directly from area high schools, their numbers remain small, constituting only 12 percent of new students in spring 2008. For students to realize the maximum benefit of the fast track model, they must begin their program of study as freshmen. For the fast track programs to achieve their full potential, ways must be found to increase the number of high school students participating in these programs in larger numbers as freshmen. This will occur as high school counselors, students, and parents are made aware of the INTS program and, more particularly, the fast track option. To this end, INTS personnel are working closely with the admissions office to inform high school counselors of the INTS program and all that it offers.

A third challenge is to balance the curricular needs of two very different groups of students in the program. The first and larger group, constituting 76 percent of INTS students, have GPAs ranging from 2.25 to 2.9, and include the DIR students noted earlier. With rare exceptions, this student demographic does not aspire to graduate study and is interested in completing their degrees as quickly as possible. These students may benefit more from taking an internship and/or a senior portfolio course than writing the senior capstone research paper that is presently required of all majors. Students in the second group, constituting 24 percent of INTS students, have GPAs ranging from 3.0 to 4.0. An increasing number of higher GPA students intend to pursue graduate study at some point and would therefore benefit from having to write the capstone research paper. Students who participate in the fast track programs are required to take the capstone research paper course as well as specialized courses modeled after the integrative course Interdisciplinary Perspectives on the City, noted previously.

A fourth challenge is to use the "bridges" (to graduate programs) and "links" (to undergraduate programs) strategy to expand the INTS curriculum. The advantages of using a "bridges" and "links" strategy for curriculum development is three-fold: The partnering unit joins with INTS in requesting one or more INTS courses, the addition of new courses strengthens the program's case for additional instructional resources, and the program is less likely to develop a "silo curriculum" that is detached from other academic programs.

There are additional initiatives that the program can take beyond the "bridges and links" strategy that will further integrate it into the academic life of the university. These activities include networking with other academic units on projects of mutual interest, securing grants, partnering with disciplinary scholars in seeking grants, publishing in respected venues, engaging the community, and demonstrating the utility of interdisciplinarity as a way to learn, think, and research. Only by modeling interdisciplinary inclusiveness can the interdisciplinary studies program at UT Arlington achieve its full potential.

The greatest challenge facing the program is its growth rate. From 619 students in February 2008, the program has grown to over 750 students in September 2008. The combination of ever-growing numbers and limited resources is dictating our developing more efficient approaches to advising and teaching. The program must make the transition from the advising and pedagogical model that has proven successful thus far to a new model that will enable the program to accommodate far greater numbers of students, maintain rigor, expand its curriculum, and fulfill its interdisciplinary mission.

NOTES

1. By "*explicitly* interdisciplinary" is meant that these courses have as their primary student learning outcomes the distinguishing characteristics of interdisciplinary learning, thinking, and research which include consciously drawing on the perspectives of disciplines relevant to a particular problem, integrating conflicting disciplinary insights or expert views, and producing a new understanding that is more comprehensive than is possible to achieve using single disciplinary approaches.

2. Weatherford College Subcontract Agreement, August 26, 2005.

3. See, for example, the essay by Jeffrey N. Wasserstrom (2006, January 20), appearing in the *Chronicle of Higher Education*, in which he states that interdisciplinarity has become "so fuzzy that a university's commitment to it is close to meaningless" (p. B5).

4. These characteristics are discussed in Repko (2008b), Assessing Interdisciplinary Learning Outcomes, *Academic Exchange Quarterly, 12,* 3.

REFERENCES

Boix Mansilla, Veronica. 2005. Assessing student work at disciplinary crossroads. *Change 37* (January/February), 14–21.

Boix Mansilla, Veronica, William C. Miller, and Howard Gardner. 2000. On disciplinary lenses and interdisciplinary work. In *Interdisciplinary curriculum: Challenges to implementation,* ed., Sam Wineburg and Pam Gossman, 17–38. New York: Teachers College, Columbia University.

Budget Hearing Report. 2008, April 1.

Haynes, Carolyn. 2002. Introduction: Laying a foundation for interdisciplinary teaching. In *Innovations in interdisciplinary teaching,* ed., Carolyn Haynes, xi–xxii. Westport, CT: Oryx Press.

Henry, Stuart. 2005. Disciplinary hegemony meets interdisciplinarity ascendancy: Can interdisciplinary/integrative studies survive, and, if so, how? *Issues in Integrative Studies 23*: 1–37.

INTS Program Review. 2004. *Program Review: Interdisciplinary Studies (INTS).* (Review Team: John Campbell, Cathleen Jordan Stuart Henry, Don Stowe and Cubie Ward). Arlington, TX: University of Texas, Arlington, March 3–5.

Ivanitskaya, Lana, Deborah Clark, George Montgomery, and Ronald Primeau. 2002. Interdisciplinary learning: Process and outcomes. *Innovative Higher Education 27*: 95–111.

Klein, Julie Thompson. 1996. *Crossing boundaries: Knowledge, disciplinarities, and inter-disciplinarities.* Charlottesville, VA: University Press of Virginia.

_____, and William H. Newell. 1997. Advancing interdisciplinary studies. In *Handbook of the undergraduate curriculum: A comprehensive guide to purposes, structures, practices, and change,* ed., Jerry G. Gaff, James L. Ratcliff and Associates, 393–415. San Francisco: Jossey-Bass.

National Academy of Sciences, National Academy of Engineering, and Institute of Medicine. 2005. *Facilitating interdisciplinary research.* Washington, DC: National Academies Press.

Newell, William H. 2007. Decision making in interdisciplinary studies. In *Handbook of decision making,* ed, G. Morçöl, 245–264. New York: Marcel-Dekker.

Repko, Allen F. 2007. Interdisciplinary curriculum design. *Academic Exchange Quarterly,* 11: 130–137.

_____. 2008a. *Interdisciplinary research: Process and theory.* Thousand Oaks, CA: Sage Publications.

_____. 2008b. Assessing interdisciplinary learning outcomes. *Academic Exchange Quarterly* 12: 171–178.

Rogers, Yvonne, Mike Scaife, and Antonio Rizzo. 2005. Interdisciplinarity: An emergent or engineered process? In *Interdisciplinary collaboration: An emerging cognitive science*, ed., Sharon J. Derry, Christian D. Schunn, and Morton Ann Gernsbacher, 265–285. Mahwah, NJ: Lawrence Erlbaum Associates.

Rogers, Steve, Michael Booth, and Joan Eveline. 2003. The politics of disciplinary advantage. *History of Intellectual Culture* 3 (1). *http://www.ucalgary.ca/hic/website/2003vol3no1/framesets/2003vol3no1rogersarticleframeset.htm*. (accessed August 28, 2007).

Schilling, K. L. 2002. Interdisciplinary assessment for interdisciplinary programs. In *Reinventing Ourselves: Interdisciplinary education, collaborative learning, and experimentation in higher education*. Barbara Leigh Smith and John McCann, 344–354. Bolton, Mass.: Anker Publishing Company.

Vess, Deborah, and Sherry Linkon. 2002. Navigating the interdisciplinary archipelago: The scholarship of interdisciplinary teaching and learning. In *Disciplinary styles in the scholarship of teaching and learning: Exploring common ground*, ed., Mary Taylor Huber and Sherwyn P. Morreale, 87–106. Washington, DC: American Association for Higher Education and the Carnegie Foundation for the Advancement of Teaching.

CHAPTER 9

Interdisciplinarity Within Emory University's Academic Community

Peter W. Wakefield

"I want to make it clear that this is something I *do*, not something I *am*."

> *— quote from colleague in Emory University's Graduate Institute of Liberal Arts about her involvement in emerging faculty research themes*

If undergraduate interdisciplinary studies programs are under attack, one wouldn't know it at Emory University. Nor, for that matter, are staunch defenders of traditional disciplines all that easy to find. If there's any problem, it's that undergraduates don't really distinguish interdisciplinary from any other studies, and encompassing definitions of the interdisciplinary program — its role within the liberal arts college and its promise to students — are hard to agree upon. Current efforts at revision aim to increase structure within the undergraduate major, to provide a critical understanding of disciplines to undergraduate non-majors, and to draw on a tradition of outreach and innovative pedagogy. Such principles, I would submit, are what interdisciplinary studies are all about — more a practice, an openness, a hunger, than a methodology or finite body of knowledge.[1]

Emory's Graduate Institute of Liberal Arts (ILA), administrative home to undergraduate majors in both Interdisciplinary Studies in Culture and Society (IDS) and American Studies (AMST), traces its origins to the 1950s and is one of the nation's oldest graduate programs in interdisciplinary studies. The ILA's long and distinctive history engenders a general, if not always explicit, pride in the ILA among Emory administrators and faculty, especially those aware of the ILA's early outreach efforts and exchanges with neighboring Morehouse and Spelman colleges, part of a broader tradition of public scholarship and community engagement that has found a conceptual home in the ILA's graduate program. The ILA has in recent years enjoyed steady institutional support, a growing faculty (now at 19, of whom two are seconded to the office of the dean of Emory college[2]), and positive interactions with colleagues in other departments, who frequently offer courses, team-teach, or cross-list with the ILA.

But the commitment to graduate education enshrined in the very name of the ILA has meant that the undergraduate program has lived, here in the heat of Atlanta, in the mostly refreshing shadow of graduate research and teaching agendas of ILA faculty. The IDS major is the successor to two previous programs founded on interdisciplinary principles. A humanities concentration, that was available as far back as 1970[3] evolved into a Liberal Studies major (LS)[4] that appeared in 1980 and had early funding through NEH. Whereas the humanities concentration was staffed interdepartmentally by faculty in the Humanities Division, liberal studies courses were all taught by faculty from the ILA, who, though part of a graduate institute, took on the program as a contribution to the undergraduate college. The change in name from humanities to liberal studies was meant to mark the broader, mostly social science, backgrounds of ILA faculty who were not part of humanities. The 1980 organization of LS under the ILA made further sense in that the graduate programs in the ILA at the time were divided into an American studies track and a focus in "Culture, History and Theory" (CHT — a rubric broad enough to fit the interdisciplinary work of ILA faculty and graduate students who were not working primarily on the US). AMST faculty in the ILA at the time were supporting an undergraduate AMST major, so the LS undergraduate major constituted a similar service to the undergraduate college for CHT faculty in the ILA. Essentially, the LS major became an undergraduate version of the graduate program in CHT that was then part of the ILA. To this day, undergraduate interdisciplinary studies aims to shape itself around structural changes emerging in the graduate programs of the ILA.

In 1996, a name change occurred, and LS became the current IDS. I have heard various reports from colleagues who were involved in the name change about its motivation. Some say that "IDS" was seen by faculty in the ILA as broadening the connotation of the major beyond traditional "great books" or "liberal arts" curricula, a reflection of the ILA's significant emphasis on non–Western, post-colonial, and critical literature and research. Others say that a rumor was current at the time that a student or students, possibly apocryphal, presumably conservative, had complained about the political sense of the word "liberal." In any case, to judge from the college catalogs of those years, the name change to IDS brought no substantive changes to the LS major — it still required 3 courses with an IDS tag that had specifically interdisciplinary content, as well as seven other courses taken from any department at Emory College — the specification of *which* seven courses would satisfy the major in each individual case was to be arrived at through consultation with a faculty advisor from the ILA. This description fits the requirements of the IDS major today as well — seven, self-designed "concentration courses," and an array of specifically interdisciplinary "frame courses" (though today the frame courses number five — the two additions focus specifically on preparation and writing of the IDS senior research project).

To speak more of recent practice, in undergraduate IDS courses students have been exposed to the emerging research of ILA graduate students and to special topics courses that reflect the expertise of a faculty whose interests range from the history of disease to digital archives and the music of the American South. But, like its LS predecessor, the IDS major remains small (currently there are a dozen majors, down from a 2005 high of 28 — contrast French's 44), with only a general commitment from ILA faculty whose publishing agendas and close work with graduate advisees demand much of their attention. A dozen undergraduate IDS courses are fielded each semester, staffed, in roughly equal numbers, by ILA faculty, ILA graduate students, and faculty from other departments. The latter are drawn to the ILA when they have a course topic that falls outside of what their home departments would approve, or simply when they want to cross-list. Graduate students get teaching experience in a small number of courses (most notably "Politics of Identity" and "Visual Culture") that are routinely over subscribed and that have been offered every semester for the last several years because these courses satisfy college-wide general education requirements. ILA faculty, on the other hand, have explicitly raised the question (in a recent department meeting, for example) of why they should offer IDS courses at the undergraduate level — there are few majors to be served by faculty IDS courses, and offering a graduate course or an undergraduate course through another department is often either more interesting or more popular among students, or both. The few undergraduate courses currently taught by ILA faculty are offered mainly because the professor in question likes the topic of the course (which is often experimental) or likes the undergraduate format, or the two together. While there is general *encouragement* from Emory College and the ILA chair that ILA faculty offer undergraduate IDS courses, there has been no enforcement or anything like yearly quota of undergraduate IDS courses for ILA faculty. The reason for this derives, in part because of the unique situation of many ILA faculty, some of whose undergraduate teaching is exclusively in the American Studies (AMST) major, and many of whom have joint appointments or other connections with other departments and entities within Emory (some of these joint or special appointments involve reduced teaching loads to facilitate research). Thus, in any given semester, the majority of ILA faculty will be found teaching graduate courses or undergraduate courses in AMST.

In part, faculty hesitation to offer regular undergraduate IDS courses can be traced to the form of a major that is amorphous by definition, and occasionally unruly in practice. As I mentioned above, the major is student-designed, requiring twelve courses (48 credits), seven of which can be taken from any department in the college. Guidelines state that students should elaborate the content of the major in consultation with the undergraduate advisor for IDS. But until recently, the person filling the advisory shoes has changed upon season and semester, with the result that students, if not exactly gaming the system, took their frustrated efforts at finding sustained advising to the drawing board, where they collected courses from their transcripts or stretched notions of cohesion to constitute their major. In the rare, sad case, the IDS major became a retrospective "catch all" way to graduate for students who hadn't satisfied major requirements in any other department.

Further, the major has required a substantial senior project — generally a 50+ page research project that synthesizes the knowledge gained in disciplinary coursework on a specific interdisciplinary question or problem. The best IDS senior projects have frequently included a comparative and international dimension. As recent examples, take: Iranian ex-patriot literature as a genre; funding mechanisms and societal perceptions of Islamic schools in Senegal; or cultural perceptions and self-presentations in the marketing of the Beijing 2008 Olympic Games. The worst IDS senior projects, however, have gone begging for an ILA faculty advisor. Since IDS majors can take the majority of their required courses outside the ILA, and often light upon ILA graduate students or cross-listing faculty when they do take IDS-labeled courses, an undergraduate major could conceivably take all of her required courses without ever meeting one of the regular ILA faculty who are supposed to supervise the senior project. Add to this the need to correlate senior projects with the expertise of ILA faculty, and the spring semester of senior year can become a big headache for student and faculty alike.

Few undergraduates demand the interdisciplinary independence of a self-designed major because of frustration within disciplinary majors. More often, students are looking to compensate for disciplines or fields that, for intellectual reasons, find no place in Emory College (e.g. communications, conflict resolution, fashion, architecture). In some cases, students' vague preconceptions have been valuably shaped by faculty research interests — architecture merges with urban studies and the history of Atlanta, or communications reconfigures under the dimension of critical media and film studies. In a case where the sophistication of a student's love for fashion doesn't rise to the level of intellectual critique, however, the academic home provided by a student-designed major has been less happy.

The vast majority of students interested in the IDS major over the past two years have been individuals excited about some aspect of their personal experience — e.g. work with NGO's in Pakistan or Vietnam, training in performance music, or tutoring to immigrants in public schools — who are looking for a way to translate that excitement into a theoretical and critical context. These students are motivated and a joy to their advisors, but they are not disciplinary iconoclasts. Such students usually have defined interests in a number of fields, such that the process of shaping a cohesive major and a committee for the senior project is easy, especially when, as happens on occasion, the main advisor can be drawn from a field like global health (which offers only a minor at Emory College and whose faculty frequently collaborate with the ILA).

On the other side of the student-faculty divide, as the case of global health indicates, Emory professors in an array of departments are incorporating interdisciplinary dimensions into their teaching. Colleagues in English, for example, draw on museum culture and social history; comparative literature has a strong philosophic focus, with many faculty from French; anthropology at Emory has a strong medical focus, with ties to Emory's Schools of Public Health and Medicine; a university-wide strategic initiative in religion and the human spirit brings together faculty and students from religion, the arts, natural sciences and law; and the ILA itself has served in different capacities as an incubator for a number of forms of intrinsically interdisciplinary inquiry that now have their own departments: Women's Studies, Comparative Literature, Film Studies, and African American Studies.

Other, special cases of interdisciplinary study thrive largely beyond the ILA at Emory. An undergraduate major in Neuroscience and Behavioral Biology (NBB) is very popular (with over 300 majors) as a pre-med track and involves faculty from psychology, anthropology, and biology, among others (including some ILA faculty). Similarly based in natural sciences, a theme of a recent university-wide strategic planning process is computational and life sciences, which links medicine, biology, math, and computer science.[5] An Emory College assistant dean for undergraduate education is herself a chemist who has spearheaded efforts to introduce experiential learning and study abroad experiences to the natural science curriculum.

Thus, the broad culture of Emory College is one that not only supports, but even assumes interdisciplinary initiatives. Even practical aspects of interdisciplinary collaboration — such as team-teaching or innovative course offerings — take place under general administrative support, requiring only departmental approval. The perennial bane of departmental planning at many institutions, student enrollment numbers are not a pressure at Emory, as the institution strives to climb in national rankings against top–20 peers, in part by lowering student-teacher ratios. The ILA has traditionally enrolled large numbers of students in courses like "Visual Culture" and "Politics of Identity" that serve as an introduction to interdisciplinary studies for majors and fulfill broader general education requirements, but the pressure that comes from *US News* has rather been to keep even sections of these courses small, typically capped at 18. Likewise, given the privilege implicit in a student-designed major such as IDS, the desire of ILA faculty, with support from the college dean's office, is to emphasize the need for exceptional motivation and academic competence in IDS majors,[6] rather than to expand the number of IDS majors; the major will likely remain modest in size for the foreseeable future.

Articulations of Interdisciplinarity

A richer imagination withholds "paradise," but I expect the situation at Emory is one that colleagues at other institutions would envy. Nonetheless, there is work to be done, and not just because departmental meetings traditionally evoke the fretful veil. As director of the IDS major, I am involved in revisions that I would like to discuss at a more conceptual level. Briefly, the structure of the revisions to the undergraduate major in interdisciplinary studies is as follows:

- IDS 200: Foundations toward Interdisciplinary Study — a team-taught, lecture-style course addressing the question "What is evidence?" across various disciplines. Team teachers for this course will be drawn primarily from ILA faculty, who will thus have greater exposure and more flexible teaching opportunities with undergraduates, both IDS majors and others. The director of IDS will provide continuity as various sections of this class evolve over time, participating in the planning even when not team-teaching a given section. Guest visits to class by other members of the ILA faculty to talk about the question of evidence in their own research will be a regular feature of IDS 200.
- IDS 201 Special Problems in Interdisciplinary Studies: smaller, problem-based developments of the question of "What is evidence?" applied to particular research problems central to on-going faculty and graduate student instructors' research. Themes will vary across sections of this class that will be taught by ILA faculty, graduate students, or teams of faculty and graduate students. The motivation

is to allow researchers, including graduate students, to design an undergraduate class that reflects on issues in their current research, yet plays to the unifying theme of evidence. IDS majors will be required to take both IDS 200 and 201; other students will be strongly encouraged to take IDS 201 in conjunction with IDS 200.

- IDS 300/700-level: flexible in theme, these courses reflect at an advanced level on-going research interests of the faculty; frequently team-taught, involving both undergraduate and graduate students (course work for enrolled graduate students would include an instructional component with the enrolled undergrads)
- IDS 400: Capstone Seminar, possibly in conjunction with AMST senior seminar, when numbers permit: involving a substantial writing component that will replace the independent senior project.

Note: IDS 400- and IDS 300-level classes would be taught primarily by the faculty of the ILA and the role of the director of undergraduate students would be either to team-teach these sections or otherwise to provide structural and intellectual continuity to the course offerings by close consultation with and administrative support the faculty teaching these courses.

The preceding courses will replace current five "frame" course requirements that each IDS major must fulfill in addition to 28 credits (seven courses) of the student-designed "concentration" courses. In particular, "Politics of Identity" and "Visual Culture" will probably fade from the graduate student teaching experience, in favor of IDS 201. The structural changes that the preceding courses carry with them are the outcome of discussions both private and in committee with ILA colleagues and are meant to address various principles that effectively articulate a shared conception of interdisciplinarity:

1. Curricular content: "eating" great books[7]
2. Collaborative conversation: interdisciplinarity embodied in practice
3. Critical organizing problem: shared questions that divide us
4. Traditions of engagement: positioning of student in class, university, society

I develop each of these points now with implicit reference to the IDS 200 gateway course that launches in fall 2008, though these themes could be traced through any of the levels of the revised IDS major outlined above.

1. Curricular Content

At the level of curricular content, I have rather sheepishly worried whether my collaborative efforts in designing IDS 200 are not a reinvention of a great books course. Just as quickly, I wonder at my sheepishness. The course in question takes the question "What is evidence?" as a theme that will allow texts and faculty colleagues to speak to each other: *A Study in Scarlet, Antigone, Republic* VII, *Consolation of Philosophy, Wife of Bath's Tale, Franken-stein, Starry Messenger, Hard Times, Great Gatsby, Midnight's Children,* etc. While I admit to myself in private moments the musty core of me that wants to die among the stacks, straining toward the silent, eternal song of words — "then what else but great books?" — this course takes its pitch not from reverence or ageless resonance, rather empowerment, the questions asked — asked by students, asked by faculty who love and live with these texts. Students are aware that they frequently lack the cultural reference of their own favorite satires; they know the joke's against them, their own faults in history. For all that, they are no less skilled in satire or sampling or historical memory of their own design. IDS 200 aims to open the texts studied as historical and human tools toward understanding ourselves and the enforced intellectual practices — the disciplines — that have surrounded these texts. "Is Sherlock Holmes a work of science or of art? For the scientist, there is a deeper irrational space revealed in Holmes' addiction," explains Elena Glazov-Corrigan, Emory, Russian Studies, who will team-teach the class with me in fall 2008.

Having read the works that whisper nightly to their teachers, the class will invite colleagues from across Emory, but primarily from the ILA, to the world of imagination opened by these readings, to see how evidence emerges differently for different questioners of these texts. *Antigone* as form of daughter, family, desire, and deeper soundings of the human psyche; *Frankenstein* embodying memories, personal and national, of mothers lost — nurturing given over to obsessive rationality without imagination; *Great Gatsby*'s valley of ashes as an insight into Atlanta's own rise from ashes and the social, racial, class-related costs of the phoenix.

Students will come to see credentialed texts not only as keys to historical moments, but also at play across disciplines, and ultimately consumable for their own social, educational, moral projects. Guadeloupean writer Maryse Condé speaks of a writerly reading process of *cannibalism*, which in essence breaks taboos, uses icons to outrageous purpose, and transforms imposed texts into one's own life — the forms, the themes, the language of great books, but consumed, digested and turned into something proper to oneself. What concerns can this text serve for each student? What experiences shape each student's own interrogation of the text? What do they see as their own here? We want to sample, to eat the canon, to come away with a full feeling of discipline — those who represent it and how — that will embolden student choices in their own majors. This seems a worthy purpose for an undergraduate interdisciplinary program.

2. Collaborative Conversation

The practice of collaborative conversation will be built into this course and central to learning outcomes. A modest number of faculty colleagues (roughly six per semester), chosen for their disciplinary breadth, appreciation of interdisciplinary projects in general, and of this course in particular, and sustained excitement for one or more of the course texts, will visit class. The purpose of such visits will not be authoritative presentation, rather, to open the texts, to establish another voice. Visitors will face interrogation on their method and use of the course text, but also on their stake — the place this book finds in their library, their home, their thinking. How does this established scholar conceive of her reading of the text in relation to her field and her imaginative life? What history — personal, professional, or human — does this text carry for this scholar before us? There is an embodiment of interdisciplinary method — perhaps the most genuine — in the unscripted, varied associations of simple, serious conversation about books and ideas. In an atmosphere of strategic planning, tenure case-building, and paper-grading, we can forget to talk to each other, to stand defenseless before texts, to share our minds. But this is the reason why we love our colleagues; this is where interdisciplinarity is most at play. We must avoid the disciplinarian's mistake: Method must not precede its ground, namely a habit of mind.

Further, recall the challenge I outlined above — that undergraduates at Emory have a limited number of opportunities to work directly with ILA faculty, due to the graduate focus of research. One ramification is that the IDS program and the ILA generally are poorly understood as entities, even by graduating IDS majors. The interactions with ILA faculty accomplished by IDS 200 will put faces and ideas to the Institute of Liberal Arts. Visiting faculty will not only implicitly advertise the other courses they teach, but will enter a relationship established by IDS 200 as a venue — for future visits, for possible team teaching, or for potential design of their own versions of IDS 200 around other organizing themes. IDS 200 is meant to serve as a "green space," not only for undergraduate introduction to the ILA and the IDS major, but also for faculty collaborations and intellectual engagements.

3. Critical Organizing Problem

The closest that IDS 200 and other aspects of the revision of the IDS major come to structuring the interdisciplinary experience is in specification of a critical organizing problem. What questions are shared across disciplines, such that the different answers, and *methods* of answering, mark the boundaries of current university departments? In the planning stages of IDS 200, this question was at the center of discussions in an undergraduate planning subcommittee of ILA faculty, and it is a question that has traditionally shaped ILA colloquia. Examples of shared questions are that of IDS 200 in its first incarnation: What is evidence? But the course is conceived to allow for structuring around other such questions: What is the past? What is death? What is reproduction? To explore notions across artistic, literary, political, social, legal, and religious perspectives can make for rich understandings out of the most meager of conceptual beginnings. *We simply slow down.* Is this the interdisciplinary method stated anew?

Again, what new insights and questions emerge when the ways of answering a question are applied to another discipline's question? Students in IDS 200 will look at Jared Diamond's *Guns, Germs, and Steel,* which in part explains history via geological coincidence, availability of resources, and disease. Diamond's method, his radical rethinking of historical explanation, will serve students as an intellectual site — a model of inquiry to which they can compare new insights reached through the understanding of history that emerges from the study of other course texts and from visitors' interpretations of these texts.

If Diamond looks at history through the lens of disease, equally interesting questions arise if you flip and ask whether disease can be explained by history — e.g. the history of particular doctors investigating, treating, experiencing, and characterizing certain diseases.[8] IDS 200, and the related set of more intensive, problem-based courses that will fall under the rubric of IDS 201: Special Problems in Interdisciplinary Studies, attempt to provide an ongoing framework within which such curving questions can be raised. This, too, seems to be distinctive of our interdisciplinary institute here at Emory: Where interdisciplinary investigations are common across many departments at Emory, the ILA is attempting to create forms for classes that themselves shuffle disciplines, rub them together, and challenge assumptions that fall out of them.

4. Traditions of Engagement

I feel compelled to recognize *liberation* as the principle behind the ILA's traditions of engagement — engagement across Atlanta, across racial and class divides, and across traditional academic forms that can be exclusionary of those outside the academy. By the 1970s, ILA faculty had set up NEH-funded joint programs and exchanges with the traditionally black colleges of Spelman and Morehouse. The ILA was the original administrative home of African-American studies at Emory, and several faculty currently hold joint appointments. Emory's Center for the Study of Public Scholarship was founded by an ILA faculty member, and has opened Emory university to a wider range of knowledge than the academic, through its focus on the connections among academia, museums, and the arts, as well as between the U.S. and South Africa. The ILA is aware of its more public role than other departments, a theme that has explicitly shaped recent institutional planning.

At the undergraduate level, revisions to the IDS program, and IDS 200 in particular, attempt to take up this tradition of engagement under a spatial metaphor of positioning. The pedagogy of an interdisciplinary class must not leave learning models implicit or unchallenged. Students are neither banks, made fungible through deposits of information, nor disembodied minds fallen from brilliance but for critical reading skills, nor immaculate seeds scattered on the wind of curiosity and in search of fertile soil in the economy of the post-graduate workplace. Emory stands geographically and socially on the side of Atlanta, and too few students (not just at Emory) are challenged academically to acknowledge the urban and historical space they occupy. The Trail of Tears passes through Georgia. The history of civil rights, likewise, tends to stick too thoroughly to the amber past in this too-busy city. Racial and social justice cannot be enshrined in national historical sites, when the dirt and trees themselves call for more. In a Ntozake Shange poem, the poet relates the experience of a child who is black and poor, nameless and unloved. In the poem, one day he is gone, "& his blood soaks up what's awready red / in atlanta."[9]

Students will read Shange's poem, which takes its spark from the series of murders of children that occurred in Atlanta in the late 1970s, but which speaks truths of other sorts of racial and social effacements. Do students know that the dirt beneath the quad is red — a staining red that has demanded labor? This will be a starting point: for students to understand what is "awready red" about this earth, this city, this state.

IDS 200 will support and coordinate with other extra-curricular projects going on at Emory, including the Transforming Community Project (TCP) and the Piedmont Project. The former initiative has over the past three years responded to racial injustice on campus and beyond by organizing a structured series of conversations across faculty/staff/student divides. TCP also supports research projects addressing race at Emory, including the racial history of the institution and the campus itself. What histories of injustice besides the Atlanta Child Murders are hidden in local geographies? Where has Emory stood in these histories? Where can students now take Emory with regard to the very social dynamics they are a part of as students at this institution?

The Piedmont Project similarly calls the university community to reflect on its physical location and practice, but under the lens of sustainability and the institution's relation to the natural environment. Students in IDS 200 will leave the classroom on certain days to walk in Emory's surrounding forests, to understand simple natural phenomena, such as native plant species and the watersheds that traverse the campus mostly unnoticed. They will also investigate Emory's role as the largest private employer in Metro Atlanta, specifically what this means for the communities and the natural spaces occupied and traversed by Emory's 21,000 employees. Attending to the natural environment will not only generally stretch students to place their education in an ecological context, but will also support the curricular units of IDS 200 on romanticism and imagination of the natural and sensual world.

Both of these projects and the broader emphasis on engagement present a challenge to students in IDS 200 to understand their scholarship as a public act. Students are agents in a particular social and historical network, and their first responsibility to this fact is awareness. The knowledge and skills they gain through the course are also power and potential. Students will be presented with the puzzle of conceiving of their course work under the category of broader social implications — where will they take this course? With whom will they share it? How will it change the world through the changes wrought in them?

In many ways and quite explicitly, the notion of public scholarship is one that Emory University's ILA has endorsed, not just as a historical dimension of our work, but, when conceived expansively, as the principle and desired outcome of all our work. To be responsible publicly for our work, we must be aware of our institutional and social privileges, located in an urban and moral history, and open to ways of communicating the significance of what we do to audiences expected and unexpected.[10]

Conclusion

Far from being faced with a choice between dissolution or definition along the lines of a discipline, Emory University's Graduate Institute of Liberals Arts and the related undergraduate major in Interdisciplinary Studies in Culture and Society are, rather, enjoying institutional support in our efforts to provide a model and venue for explorations and conversations already taking place that constitute the intellectual curiosity of colleagues across departments. The ILA will continue to foster an academic "green space" that opens unexpected vectors in the encounter between student passions and faculty expertise. Team-teaching experiments, a critical understanding of the social, moral, and historical geography of academic knowledge, and a commitment to understanding scholarship as a public act define our practice of interdisciplinarity at Emory University.

NOTES

1. My understanding of Emory's Graduate Institute of Liberal Arts and the vision of interdisciplinarity outlined in this chapter have benefited greatly from conversations with many colleagues at Emory. Thanks goes to my colleagues in Emory's Graduate Institute of Liberal Arts, especially Angelika Bammer, Edna Bay, Kevin Corrigan, Elena Glazov-Corrigan, Walt Reed, and Dana White. Walter Adamson, History, and Gretchen Schulz, Oxford College also helped my understanding of the history of the ILA. The approach to interdisciplinary studies embodied in revisions to Emory's IDS program, including the new .course IDS 200, which I discuss below, and my general project in this paper of articulating a definition of interdisciplinarity from actual practice, find theoretical support in scholarly discussions of interdisciplinarity. Cf. Joe Moran (2002): "My main argument will be that we cannot understand interdisciplinarity without first examining the existing disciplines, since interdisciplinary approaches are always an engagement with them, and the modes of knowledge that they exclude by virtue of their separation from each other." By the same token, I argue that interdisciplinary approaches must be understood through the practices of those teaching and engaged with disciplines through interdisciplinary research. My approach is also consistent with Julie Thompson Klein's assertion that two ways in which the modern concept of interdisciplinarity have been shaped are "by the emergence of organized programs in research and education;" and "by the emergence of identifiable interdisciplinary movements" (see Julie Thompson Klein 1990) My location, intellectual and professional, is in one of the latter "identifiable movements."

2. One is the dean himself—a coincidence that has not hurt the ILA in institutional planning.

3. *Emory College Bulletin, 1970–71* describes the humanities concentration as a "Divisional Program ... of human studies distinctive to individual studies in the ancient world, the medieval world, and the modern world" (*Emory College Bulletin 1970–71*, 73). By 1975, this conception had been broadened: "An alternative to concentration in one of the departments of the College [that] provides the student with an opportunity to develop an interdisciplinary emphasis rather than concentrate in a single department and a broad education especially for the student who intends to enter a professional school upon graduation" (*Emory College Bulletin 1975*, 66–67).

4. *Emory College Bulletin, 1980–81* describes the Liberal Studies *major* along the lines of the Humanities *concentration* of preceding years, but with the modification that the LS major required 10 courses, including "a group of interdisciplinary course offerings," such as "LS 112: Youth, Identity, and the Self" (*Emory College Bulletin 1980–81* 90). By 1994, the *Emory College Bulletin* described the imagined LS student more specifically, if still somewhat vaguely: "The major in Liberal Studies is particularly suited for the intellectually adventuresome student whose interests cut across a variety of disciplines. Concentrators normally combine a core of discussion-intensive interdisciplinary liberal studies courses with more specialized courses taken from different departments" (*Emory College Bulletin* 1994, 143). Among the LS courses in 1994, one finds "Interdisciplinary Perspectives," and "Old World/New World." Liberal Studies faculty in 1994 were the members of the ILA.

5. The practical separation of interdisciplinarity in the natural sciences and elsewhere at Emory might map on to Moran's (2002) distinction between "competing impulses behind the term" 'interdisciplinary': "On the one hand it forms part of this traditional search for a wide-ranging, total knowledge; on the other it represents a more radical questioning of the nature of knowledge itself and our attempts to organize and communicate it" (Moran 2002, 15).

6. Five of seven IDS majors graduating in May 2009 are aiming for honors.

7. I elaborate below, with reference to the work of Maryse Condé, on how this course

attempts to draw on literary notions of cannibalism and internalization. A concise exposition of Condé's theory of literary cannibalism can be found in Dawn Fulton (2008), who quotes Condé's "*Des héros et des cannibales*": "For Oswaldo de Andrade and the modernists of the early twentieth century, it is not enough to simply eliminate intellectual colonization, to simply reject Western culture. Instead Western heritage must be desacralized and then ingested. We must subvert Shakespeare, the canonical European author par excellence, and ridicule his her Hamlet so as to better appropriate him" (quoted. in Fulton, 124; Fulton's chapter is entitled "Unfamiliar Cannibals").

    8. The work of ILA colleagues Sander Gilman (1982) and Howard Kushner (1999), who will visit IDS 200, exemplifies this description.

    9. Excerpted from Shange (1983, 45).

    10. A key feature of broader responsibility for the scholars we send forth must be greater tracking, communication, and involvement with IDS alumni. A survey is currently being prepared to gather better alumni data, which has been sorely lacking to date. The most recent program assessment, in 2005, focused primarily on structural problems with the IDS major, outlined above. Student data in the assessment refers primarily to students who were then-current in the program.

References

Emory College Bulletin, 1970–71.
Emory College Bulletin, 1975.
Emory College Bulletin, 1980–81.
Emory College Bulletin, 1994.
Fulton, Dawn. 2008. *Signs of dissent: Maryse Condé and postcolonial criticism.* Charlottesville, VA: University of Virginia Press.
Gilman, Sander. 1982 [1996]. *Seeing the insane.* New York: John Wiley and Sons.
Klein, Julie Thompson. 1990. *Interdisciplinarity: History, theory, and practice.* Detroit: Wayne State University Press.
Kushner, Howard. 1999. *A cursing brain? The histories of Tourette syndrome.* Cambridge, MA: Harvard University Press.
Moran, Joe. 2002. *Interdisciplinarity.* New York: Routledge.
Shange, Ntozake. 1983. About Atlanta. In *A daughter's geography.* New York: St. Martin's Press.

CHAPTER 10

Turning Points:
New Century College at
George Mason University

Janette Kenner Muir

New Century College (NCC) at George Mason University is a story of challenging tradition, surviving difficult times and educational innovations. The story is somewhat comic, certainly tragic, but in the end, heroic. It is a story worth telling as it provides several lessons for how to do interdisciplinary research and pedagogy in a research institution accustomed to privileging disciplinary teaching and scholarship. The issues surrounding the evolution of New Century College are complex, and must be considered within the context of the campus community and changing trends in higher education. Despite its successes, early reports about the college raised several issues of concern for the university. Discussions focused on concerns about faculty development, credit evaluation, course duplication, and the overall rigor and utility of integrative and interdisciplinary studies. Some administrators believed that the value of the college, strongly evidenced by a variety of indicators of student support, student performance, and faculty scholarship, was not maximized for the benefit of the university as a whole. Yet many leaders recognized that the face of higher education was changing, and universities needed to find ways to structure educational experiences to adapt to changing technologies, evolving marketplaces, and shifting public expectations. The university of the 21st century, many knew, must develop processes for identifying and facilitating the adoption of techniques and strategies that work. However, there were skeptics who found much to criticize. In order to understand the various political ramifications, in this article three major turning points will be described: a shift in college oversight, an example of non-consultative decision-making, and a reorganization of college structures. But first it is important to describe NCCs formation and contribution to George Mason's interdisciplinary education.

NCC was formed in the mid–1990s as a response to questions being asked nationally about the quality of the college experience for students, both academically and socially. Numerous critiques about higher education such as Allan Bloom's *The Closing of the American Mind,* challenged the intellectual standards and rigor of institutions of higher learning and the lack of a common purpose. These critiques were echoed by then Department of Education Secretary William Bennett and Lynne Cheney, head of the National Endowment for the Humanities, who also called for reform proposals.[1] As university costs climbed, many critics were concerned about the quality of education that students received and questioned the overall benefits they gained from earning college degrees from research institutions. Many students would claim that their main motivation for college, bolstered also by employer demands, was to earn the necessary credentials to make money and succeed in one's career; fewer students were concerned with "acquiring a meaningful philosophy of life."[2]

At the same time, a movement was afoot to rethink the college experience. Already in place were successful college examples such as Evergreen and Alverno, and conversations were happening across the country about how to deepen the experience for college students. The Carnegie Foundation for the Advancement of Teaching supported numerous initiatives to enhance teaching in higher education, and Ernest Boyer's *Scholarship Reconsidered* was an effort to rethink faculty expectations around scholarship and teaching. In response to concerns about the quality of colleges and universities, in 1993 the State Council for Higher Education (SCHEV) offered grants to Virginia institutions to develop new curriculum for student learning. Known for its innovative spirit,[3] George Mason University responded to this charge, and a group of interested George Mason faculty gathered to consider what kind of learning would be most valuable for students as they approached the 21st century. In 1994, the "Zero-Based Curriculum" project asked faculty, staff and administrators to consider the following question: If we started again from scratch, with no preconceived ideas about what an educated college student should look like, what would we, as informed and experienced faculty, create?[4] After more than two years of work, a great deal of intellectual energy, and a hefty commitment of resources, New Century College was born.

Creating a College

NCC began in 1995 with its first freshman class of two hundred students. After almost fifteen years in existence, through some tough political challenges and reshaping in terms of administrative structures and curriculum offerings, the college now flourishes, offering an integrative studies major with interdisciplinary concentrations, four interdisciplinary minors, a unique freshman experience, a living/learning residential program, experiential and service-learning programs, and areas of excellence in education, multimedia/ information technology, leadership and conservation studies. Seminar-style learning communities and field-based classes provide educational experiences that deepen connections for students. Essential facets of the NCC program will be briefly discussed by describing key pedagogical and curricular innovations.

Innovative Pedagogies

COMPETENCY-BASED LEARNING

As a key facet of learning in an integrative environment, a focus on competency-based education is a critical part of NCC's pedagogy. Patterned after programs such as those offered by Alverno College, nine competency areas currently frame the curriculum: communication, group interaction, critical thinking, strategic problem solving, effective citizenship, aesthetic awareness, global understanding, valuing and information technology.[5]

Recognizing that competency development can be challenging to assess, the idea of portfolios was introduced and has become an essential part of NCC learning. As a measurement of learning, a portfolio provides a compilation of student work either in a class or in the overall program. Reflective writing and evidence of learning are staples in this development. Students complete portfolios in their first year of college addressing their learning in several competency areas and providing evidence such as papers, photographs, email missives, and faculty feedback to provide a robust picture of themselves as learners. These portfolios are stored electronically and are available to students when they reach their final year in NCC.

In order to graduate with an integrative studies degree, students must show competency development through a final graduation portfolio where they are asked to provide evidence of learning throughout their college years, around the competency areas and their chosen academic path. Evidence of learning can be through actual course assignments, learning experiences outside the classroom, such as internships and study abroad, and experience in campus life activities.

EXPERIENTIAL LEARNING

Another important facet of NCC's pedagogy, experiential learning best supports the NCC motto of "connecting the classroom to the world." Recognizing this to be such a valuable part of learning, students majoring in

Integrative Studies must complete at least 12 hours or 10 percent of their college education in learning that moves outside the classroom and provides lasting connections for students.

Incorporating experiential learning activities in classes is not an easy proposition for faculty who need to cover course content and also think about ways to enhance competency development for students. Realizing that committed faculty and program support are essential to successful experiences for students, NCC sponsors two campus centers — the Center for Leadership and Community Engagement (CLCE), and the Center for Field Studies (CFS). These centers provide resource and informational support for experiential classes and individual learning activities. CLCE, for example, supports a variety of campus programs on leadership development, service learning, and alternative break activities such as helping rebuild homes in New Orleans after Hurricane Katrina, or working with inner-city children in New York City. CFS supports field-based courses such as scuba diving in the Bahamas, geography lessons in the Shenandoah region, and fieldwork observing the 2008 New Hampshire primary campaign. These centers facilitate the logistics of travel and work outside the classroom, thereby supporting faculty teaching and helping to improve student learning.

LEARNING COMMUNITIES

Another important facet of NCC pedagogy is the use of learning communities and team teaching. Much work has been done around this concept, and the National Resource Center for learning communities, sponsored by Evergreen State College, serves as a useful place to seek information on this type of pedagogy. The Center's website describes learning communities in higher education as:

> [C]lasses that are linked or clustered during an academic term, often around an interdisciplinary theme, and enroll a common cohort of students. A variety of approaches are used to build these learning communities, with all intended to restructure the students' time, credit, and learning experiences to build community among students, between students and their teachers, and among faculty members and disciplines.[6]

NCC's learning communities are structured with many of these ideas in mind. Classes vary in credits from 2 to 8, are often team-taught, and focus on problem-based inquiry and the integration of disciplinary content. For example, a course on youth advocacy combines elements of family communication, community psychology and political science to think about ways to empower future teachers and young people; or a course such as conservation studies will combine a biologist with a nature writer to explore issues that impact the environment.

In NCC, learning communities are interdisciplinary, team-taught and collaborative. By combining disciplinary perspectives around problem-based inquiry, these classes attempt to provide structure to the often-fragmented learning that students experience as they work their way through unconnected courses. Active participation and interactions between students, faculty and the wider local community are emphasized.[7]

Learning communities, experiential learning and competency-based learning are important pedagogical facets of the program. Each facet is a college graduation requirement for the college, and together these aspects frame a vital way to engage students and encourage lifelong learners. These facets are also important for preparing students directly for the workplace, responding to the increased demands for marketable skill sets. How these pedagogical innovations impact actual curricular reform will be discussed in the next section.

Curriculum Development

The First Year Experience

NCC's First Year Experience (FYE) was developed based on a recognition that the freshman year of college is often the most crucial for students in establishing good academic habits and making connections to the institution and to social communities. The idea behind this first year curriculum is that the courses are integrative, combine academic coursework with student life, and provide a place where students make lasting connections both socially and academically. Collectively, this year serves as an important foundation for the remaining college years by providing much of the course content intended for the general education requirements at George Mason.

FYE currently consists of four sequential 8-credit learning communities, taught by faculty teams and integrating basic course areas such as composition, math, science, the arts, world history, government, and information technology.[8] The learning communities are currently taught in six-week increments with break time in between to finish course requirements. Completion of the first year equals thirty-two credits, fulfilling most of the general education requirements for the university. A focus on intensive writing, technology integration, and off campus experiential learning activities frames learning in the first year.

In keeping with the idea of establishing a strong first year foundation, NCC also supports living/learning floors in the residential halls. Many students immersing themselves in the first year program find it helpful to live with others going through the same experience. As a result, what began as a one-floor commitment in the residence hall has now grown to almost three full floors.

AN INTEGRATIVE MAJOR

NCC's focus on interdisciplinary and integrative studies combines inter-disciplinary knowledge with workplace and lifelong learning skills. The integrative studies major requires students to engage in active learning and research, and prepare for living and working as citizens of a global community. Faculty members are committed to teaching and learning, and serve as mentors for students, often engaging in research and teaching collaborations. Integrating theory and practice, students develop programs of study that support the pedagogical innovations of the college.[9]

Both the structure and curriculum of the New Century College degree program challenge students to think deeply about the ways they learn. To do this students are asked to engage in reflective practice through intensive writing and portfolio work. This is a major form of assessment for the college and is used as a way to measure student learning and programmatic development.

Students who major in integrative studies choose an interdisciplinary concentration as a way to focus their studies. Originally, the program was comprised of over ninety different concentrations; however, criticism about duplication with disciplinary departments and lack of faculty expertise in some areas led to administrative pressure to streamline the program to twelve primary areas, while retaining the option for students to design their own degree. Each concentration integrates learning communities and experiential learning, and is created in a way that maximizes flexibility for students. Different options are provided and students are encouraged to further specialize through minors such as multimedia, nonprofit studies, sustainability and leadership studies. A final capstone course provides a space for students to reflect back on their learning during their college years, assess their experiences outside of the classroom, and think about ways to market themselves with prospective employers more familiar with college graduates who come from traditional disciplinary programs.

Given the various innovations, it is important to note that these ideas did not always find great campus support. Challenges were raised about the quality of student learning, the amount of resources needed to sustain this kind of program, and the potential "turf" issues that could develop as students chose academic paths similar to traditional departments and faculty from other departments found it more invigorating to teach in learning communities. These challenges prompted several defining moments for the college that illustrate some political implications of interdisciplinary program development.

Turning Points

As stated at the outset, in spite of being framed as a response to national and state challenges about the quality of college and university education, reports about New Century College raised issues of concern for the university regarding faculty development, credit evaluation, course duplication, and the overall rigor and utility of integrative and interdisciplinary studies. In order to understand the various political ramifications, three major turning points are described in the following section: a shift in college oversight, an example of non-consultative decision-making, and a reorganization of college structures.

Turning Point 1: Cautious Optimism

Approximately four years into NCC's program, concerns expressed by non–NCC faculty and campus administrators about resource and space allocations and program quality escalated when GMU's Board of Visitors (BOV), a group appointed by Virginia's governor to oversee university matters, began to take a serious look at NCC's curriculum and pedagogy. A primarily conservative board at the time (reflective of a highly-partisan Republican governorship) was somewhat skeptical of the type of courses offered and the possible duplication of coursework with other departments. Some BOV members were concerned that learning communities lacked disciplinary depth; yet they also were apprehensive about a learning community appearing too disciplinarily focused, thus making it seem better suited for a traditional department. Finally, there was a great deal of discussion about what students actually majored in with an interdisciplinary degree and its marketability with prospective employers.

After much debate and lobbying, despite the recommendation of a faculty review committee initiated by the president and BOV that NCC remain autonomous, the decision was made to move NCC from an independent college to a quasi-college under the auspices of the College of Arts and Sciences. This would be a "college within a college" model. NCC was to maintain its own graduation requirements and convocation while answering to the leadership of CAS as overseers. More conservative BOV members were "cautiously optimistic" about the long-term success of this move. Faculty members and others sympathetic to NCC also expressed cautious optimism, but for entirely different reasons. They worried about the lack of autonomy under this new college structure, the potential impact to NCC's resource allocations, and the possibility of curricular reform that would not match the mission of the innovative college.[10]

In 2000, NCC moved bureaucratically and structurally into CAS, under an academic dean who had previously, in a speech to the BOV, recommended closing the college. Interdisciplinary programs, he argued, lacked rigor at the undergraduate level and were generally a waste of resources. Defined as a marriage of sorts between the two colleges (some referred to it as a "shotgun wedding"), there was a great deal of frustration expressed by the NCC faculty who had to provide greater justification for teaching methodologies and content that did not fit into traditional disciplinary frameworks. Some administrators believed team teaching to be half the work and less responsibility, leaving more time to focus on research. Ideas of variable credit (thinking beyond three credits = one course), counting experiences outside the classroom, and bringing together faculty from various disciplines to focus on problem-based inquiry, were all suspect under this new college paradigm.

The move into CAS, while initially cordial and supportive, resulted in a number of administrative decisions. First, some administrators believed that too many resources were being channeled into the program, and NCC's budget was therefore reduced by more than 50 percent, moving from a million plus budget to approximately $500,000. Budget cuts resulted in the loss of faculty positions within NCC along with increased workloads for NCC faculty and staff. Previously, resources had been used to encourage faculty from disciplinary departments to teach in NCC learning communities. In turn, resources were provided to departments for full-time one-year replacement positions so that departments would not have to hire adjuncts to cover these classes. Once this budget was so substantially reduced, NCC lost the ability to engage in significant faculty exchanges with other programs. What was once a vibrant place for university faculty to come and experiment with new pedagogical methods and to work with those from other disciplines, turned into a place with limited resources and declining faculty numbers as some chose to move on to other programs in the university and beyond. With the loss of faculty, so went the ability to experience different teaching teams, to effectively handle faculty governance, and to build relationships across campus. NCC faculty were simply too busy and too stretched to make up for the losses they experienced under the College of Arts & Sciences.

A second significant decision impacting NCC focused on greater curriculum oversight by CAS. Prior to the move, as a separate college NCC had a curricular structure in place that carefully assessed each new learning community and experiential learning course. Once under the jurisdiction of CAS, the college had to provide a different level of explanation for curricular approvals. Taken at face value, this would seem appropriate, however, the problem was in attempting to explain variable credits, competency based learning, and team teaching. Faculty who worked in traditional departments had difficulty discerning how one could consider student experience outside the classroom as credit-bearing, and often argued about duplication when courses appeared too similar to what was perceived as disciplinary territory.

NCC survived this turning point, but had to make several changes in order to do so. Faculty numbers declined, leaving fewer faculty and staff to do the teaching, advising and governance needed to help the college function. Faculty morale also declined due to the belief that CAS administrators made little attempt to understand the unique design and mission of the college, not least to understand that it originated in a state mandate to improve the quality of undergraduate education. Faculty were asked to make greater university connections, but with limited staff and resources it was increasingly difficult to establish the campus relationships that would help to engage faculty beyond the college.

Turning Point 2: Crisis of Confidence

Moving beyond the initial challenges of resource and faculty losses, a second turning point occurred that resulted in increased skepticism about CAS's intent to support NCC. A dean's decision to move a program out of NCC, without any consultation with faculty or administrators responsible for the program, resulted in a crisis of confidence for the faculty and a loss of credibility for the CAS Dean.

Early on in NCC's development, interdisciplinary programs within the university shifted as administrators looked for appropriate homes for these departments. Through this process, an undergraduate social work program and an adult degree, the Bachelor of Individualized Studies (BIS), were moved under NCC's umbrella. While the fit was not perfect, the missions of each program were similar, and much work was done to integrate these programs into the college. New curricular designs, re-envisioned websites, inclusive governance and shared teaching philosophies were ways that these programs began to build synergy and create a vibrant college with a variety of programmatic options.

After some time, it became clear that the social work program needed to move out of NCC because the department was intent on building a Masters program. For accreditation purposes, social work needed to be placed in a structure where it could gain more visibility and show parity with other programs around the United States situated in stand-alone social work schools. The BIS program, however, was a different story.

Adult learners taking classes in NCC found the environment to be interesting and refreshing. Faculty enjoyed advising BIS final projects and found these students to be some of the strongest academically. Despite the thriving environment, CAS administrators determined that the BIS program would be best as a stand-alone department within the larger college. This decision was made without any discussion with those who ran the program or who were familiar with its operation. The removal of this degree from the college was also poorly communicated to students and faculty. The CAS dean wrote a letter to all BIS students, but integrative studies majors also found out about this letter and mistook it to say that NCC, as a whole, was closing. The letter made it into the GMU's campus newspaper, *The Broadside*, and many students grew concerned about the validity of their degrees and the survivability of the college.

The result of this decision and subsequent move in 2004 was that the BIS program grew increasingly isolated. After the move, the program went through three directors and experienced a physical move into smaller space. Fewer BIS students were seen in NCC classes and the synergy between the programs was significantly altered. BIS also experienced difficulty in maintaining consistent contact with NCC faculty to serve as advisors and mentors. Most importantly, this decision, and the specific way it was handled, created a crisis of confidence for faculty and staff, resulting in a great deal of ill will between CAS and NCC.[11]

Turning Point 3: Restructure and Redefinition

Despite the turning points that occurred early on in the history of NCC, the college managed to survive and thrive. The ten-year anniversary was evidence of resilience and the ability to bounce back, especially in the midst of loss and multiple changes. A final turning point worth discussing came with the restructuring of the College of Arts and Sciences into two separate colleges — the College of Science (COS) and the College of Humanities and Social Sciences (CHSS).

The impetus for larger systemic change was a combination of the need to reduce the size of CAS, provide a more concentrated focus on the sciences, and better manage the resources of what had been a somewhat unwieldy college. Faculty were mixed in their support of this division, and NCC, in particular, believed that this bifurcation would be harmful to the NCC faculty with scientific expertise. There was also concern about the impact this split would have on science-oriented NCC concentrations such as pre-medicine and conservation studies.

Despite protestations, and with a great deal of administrative support, COS and CHSS were formed. New Century College remained in CHSS, along with most other interdisciplinary programs that carried a humanities and/or social science focus. Four aspects of this restructuring turned out to be beneficial for NCC. First, the internal selection of a dean familiar with interdisciplinary learning, and the specific programs in CHSS, helped position NCC in a way that generally required less explanation and justification. Second, this dean created a structure that grouped all eleven interdisciplinary programs situated in the college in a way that provided greater synergy and support for these interests, including resources for special interdisciplinary programming.[12] Third, governance structures were created for the new college that provided greater transparency and accountability. With more committee structures and opportunities to participate in governance, NCC faculty moved to the forefront of leadership in CHSS, serving on committees such as curriculum, promotion and tenure, strategic planning, and the Dean's Council. Finally, under this college structure, a new associate dean for NCC was appointed following a nationwide search. This administrator brought work and scholarship experience in leadership studies and was instrumental in elevating NCC to a greater position of strength in CHSS. This associate dean's portfolio has expanded to working with more interdisciplinary degree programs within CHSS,[13] which has interesting implications for the future in terms of program expansion and consolidation.

Living within the new college structure has ultimately been beneficial to New Century College. Programs continue to grow and NCC is starting to prepare for its 15th anniversary. New faculty members (replacing those who have retired or moved on to other jobs) have joined the college bringing fresh energy and ideas. They have heard stories of NCC's earlier years and recognize the potential problems the college could face with administrative changes and budgetary challenges. However, they seem willing to commit to the college's mission and recognize the political and administrative work that needs to be done to thrive in this innovative interdisciplinary environment. Although the initial move was faced with skepticism, and while it is still challenging for those with scientific expertise to live in this college, it seems clear that the restructuring and the administrative shifts have, at least in the short term, been beneficial.

Lessons Learned

Through almost fifteen years in existence, New Century College has experienced definite highs and lows. The three turning points described above are moments in time that significantly impacted the direction of the College and the morale of the faculty and students. The question to ask, especially in light of the politics of interdisciplinary studies, is what lessons have been learned in the process and what best practices are in place to help NCC continue to move forward?

Students Matter

Early on in NCC's development it became clear that unique students were attracted to the college. With its focus on leadership development, for example, NCC plays a distinct role at George Mason in attracting and developing student leaders. Opportunities available for students, along with the support from the Center for Leadership and Community Engagement, cultivate a student body engaged in leadership and service activities around the campus. Some of the positions that have been held by NCC students include: president of student government; speaker of student government; managing editor of *Broadside*; president of the Golden Key Honor Society; president of the Delta Sigma Theta sorority; chair of the Program Board. NCC students also serve as orientation leaders, resident advisors, and peer mentors on campus. Clearly there is a strong campus-wide presence of NCC students, an aspect of the college that has managed to gain the attention of campus administrators.

NCC students also seem to be more engaged with their academic experience. Every three years, NCC administers the National Survey of Student Engagement (NSSE) survey that compares first-year students at George Mason with students in the NCC First Year Experience. Findings tend to indicate that NCC freshmen engage in more writing and critical thinking assignments, are more likely to stay at George Mason for their college career, and report "higher levels of academic challenge, more engagement and collaboration in learning and a more positive campus environment."[14]

As graduates, NCC alumni are also making significant accomplishments. Many go into teaching and work throughout the Northern Virginia region. Others go into careers such as the Peace Corps, develop their own businesses, work for NGOs, or work in corporate settings. Recently, the NCC alumni association has endowed a scholarship for an NCC undergraduate and gives an annual award to outstanding alumni. These actions speak to the success of the college and the long-term affinity that many NCC students feel towards the program.

Throughout its turning points, NCC was always concerned about the significance these changes would have for students and the long-term impact on their undergraduate degrees. There were times when students lifted morale for faculty and staff who were discouraged and disillusioned by college changes. In the sharing of intellectual authority and collaborations, NCC has managed to foster a vibrant collection of students willing to take active roles in shaping their academic experience and supporting the college's long-term goals. These examples of student and community support show that while senior administrative leadership is crucial, if a program can show clear evidence of student learning and community support, it may survive leaders who do not fully support the program.

Assessment Matters

Early on in NCC's existence, it became clear that the college would need to provide continual evidence of its effectiveness in order to receive ongoing administrative support. NCC had to prove that its teaching and learning methods were essential for student development and that the pedagogical focus was "cutting edge." Given the resources needed to manage a program such as NCC and the amount of work faculty accomplish in teaching within the college, assessment matters significantly for evaluating student and programmatic development.

Evaluating Students

As noted earlier in the discussion on competency development, portfolios are used extensively as a means for evaluating student learning. These portfolios begin in the freshman year and are built upon throughout the student's college career, culminating in a graduation portfolio that assesses competency development and student preparation for life after college.[15] Work is currently in progress to develop an online repository where students can collect materials from each learning community in a secure, easily accessible place. Students will be asked to engage in on-going reflective practice so that, by the time they are ready to complete their Capstone requirements, the process will be more manageable given that materials have already been collected in one place.

There are many other forms of assessment for NCC students beyond the portfolio process. Given the learning community focus, a great deal of collaborative work takes place through group research and presentations. Nearly every learning community has some kind of group experience integrated into the curriculum and this type of collaborative learning is often noted by students as a major aspect of their learning. Writing is also a large area of assessment in the college. Given that learning communities satisfy the composition requirements of the university, they are generally writing intensive with multiple drafts and peer review integrated into the coursework.

Evaluating Program Requirements

Beyond the student evaluative process, it is also essential for the NCC program to be continually evaluated for its effectiveness. Part of the rationale for the yearly NSSE survey is to gather information about student learning and the programmatic elements that need to be carefully considered.

Outside evaluators have visited NCC to assess its effectiveness in specific areas such as student engagement and competency development. Several dissertations have also assessed various programmatic aspects.[16]

In 2008, NCC has undergone an extensive program review as a requirement for Southern Association of Colleges and Schools (SACS) accreditation. In this process, several surveys have been conducted with current students, faculty and staff and alumni. Once this program review is completed, NCC will have a more thorough picture of areas that need possible restructuring.

As students are asked to be thoughtful and reflective about their learning, NCC must also do the same. Given its focus on innovation and interdisciplinarity it is critical for the college to think about ways to grow and change as the student body changes. Integration of new technologies, consideration of new ideas for experiential learning and developing ways to better deliver learning communities are always at the forefront of how work is accomplished in the college.

Building a National Reputation

Though often feeling like "strangers in their own land," New Century College has managed to build a national reputation for innovative pedagogy and interdisciplinary development. Participation in national conversations about learning community pedagogy and serving as a programmatic model for other schools are ways that the program has built a national reputation. Some of these activities are described below.

PARTICIPATION IN NATIONAL STUDIES

As NCC developed, others began to take notice. One striking example was the NSSE Disseminating Effective Educational Practices (DEEP) project. Representatives conducted a campus site visit, and spent a great deal of time learning about NCC. The team found that although the whole campus focuses on the incorporation of collaborative and active learning, NCC serves as a national model for the ways in which an experiential approach to teaching can enhance student learning.[17]

The success of that visit, in large part, led to NCC's selection for the Boyer Center Partner Assessment Project, a national study looking at eight programs around the country that emphasize strong relationships between academic and student affairs. NCC was also chosen to participate in national curriculum projects such as SENCER (science education and civic engagement), Diverse Democracy (increasing civic engagement on campus) and the national Learning Communities dissemination project funded by Pew Trusts. NCC has also joined groups such as the Council for Innovative Educational Learning (CIEL), and is currently participating in a study with Washburn University.

NCC MODEL

In 2004, George Mason's *US News & World Report* ranking of 18th in the nation for learning community pedagogy was due, in large part, to the work that was accomplished in NCC.[18] Offering freshmen and upper-level learning communities every semester, available to all GMU students, NCC is now a campus leader on how to create learning environments that improve student satisfaction and academic results. As the last SACS accreditation report noted: "NCC may serve as one of the best models of what George Mason means by learning centered."[19]

NCC innovations have also been modeled in other parts of the country. College and universities around the country have inquired about NCC pedagogy and many people come to visit the campus to learn more about the program. International visitors from the United Kingdom and Russia have also come to learn about new innovations in higher education, and the NCC model. NCC curricula is gaining attention as the freshman syllabus for Unit 4 (NCLC 140) was selected by the American Political Science Association as one of ten best syllabi for teaching about democracy, and science curriculum in the conservation studies concentration has been noted by the SENCER Institute (Science Education for New Civic Engagements and Responsibilities) as a national model for teaching about issues impacting the environment.

These brief examples are important illustrations of the ways NCC has intentionally worked to build a reputation beyond the university borders. Establishing this reputation has been an important part of illustrating the college's impact and gaining the attention of campus administrators. Showing examples of other institutions interested in the NCC model is helpful for navigating the internal politics of the program and proving the staying power of interdisciplinary studies.

The NCC Faculty: Committed to Teaching and Learning

Despite budget changes over the years and reduced faculty numbers, NCC has continued to build a program in which faculty members can thrive. While there are fewer faculty from around the university participating in the college, there are now more full-time faculty with NCC lines. The faculty currently consist of a full professor, several associates, and at least five in tenure-track positions. There are also several "term" faculty renewable every one to three years, graduate teaching assistants who teach in learning communities and advise for the college, and several staff administrators who also help to manage the program.

Every year since 1996, at least one faculty member teaching in NCC has won a university teaching award, more than any other unit or department on campus. Two NCC faculty members have been the recipients of the prestigious David King teaching award, an award that recognizes long-term teaching and commitment to George Mason University. NCC faculty members have held senior scholar positions at the American Association for Higher Education (AAHE) and the American Association of Colleges and Universities (AAC&U). They have served as national journal editors, as lead investigators on several teaching-oriented grants, and NCC faculty members have been recognized at the state and regional levels for teaching excellence.

Additionally, faculty and administrators connected to NCC have found value in working with colleagues doing similar work across the country. In 2005, NCC hosted a joint national conference Association for Integrated Studies (AIS) and the Association for General and Liberal Studies (AGLS). This conference brought together national scholars grappling with issues around integrative learning, general education and interdisciplinary foci. NCC is also committed to working with CIEL schools that are geared toward innovative learning techniques for the classroom.

As mentioned earlier, NCC faculty are highly committed to campus governance, serving on the Faculty Senate and several university committees. Nearly every full-time faculty member is involved in governance within the new college structure. What we have learned from these political and organizational experiences is that to deal with the politics of interdisciplinary learning we must be engaged, working from within to impact organizational and structural change for the benefit of student learning. In this way, those who express skepticism about the college begin to gain clarity because they have worked with NCC faculty and thus have a better understanding of how the program works and the commitment necessary to make it happen. Thus, working from within can transform attitudes and begin to change behavior, albeit sometimes more slowly than some would like to see.

Towards the Future

As NCC moves ahead there are many unknowns about the future, in particular about programs and about next steps. The college now operates from a place of strength and faculty continue to find new ways to engage students in interdisciplinary and integrative aspects of teaching and learning. However, recognizing what has worked in the past is simply not enough. NCC is a program founded on innovation; therefore, it must always be forward-looking, seeking new methodologies and pedagogies to engage students of the 21st century. There is never time for complacency in interdisciplinary learning — NCC must continue to seek ways to more fully engage with students, in a rapidly changing educational environment; at the same time it must be resilient in defending its proven core educational values.

NOTES

1. For a discussion of early higher education critiques see Bok (2006).

2. See statistical note offered provided by Bok, p. 26.

3. George Mason was chosen by the American Association for Higher Education (AAHE) as an innovative institution to be studied for best practices in student learning. The work in NCC was an important part of this study. See. Kuh, et al., 2005).

4. John O'Connor, "Zero-Based Curriculum Proposal."

5. For a more thorough discussion of each competency area, consult NCC's website, *http://ncc.gmu.edu/competencies.htm*. Retrieved 25 June 2008.

6. Learning Communities National Resource Center, Evergreen State College Washington Center. *Http://www.evergreen.edu/washcenter/project.asp?pid=73*. Retrieved 25 June 2008.

7. More information on learning communities in NCC is provided on the college's website *http://www.ncc.gmu.edu/learncomm.html*. Retrieved 25 June 2008.

8. It is important to note at this juncture that a task force is reviewing the first year curriculum with a goal to revisit the initial assumptions and keep abreast of innovations in higher education. Recognizing the need to always look to the horizon and be responsive to student learning needs, the task force is in the process of making suggestions for how this First Year Experience may look in the next decade. Some suggestions currently being considered are shortening the amount of credits per learning community, revisiting the current time frame for classes, developing a program that will appeal to students with AP and IB credits and rethinking the combination of general education requirements integrated into each current unit. The new framework is slated to be rolled out in Fall 2009. For an update on the new requirements, please consult the NCC website: www.ncc.gmu.edu.

9. See NCC website.

10. These issues were raised in a transition report that was developed at the time of the move into the College of Arts & Sciences. Members of the transition task force directly addressed these concerns by attempting to establish guidelines for how CAS and NCC would work together. This lengthy report evolved into a two page synopsis that laid out a basic structure for the initial transition. Much of the details of the plan would be worked out as NCC settled into its new structure.

11. It is interesting to note that the program now has a new director who is supervised by the associate dean for New Century College, also the overseer for other interdisciplinary programs in the college. Therefore, it is possible that there will be more synergy between the programs in the future.

12. For a description of all the programs situated in the College of Humanities and Social Sciences and the ways interdisciplinary programs are defined, consult the CHSS website at *http://chss.gmu.edu/chss/about/index.cfm*.

13. CHSS interdisciplinary programs include: New Century College, the Program for Higher Education, Masters of Arts in Interdisciplinary Studies, the BIS program, to name just a few examples.

14. "NSSE Report," 2004, George Mason Office of Institutional Assessment.

15. For an example of graduation portfolio guidelines, consult the NCC website noted above.

16. One example of programmatic research can be found in Adina Elfant's dissertation: A Study of the Relationship Between Integrative Studies Freshmen Learning Styles

and Their Instructors' Learning Styles Represented By Students' Course Achievement. George Mason University, 2002.

   17. Kuh, et al., 198.
   18. "America's Best Colleges Guide — Top Rankings for Learning Communities." *United States News and World Report*, 2004.
   19. George Mason University SACs report, 2000.

REFERENCES

Bok, Derek. 2006. *Our underachieving colleges.* Princeton, N.J.: Princeton University Press, College of Humanities and Social Sciences. 2008. *http://chss.gmu.edu/chss/about/index.cfm* (accessed 18 August 2008).

Elfant, Adina. 2002. A Study of the Relationship Between Integrative Studies Freshmen Learning Styles and Their Instructors' Learning Styles Represented by Students' Course Achievement. *Ph.D. diss.* Fairfax, VA: George Mason University.

Kuh, George D., Jillian Kinzie, John H. Schuh, Elizabeth J. Whitt and Associates, eds. 2005. *Student Success in College: Creating Conditions that Matter.* San Francisco, CA: Jossey-Bass.

Learning Communities National Resource Center. 2008. *http://www.evergreen.edu/wash center/project.asp?pid=73* (accessed 25 June 2008).

New Century College Website. 2008. *http://www.ncc.gmu.edul* (accessed 25 June 2008).

NSSE Report. 2004. Internal Document. Fairfax, VA: Office of Institutional Assessment, George Mason University.

O'Connor, John. 1994. Zero-based curriculum proposal. Internal Document. Fairfax, VA: George Mason University.

SACs Report. 2000. Fairfax, VA: George Mason University.

US News and World Report. 2004. America's best colleges guide: Top rankings for learning communities, *U.S. News and World Report.*

Barriers and Solutions to Launching an Interdisciplinary Movement: The University of Massachusetts–Lowell

Diana C. Archibald

The University of Massachusetts–Lowell (UML) faces some unique challenges regarding interdisciplinary initiatives due to its geographical location and history. The University of Lowell was formed in 1975 when two separate higher education institutions on different sides of the Merrimack River in Lowell, Massachusetts, were merged into a single entity. Lowell State College on the south side of the river specialized in training teachers and nurses, thus focusing more heavily on the liberal arts and health. Lowell Technological Institute, on the north side of the river, was originally formed to train engineers for the local textile mills and thus emphasized engineering and the sciences. University of Lowell joined the University of Massachusetts system only in 1991.[1] While UML today is one institution, on paper, for all practical purposes, the institution still feels the effects of its fragmented history. Faculty seeking to make connections across disciplines must often literally cross over to the other side to meet. Lack of physical proximity is sometimes crippling to efforts to create interdisciplinary connections, and at best has been the cause of much frustration and delay. We have found that such barriers can nevertheless be surmounted, if knowledgeable and committed leaders exist within *both* the faculty and administration. Perhaps this conclusion is not so very surprising. Yet the lessons learned at UML while we attempt to implement a campus-wide interdisciplinary initiative highlight the particularly crucial linchpin of leadership.

Chancellor William Hogan, the UML head for twenty-five years, was, according to former Provost John Wooding, "a strong believer in interdisciplinary work — he said many times that knowledge now does not come in discrete parcels and that both research and learning should reflect this."[2] Chancellor Hogan put his commitment to interdisciplinary engagement into practice by forming a controversial new interdisciplinary department in 1997: the Regional, Economic and Social Development (RESD) Department. Hogan asked Wooding to lead the effort to establish that new department because he knew that Wooding shared his strong commitment to interdisciplinary teaching, research, and service. In 2003, when then Provost John Wagner retired, Chancellor Hogan hired Wooding to fill the chief academic officer position for the campus. When Wooding came on as provost, "Hogan instructed [him] to develop a transformation plan for the university, based, in part, on the recommendations of The Task Force [on Deepening the Pool of Students] and other committees." Wooding presented his ideas to the senior leadership team (deans and vice-chancellors) in the summer of 2003, and he notes, "All parts of what was to become the transformation plan were referred to at that presentation (interdisciplinary education was a core part, outreach, collaborative research, and a focus on undergraduate education were also part of this). It had Hogan's complete endorsement and support, and the following year he allocated funding for the whole project."

At a retreat for the new leadership team in 2004, the "embryonic plan" for the transformation project was discussed, and the following year faculty and staff were consulted in a series of "critical issues" sessions. Finally, ten committees, or "teams," were formed to determine how to effect this campus-wide change.

In the fall of 2005, Provost Wooding asked me to chair one of these committees, charged with "examining interdisciplinarity and making recommendations about institutionalizing support (structures and mechanisms and activities) for quality interdisciplinary outcomes in learning, discovery, and engagement." The provost and I assembled a team comprised of seven tenured faculty, one from each of UML's Colleges/Schools/Library. Anticipating considerable resistance in our efforts to institutionalize support for interdisciplinary activities, we chose members carefully, selecting only tenured faculty who were known across campus as fair-minded and collegial, with extensive leadership experience in interdisciplinary initiatives and involvement in a number of campus organizations. Further, we determined that the team would make decisions by consensus alone, not majority rule. I felt strongly that the voices of each of these faculty members must be respected, for if anyone dissented, it was likely there would be many others who would be of that same opinion. For our plan to be successful, each of us had to be willing to stand behind our recommendations. But to reach consensus, the team had to delve more deeply into the scholarship of interdisciplinarity and talk through our findings and our fears at multiple meetings over the course of two years.

Since part of our charge was to make data-driven decisions, we spent the majority of our time as a committee conducting and analyzing research, including but not limited to such tasks as the following:

1. reviewing the literature on interdisciplinarity (not merely IDS teaching and learning but also theories of interdisciplinarity and interdisciplinary research and collaboration, etc.);

2. studying interdisciplinary programs at a variety of other institutions and interviewing interdisciplinary administrators at those institutions to learn about the barriers they have faced and how they have overcome those barriers;

3. creating UML faculty survey questions and analyzing those results;

4. contacting the national organization for interdisciplinary studies, the Association for Integrative Studies (AIS) and soliciting board members' assistance at various stages in our process; and

5. meeting with various campus groups and individuals to learn more about the issues interdisciplinary practitioners face at UML.

On June 1, 2007, we presented our final report, the culmination of two years of research, analysis, and discussion. The report attempted to articulate first, the barriers to interdisciplinary activities that we discovered (i.e., what problems interdisciplinary practitioners encounter at UML and elsewhere), and second, what we believe the University of Massachusetts Lowell needs to do to support high-quality interdisciplinary research, teaching, and service over the long-term.

Unfortunately the UML chancellor, William Hogan, who first set this process in motion, retired halfway through our process, leaving the fate of the university's "transformation project" unclear. By the time we submitted our final report, a new permanent chancellor, Martin Meehan, had taken office. Chancellor Meehan replaced Provost Wooding with an acting provost to serve until a permanent provost could be hired. When Provost Wooding was, in his words, "fired," it was unclear if his activities, such as the Transformation Project (and our Interdisciplinarity Team, with which Provost Wooding was particularly involved) would suffer by association despite the intimate involvement of over a hundred faculty and staff in these ten committees. Many on campus, especially those most heavily involved in interdisciplinary programs, have interpreted what happened to Dr. Wooding as a victory for the anti-interdisciplinarity faction on campus (for example, those who had opposed the formation of the interdisciplinary department, RESD).

Whether or not this interpretation represents a fair assessment of motivations and power shifts, it reveals the sort of political climate in which advocates of interdisciplinarity at UML have been working and the recent state of morale among this group. Certainly a lack of communication about the new administration's goals and priorities has led to much uneasiness.

Our team received feedback on only one occasion after our report was submitted. The UML deans met with the ten transformation project committee chairs a few months after they received our final reports to tell us how they had decided to respond to our recommendations. The new administration and the deans at this meeting were positive, in general, about our work, and they all expressed "support for interdisciplinarity." Clearly, though, not everyone at the meeting had taken to heart the section of our report that discussed the need for clarification of our terms, for example, appropriate usage of the notion "interdisciplinary" versus "multidisciplinary." One Dean at the meeting cited, as proof of his support for interdisciplinarity, his college's new "interdisciplinary program in forensic science," a program which, when I asked for clarification, he admitted was a degree in chemistry with what amounts to a minor of five separate criminal justice courses with no integration of the two disciplines. I came away from the meeting with the sense that very little would change as a result of our efforts. Without administrative leadership fighting for high-quality, sustainable interdisciplinary work, we would continue in the same vein.

The ensuing year demonstrated how crucial leadership is to moving any initiative forward. Not only did the new administration not accept our major recommendation of a hub for coordinating interdisciplinary and integrative teaching and learning, research, and service at UML, but they also failed to act on the simplest, no-cost recommendations to improve visibility and functioning of campus interdisciplinary programs. I had received personal assurance that as many no-cost, low-cost operational recommendations would be implemented as possible and within the year, and I was told that these recommendations were reasonable. I left for my year-long sabbatical hoping this promise would be kept. It wasn't. Interdisciplinary activities were valued insomuch as they could be touted as one of our strengths at UML (and it is true that many at our institution are engaged in excellent interdisciplinary research and teaching), but it would take new leadership in the provost's office if we were to see long-term institutional support for interdisciplinary activities on campus — not merely the neglected IDS programs, which were cut back even further the year after our report was submitted, but also thriving interdisciplinary research initiatives that we had begun and which were abandoned. The stated rationale for every cut was always the same: budget.

Budgetary Concerns at UML

UML is a state institution in a commonwealth where dozens of high-powered private universities and colleges receive millions in public funding while the state university system's funding has declined steadily over the last two decades, more or less, hovering in recent years at around 37 percent state revenues for our yearly budget, leaving the majority to be raised from tuition and fundraising (Eiranova 2007, 2). When Chancellor Hogan retired from UML in 2007, he left a multi-million dollar budget deficit, one of the first years he ever did so. Previously a scrupulous fiscal steward, Chancellor Hogan had kept UML afloat for decades without laying-off any employees. Current Chancellor Meehan has been attempting to balance the budget, but a continued crisis in public higher education funding has made it difficult for him to dig UML out of the red. For the first time in 25 years, staff and faculty began being laid-off in 2007, and the director of human resources says there are more lay-offs to come.

For all of the legitimate budgetary concerns that UML faces, money has still been found for special projects. Anyone familiar with budgets in academe knows that there is always a certain amount of flexibility in the budget. The new chancellor completed renovations of an historic building on the State College part of the campus, a building with a lovely view of the Merrimack River, and he moved the chancellor's office to that building. In the summer of 2008, the athletic fields below his office were also renovated. Money was found for academic initiatives in anti–RESD departments and colleges, and money was found for high-profile, press-filled events. Interdisciplinary programs such as gender studies, a thriving program for over thirty years, saw a complete withdrawal of support from the new administration in 2007–08, with the director's one-course release per year taken away and a popular interdisciplinary teaching training program de-funded. There was no programmatic budget to take away since the gender studies program was funded through individual requests for support from various campus entities to finance its activities every year. Most other interdisciplinary programs saw little or no support the first year of Chancellor Meehan's administration, as well.

Certainly this lack of financial support will come as no surprise to those well acquainted with the history of interdisciplinary studies in American universities. Interdisciplinary studies programs are often seen as expendable, as a nice add-on but not rigorous or academic enough to warrant any real commitment from the institution, especially when budgets are being slashed. Traditional department structure, and faculty governance based on that structure, determines that the disciplining of the institution continues. Thus even when money is taken out of the question, interdisciplinarity is not supported because of the further entrenchment of the disciplinary power structure (Henry 2005). Certainly in the case of UML, interdisciplinary studies received little or no support from the administration during the 2007–08 academic year, at least in terms of adopting our committee's recommendations, despite the fact that these recommendations were based on meticulous research (including much data on interdisciplinary studies at UML), an incremental plan for implementation that spread out the cost of implementation over five years (with increasing self-sufficiency of our proposed changes), and a slate of no- and low-cost recommendations that we were assured would be addressed this past year.

Why Interdisciplinary Studies Matters to UML and the Barriers We Discovered

When the Interdisciplinarity Team began meeting in 2005, we took nothing for granted, even the notion that interdisciplinarity is desirable or necessary. Indeed, all of the committee members at one time or another encountered skepticism from colleagues about the value of our work, so we were keenly aware of those in our faculty survey who said that interdisciplinary activities are "not rigorous"/"watered down," "fluffy"/"fuzzy," or a "joke." We also heard from many more colleagues who expressed their gratitude to us for undertaking the monumental task of identifying barriers to interdisciplinary teaching, research, and service at UML and proposing changes to help sustain high-quality interdisciplinary activities over the long-term. Indeed, we discovered much more interdisciplinary work going on at UML than any of us had realized. With so many counting on our help and yet such a range of reactions to interdisciplinarity, we felt it particularly incumbent upon us to ensure that our decisions were based on good data and best practices, rather than whim or fancy. The Interdisciplinarity Team thus repeatedly circled back to the question of whether interdisciplinarity, in all its manifestations, really is important to UML, as we attempted to fulfill our charge: "to examine interdisciplinarity and make recommendations about institutionalizing support (structures and mechanisms) for quality interdisciplinary outcomes in learning, discovery, and engagement."

Our faculty survey demonstrated interdisciplinary studies' importance.[3] Further, our committee found broad, national consensus on the value of interdisciplinarity in organizations from the sciences and professions and from the humanities and social sciences, in government and industry, and from town and gown. These points of consensus, and their relevance to UML, are outlined below.

1. *Interdisciplinary Studies Equates to a Better Prepared Workforce.* Employers want to hire graduates who can work collaboratively in interdisciplinary teams, and they need graduates who are flexible and can think outside a narrow academic discipline to solve "real world" problems. According to a report by a research firm acting on behalf of the Association of American Colleges and Universities, "Fully 63 percent of business executives interviewed agree that too many recent college graduates do not have the skills to be successful in today's global economy" (Peter D. Hart Research Associates 2006, 7). What, in particular, college graduates need is a greater facility with "integration and application of learning" (ACC&U 2007). AAC&U President Carol G. Schneider remarked, "It's time to stop channeling students into narrow tracks that prepare them for an initial job but not for tomorrow's challenges" (ACC&U 2007). The AAC&U's LEAP report contends that, "whatever their field of study, all of today's students need a liberal education that integrates knowledge, skills, and practical applications. The academy's traditional divisions of 'liberal arts' and 'professional' fields stand in the way of students' and the nation's long term interests" (ACC&U 2007).

2. *Interdisciplinary Studies Equates to Fundable Research.* Funders, especially governmental agencies such as the NSF and NIH, frequently issue RFPs requiring collaborative, multidisciplinary teams, and see interdisciplinary approaches as necessary to solve complex, real world problems. According to the National Academy of Sciences (2005, 2): "*Interdisciplinary thinking is rapidly becoming an integral feature of research* as a result of four powerful 'drivers': the inherent complexity of nature and society, the desire to explore problems and questions that are not confined to a single discipline, the need to solve societal problems, and the power of new technologies" (emphasis added). Hackett (2000, 148–49) notes a "rise in the level of interest in interdisciplinary teaching and research" due to perceived "intellectual opportunities, converging lines of inquiry, administrative mandates, the desire to solve practical problems or to reap economic benefits," etc. Further, "the current interdisciplinary drive ... is clearly in evidence within the walls of NSF," with a "variety of interdisciplinary activities ... proposed and funded."

3. *Interdisciplinary Activities as an Essential Component to Meet Other Goals.* Certain accrediting agencies, such as ABET [Accreditation Board for Engineering and Technology] explicitly ask for interdisciplinarity and integration. Furthermore, interdisciplinarity and integration are necessary for many efforts that we value, such as diversity, sustainability, community engagement, international connections, and first year experience, etc. The 2007–08 ABET Criteria for Accrediting Applied Science Programs overview states, "Baccalaureate degree programs must demonstrate that graduates have ... an ability to function on multi-disciplinary teams," and "the broad education

necessary to understand the impact of solutions in a global and societal context" (ABET 2007–08, 1).

4. *Interdisciplinary Studies Produces High Student Engagement.* Interdisciplinary and integrative pedagogy that follows best practices makes use of active learning and student-centered learning approaches, known to help student engagement. To master integration, students need hands on experience in trying to synthesize multiple perspectives. Since ID/IN learning opportunities help students to make connections across their coursework, students gain a stronger sense of cohesiveness in their program of study. As Braxton and Hirschy (2005, 78) claim, "Faculty who intentionally" employ active learning techniques in class and foster "critical thinking ... contribute to student persistence." In addition, students enrolled in these courses " are more likely to experience great degrees of subsequent institutional commitment."

5. *Interdisciplinary Approaches Require Students to Engage in Higher Order Learning.* Students in interdisciplinary courses acquire sufficient content knowledge — and they learn synthesis, analysis, and evaluation, due to the very nature of what interdisciplinary approaches demand. Critical thinking skills are thus improved. The AAC & U survey of employers and recent college graduates mentioned above showed that 73 percent of employers surveyed want "colleges and universities to place more emphasis" on "critical thinking and analytical reasoning skills," and 70 percent desire a greater emphasis on "the ability to be innovative and think creatively" (AAC&U 2007, 3).

6. *Interdisciplinary Studies Produces Increased Faculty Engagement.* Retention and satisfaction of faculty, especially junior faculty, is increased through interdisciplinary work (which, according to our UML survey, the majority of this rank desire to pursue), and successful collaboration combats isolation and increases morale. New directions in interdisciplinary teaching may lead to new directions in research and service and vice versa. UML has hired faculty in the last several years specifically to facilitate interdisciplinary collaboration. The influx of fresh perspectives and faculty who are excited to work on interdisciplinary projects is leading to a sea change in the way UML sees itself. Junior faculty at UML are the most eager to increase their engagement in interdisciplinary activities, with a full 60 percent in our survey claiming they are "very interested" in increasing their interdisciplinary activities and another 33 percent being "somewhat" interested in doing so. Yet assistant professors are the least connected faculty on campus because the traditional structures of the university do not facilitate cross-departmental collaboration and exchange. The desire to do interdisciplinary work is strong in other faculty as well. Faculty, in the 2006 UML survey, saw the following benefits to interdisciplinary work: "higher quality research outcome," "new ideas, visions and

insights into problems," "intellectual stimulation, " and "more meaningful, holistic and maybe transformative," "liberating," and "exciting."

Having established the importance of interdisciplinarity for UML, our committee turned to the question of how to institutionalize support for such interdisciplinary activity. While designed for our own institution, our recommendations have a wider application. Indeed, many of the challenges that UML faces are so common that a great number of the recommendations in our report would be of use to other institutions with similar issues. The 2006 UML Faculty Survey revealed a number of barriers to interdisciplinary teaching and research at the University and a significant amount of frustration on the part of faculty. Overall, 30 percent of faculty respondents indicated that they do a great deal or quite a bit of interdisciplinary teaching, with another 32 percent doing some. About 44 percent of faculty are engaged in a great deal or quite a bit of interdisciplinary research, with another 27 percent engaged in at least some. While a few respondents either said they did not experience or could not identify any barriers to interdisciplinary teaching or research, most faculty broadly agreed on significant barriers.

The single biggest problem or barrier to interdisciplinary teaching respondents identified was *time and workload*, at 21 percent. As one survey respondent put it, "The senior administration doesn't know what it means; the time demands are enormous." Faculty realize that to undertake interdisciplinary teaching effectively, they need to have time available to devote either to study of pertinent insights from another field (if teaching an interdisciplinary course alone) or to work with one or more colleagues to develop a team-taught course. Participants in the pilot Gender Studies Teaching Fellowship Program remarked, quite pointedly, that the single course release they received enabled them to innovate and develop their teaching in ways not possible when bearing a full 3/3 teaching load. One junior faculty member remarked, "The fellowship offered the time and structure to develop an interdisciplinary intellectual community that will bear fruit for years to come in teaching and scholarship." Clearly, if UML wishes to support high-quality interdisciplinary teaching and learning, the issue of time must be addressed.

The second most frequently mentioned barrier (18 percent) by our survey respondents was the *difficulty of coordinating between disciplines and the isolation and separation of departments or disciplines*. Respondents mentioned feeling "compartmentalized" and "fragmented" within the traditional department structure at the university, citing lack of "contact between faculty of various colleges" and "interaction [between] different departments." As one respondent put it, "[It's] hard to bring people together, and hard to find appropriate projects." It is not just the logistical difficulty of meeting potential collaborators that worries some faculty; it is "communication issues [such as the] language barrier between people of different disciplines" and the difficulty of overcoming that barrier in order to be able to work together effectively.

Regarding the third most common barrier, *institutional structure issues* (receiving 17 percent combined Administrative Structure and Department Rigidity), one faculty member said, "There is no culture or structure [in place] for people working with others from other departments." The "lack of infrastructure support" for interdisciplinary teaching collaboration clearly hampers some actual and would-be interdisciplinary practitioners.

Other issues cited by respondents included: lack of knowledge of interdisciplinary teaching approaches (8 percent), inadequate rewards and incentives structures like tenure and promotion (5 percent), lack of funding sources (4 percent), lack of student preparation (4 percent). Interdisciplinary teaching is difficult, and faculty, such as this respondent, know that it takes "depth, preparation and pedagogical skills ... [for] a faculty person to teach in a truly interdisciplinary way." Clearly, it is not "faculty willingness" that is standing in the way; as only 4 percent of respondents stated this. Rather, one respondent summed up the problem beautifully: "Interdisciplinarity does not have a home."

The single biggest problem or barrier to interdisciplinary research respondents identified was the *difficulty coordinating between disciplines and the isolation and separation of departments or disciplines* (19 percent). As with interdisciplinary teaching, finding suitable partners for collaboration was a big concern for faculty, who remarked on the difficulty of "understanding different disciplines" and "establishing communications and contacts." They cited the "isolation of people working in too narrowly defined areas" and a "lack of awareness of other people's talents" or a "lack of mutually shared goals." As one respondent put it, "You don't know people in other departments, so if you don't know what their research interests are, it's hard for me to apply [theirs] to mine." Faculty who attended the Interdisciplinary Collaboration Workshops in the fall of 2006 indicated that the top reason they came was to get connected to other faculty and discover their interests. Without a faculty lounge or club on campus or some central locale where needed "proximity" can be achieved, many faculty will continue to feel somewhat isolated.

The second most frequently mentioned barrier to interdisciplinary research (by 16 percent of survey respondents) was funding/resources. While some indicated that they thought there was little or no funding available for interdisciplinary research, others recognized that there may be funding sources out there but that they either do not know how to access those funds or have attempted to do so and encountered difficulty. This issue is not surprising, as the funding landscape is constantly changing. Major governmental agencies such as the National Science Foundation or the National Institutes of Health regularly release CFPs for interdisciplinary and integrative projects. Faculty seem to want more help specifically in finding and applying for such interdisciplinary external funding opportunities, but they also need help in finding suitable partners for such projects to begin with and "help with training" in interdisciplinary research processes (reported by 8 percent of respondents).

Following closely on the heels of funding issues, the third most frequently mentioned barrier was time and workload (15 percent). One faculty member suggested, "It takes time for faculty members to become competent in other fields," and another respondent added, "We are time bound by tenure and other time requirements as well as your own exposure to and perception of research." About 7 percent thought that the "university reward program and structure don't support [interdisciplinary research]." And 8 percent saw administrative structures and department rigidity as top barriers. Only 6 percent indicated faculty willingness as the biggest barrier.

In the survey, faculty identified four main areas of change with potential for increasing their level of interest in engaging in interdisciplinary activities or their satisfaction with pursuing their interdisciplinary work: time (28 percent), funding (22 percent), infrastructure (19 percent), and credit (tenure/promotion, 10 percent).

While some faculty felt no incentives were needed (either because they did not perceive any barriers to their interdisciplinary work or because they did not intend to do any interdisciplinary work and thus no incentives would induce them), a significant majority (79 percent) want changes: "time and funding for professional development to develop interdisciplinary skills," a reorganization "to make it easier to get together," and greater "cooperation and ... infrastructure support."

Interdisciplinary program administrators with whom we spoke over the last two years also agree that time, funding, and infrastructure are their top concerns. While these concerns manifest themselves differently for programs, the issues are the same. For example, lack of infrastructure may mean, for some interdisciplinary programs problems with visibility and communication. Those interdisciplinary programs, in particular, which are not departments but coalitions of faculty from across campus, are often left out of decision making because interdisciplinary program directors are not chairs. Many interdisciplinary programs:

- do not have their own program course prefix (a fact which leads to a lack of control over their own curriculum, as well as problems with dissemination of information to students)

- are not included in the registrar office processes and, thus, are unable to monitor adequately which cross-listed courses are being offered each semester
- are not consulted or even informed about departmental and college initiatives affecting them
- do not have a dedicated office or even their own bulletin board (thus perpetuating their invisibility to students and colleagues alike).

Several interdisciplinary administrators also mentioned the difficulty their programs had helping even their own faculty to connect because of the difficulty in bridging departmental divides. And some perceived a lack of university recognition of the program's existence, as evidenced by omissions from lists on websites or lack of invitations to table at open house. Many interdisciplinary administrators and many of the faculty who participate in these programs also indicate the need for more "faculty training," especially in interdisciplinary pedagogy and theory as well as "forum[s] where faculty can discuss interdisciplinary activities." While these programs undertake and accomplish much, frustrations are running high for many of those participating in and administering these programs. Yes, they have been able to do much with little, but that sort of effort is unsustainable and can lead to lower morale, reduced productivity, duplication of effort, and high burnout rates of leaders.

Recommendations

Since our faculty survey and other research showed broad participation in interdisciplinary activities, along with overwhelming interest in increasing their level of engagement (85 percent) and agreement on significant barriers to doing so, we formulated the following recommendations.

Our committee drafted the final recommendations during our last two months of work with absolutely no contact with the administration and without any real sense of what sort of proposal would be most welcome. The group decided that we would present a few different sets of recommendations: a list of no- and low-cost operational recommendations meant to solve logistical problems that interdisciplinary programs were then currently facing, an overarching plan for organizing and sustaining support for all interdisciplinary activities on campus through a central hub, and several smaller entities or activities within that larger hub frame that could be implemented without accepting the whole. We put forward a proposal that we thought would be flexible enough to fit into whatever plans our new chancellor had for our institution. We worked especially hard to present some recommendations that would have a zero dollar impact on budget, and our grander recommendation came with a five-year budget to demonstrate how the plan could be implemented incrementally and become self-sustaining. In some ways, not knowing our audience's inclinations may have actually strengthened our report (and made it more applicable to other institutions), causing us to think more creatively about how to solve the real problems we were addressing, trying to anticipate every possible objection.

Given the inherent difficulty any departmentally structured institution faces in bridging the gap between disciplines, and given our own special challenges as a physically and historically divided university, our key recommendation was to create a Hub for Interdisciplinary and Integrative Activity (HIDINA) whose purpose would be to coordinate, connect, and enable interdisciplinary (ID) and integrative (IN) research, teaching, and service through (1) Resource Management, (2) Programming, and (3) Assessment and Progress Monitoring. In order to have visibility and credibility, this Hub would need to be both a physical location and an independent organizational unit. The establishment of such a Hub and allocation of office space would, among other things, signal to the University community the administration's commitment to bringing North and South campus "cultures" together to form a more connected community of scholars dedicated to innovation and collaboration.

HIDINA's aim was not only to connect faculty with one another but also to connect faculty, staff, students, the community, the corporate sphere, and potential funders who wish to pursue interdisciplinary and integrative work. HIDINA would also have crossed the traditional lines between research, teaching, and service by actively seeking ways to combine these activities using interdisciplinary and integrative approaches. HIDINA, therefore, would have served as a sort of campus-wide resource and service center for all interdisciplinary and integrative activity, potentially offering support to any group or individual engaged in such work and providing much-needed expertise in interdisciplinary and integrative theory, practice, and assessment.

HIDINA would best meet the needs of interdisciplinary and integrative practitioners first, by acknowledging practitioners' concerns and second, by creating support structures to remove barriers and facilitate interdisciplinary and integrative activity. Respondents to the faculty survey identified the following issues as the biggest barriers to their interdisciplinary research and teaching efforts: separation of disciplines/people, difficulty coordinating among disciplines, lack of release time for training and development, lack of research funding and/or staff support, and lack of knowledge of how to conduct interdisciplinary research or integrate other disciplines. Our proposed hub would have directly addressed faculty-identified barriers and concerns through meeting the following objectives: (1) coordinate interdisciplinary and integrative efforts for the entire campus, (2) connect faculty, students, and outside constituents in order to solve problems and address issues that are too broad or complex to be dealt with adequately by a single discipline or approach, and (3) enable high-quality interdisciplinary and integrative activities to thrive and be sustained over time.

We recognize that some interdisciplinary programs at UMass Lowell arose spontaneously and have survived throughout the years with little or no administrative support. The efforts of our faculty, who have dedicated many hours of service to these programs and their students, are truly remarkable and should be applauded. While some programs receive a lot of attention, others quietly do their work almost unobserved by the university community and are happy to "fly under the radar," so to speak. Notable, however, are the ways in which lack of a communication and support structure have also led to significant drawbacks like faculty burnout, low morale, and even sometimes closure of valuable programs. From the perspective of the university as a whole, this laissez faire approach has sometimes also led to:

- a lack of comprehensive and accurate information about the work taking place at our institution and thus limited awareness by administrators, students, and the public;
- a lack of support structures to assist programs in a systematic and equitable way;
- a tendency for programs to have to "reinvent the wheel" because they are not a part of a community of interdisciplinary practice (an inefficient and discouraging phenomenon that distracts programs from their important work); and
- a lack of support as well as processes (specifically geared toward the unique challenges of interdisciplinarity) whereby programs can continue to improve the quality of interdisciplinary teaching and learning, whether that program is struggling or excelling.

To address these institutional and programmatic barriers and challenges and to support the efforts of our faculty and the learning of our students, we recommended several courses of action, including the formation of an Interdisciplinary Programs Committee and an Integrative Programs Committee, a campus-wide interdisciplinary teaching training program, interdisciplinary research training seminars, events to initiate collaboration, and events to educate the campus community about interdisciplinary and integrative best practices. Some of these recommendations were based on existing programs, such as the collaboration workshops we offered in 2005–06, and the highly successful Gender Studies Teaching Fellowship Program from 2005–07 that we proposed be expanded to serve the entire campus. We also recommended several small steps that the administration could take to give interdisciplinary programs greater visibility, steps such as allowing program directors to attend chairs meetings held by college deans, thus keeping such programs informed and enabling them to provide input on college-wide initiatives.

Conclusion

As of October 2008, no official action has been taken on our committee's final recommendations. However, a new provost joined the administration at UML in July: Dr. Ahmed Abdelal, former provost at Northeastern University (2002–08). A microbiologist by training and a self-described practitioner of interdisciplinary research, Dr. Abdelal brings years of professional experience as both teacher and administrator to UML. In an interview on September 9, 2008, Dr. Abdelal indicated that he is a "strong supporter" of interdisciplinarity and that his track record shows his commitment to such efforts. As provost at Northeastern, he served as principle architect of a strategic plan that included much attention to interdisciplinary issues and as an administrator he sought to "strengthen interdisciplinary linkages." He contends that to solve real problems we need an interdisciplinary approach, and that any institution that wants to advance at a higher rate "needs to be on the forefront of interdisciplinary learning." Dr. Abdelal claims that his record demonstrates that he sees interdisciplinarity as a "priority" and has allocated funding accordingly, even launching an interdisciplinary hiring initiative. Further, Dr. Abdelal indicated that before applying for the position as provost of UML, he carefully examined our institution and was impressed, in particular, with the extent of interdisciplinary teaching, research, and service undertaken here. Looking for a new challenge, a place that is ready for the change that he is best suited to bring, Dr. Abdelal seems very excited to be at UML and to move forward with his plans to support all of our endeavors, including and perhaps especially our interdisciplinary work.

The provost had not seen our Interdisciplinary Team final report. Indeed, the website housing all of the transformation project materials has disappeared from the UML site. Dr. Abdelal has promised to read the report and consider its recommendations. Starting in the spring of 2009, the upper administration will be creating its five-year plan, and our new provost "expects to advocate strongly for interdisciplinarity here." Whether he will agree with our recommendations or be able to effect the changes that he desires remains to be seen. Meanwhile, his actions speak loudly of his intent. The present and past directors of the UML Gender Studies Program met with Dr. Abdelal to introduce him to their thriving program and to apprise him of the lack of support that has been undercutting their success. At the end of the meeting, Dr. Abdelal reinstated the director's course release (time is a precious commodity, indeed) and gave the program a $10,000 budget, the program's first budget in its thirty-plus year history. So we have reason to hope.

That's the lesson, perhaps, that the case of UML offers to academe. A representative group of stellar faculty work for two years creating an airtight case for what their institution should do to institutionalize support for interdisciplinarity. They consult the experts, they research what their own faculty are experiencing, and they bring to bear on the problem all of their years of experience and vastly different disciplinary perspectives to produce a consensus document. Every conceivable objection, every contingency is accounted for, and a flexible and multi-faceted plan is presented in a 117-page report ... that sits on a shelf waiting for an administrator with vision and knowledge to read and act on it. Without leadership on the faculty level even the most determined and competent administrator will not be able to effect lasting change. Faculty need to be excited by the prospect of doing interdisciplinary work, and they need to see its benefits for students, for their careers, and for the world. But faculty can be all of this and more, and if they are not supported by the institution, they will often experience burnout, leave the university, or retreat to their departments. For high-quality interdisciplinary work to be sustained, leaders at the faculty and administrative levels must work together. High-quality, sustainable interdisciplinary activity requires a truly collaborative effort.

NOTES

1. UML is ranked (by the Carnegie Foundation) "Doctoral Research University — Intensive," with around 11,000 full-time students, over 680 faculty, and eighty-eight degree programs at the undergraduate and graduate level.

2. Quotations from Dr. John Wooding are excerpted from an email from Dr. Wooding to me, written 6/28/08, and are quoted with his permission.

3. Our faculty survey enjoyed a 60 percent response rate and was representative of faculty at all ranks in all departments across campus. Please see Appendix at the end of this book for a summary of our findings.

REFERENCES

AAC & U (American Association of Colleges and Universities). 2007. Press Release, January 10. *http://www.aacu.org/press_room/press_releases/2007/LEAPReport.cfm* (accessed July 19, 2008).

ABET (Accreditation Board for Engineering and Technology). 2007–08. *Criteria for accrediting applied science programs.* Baltimore, MD: Applied Sciences Accreditation Commission. *http://www.abet.org* (accessed January 17, 2006).

Braxton, John M., and Amy S. Hirschy. 2005. Theoretical developments in the study of college student departure. In *College student retention: Formula for student success* ed., Alan Seidman, 61–88. Westport, CT: ACE/Praeger.

Eiranova, David. 2007. Meehan: UML set to grow. *Lowell Sun*, Sept. 29. *http://www.uml. edu/Media/News%20Articles/2007%20UML%20in%20the%20News/Meehan_Says_UM L_set_.html* (accessed October 11, 2008).

Hackett, E. 2000. Interdisciplinary research initiatives at the U.S. National Science Foundation. In *Practising interdisciplinarity,* ed., Peter Weingart and Nico Stehr, 248–259. Toronto: University of Toronto Press.

Henry, Stuart. 2005. Disciplinary hegemony meets interdisciplinary ascendancy: Can interdisciplinary/integrative studies survive, and if so how? *Issues in Integrative Studies* 23: 1–37.

National Academy of Sciences. 2005. *Facilitating interdisciplinary research.* Washington, D.C.: National Academies Press.

Peter D. Hart Research Associates, Inc. 2006. How should colleges prepare students to succeed in today's global economy? Dec. 28. *www.aacu.org/leap/documents/Re8097abcom bined.pdf* (accessed July 12, 2008).

CHAPTER 12

A Canadian and Collaborative Perspective: The Office of Interdisciplinary Studies at the University of Alberta

Rick Szostak

The University of Alberta is a large research university that celebrated its 100th anniversary in 2008. As with most large research universities, it has traditionally been organized around departments. Indeed for decades the province's Universities Act has stipulated that professors are appointed into departments. In the Faculty of Arts (College of Arts in American parlance), interdisciplinarity has been advocated for decades (at least by many, often at the decanal level), but no administrative structure existed to support its development. An ambitious effort to create a division of interdisciplinary studies (alongside divisions of fine arts, social science, and humanities) in the 1990s collapsed in the face of objections from department chairs. Some interdisciplinary programs — women's studies and East Asian studies — achieved departmental status. A program in Middle Eastern and African Studies (MEAS) survived without any official administrative support due to the dedication of a small nucleus of faculty members. A graduate program in Humanities Computing (HuCo) was created, and was administered by an associate dean in the absence of any other suitable administrative home.

In 2003, during a period of financial stringency at the university, the Faculty of Arts first created the Office of Interdisciplinary Studies (OIS). The dean's office recognized that an administrative structure was desirable to support interdisciplinarity, but had limited resources to devote to the initiative. I had the pleasure of serving as the first associate dean responsible for OIS (until 2005). The OIS when it opened had responsibility for seven interdisciplinary programs:

- MEAS (above)
- HuCo (above)
- An individualized major (such that students could design their own thematic major in consultation with an advisory committee). I created the major in consultation with other associate deans and interested faculty members, and drawing on the advice of members of the Association for Integrative Studies (AIS) experienced with such programs (especially former AIS President Don Stowe). Students pursuing this major need to write a proposal that suggests a title, theme, and set of courses from at least three departments/programs that support that theme. A committee of three faculty members from different departments adjudicates the proposal and, if it is judged appropriate (generally with revisions), serves as the student's advisory committee. Students must apply during their second or third year (to avoid the danger, observed at other institutions, of students trying to justify after the fact a mélange of courses taken). Students are required to take two courses about interdisciplinarity itself (see below). Only a handful of students have pursued this option, but they have been highly motivated and very grateful of the opportunity.
- Science, Technology, and Society (STS). I convened a committee of interested faculty members in early 2003, and it needed only three meetings and hundreds of emails to agree on a curriculum for both a Major and Minor.
- International Studies (minor) This small program had been created years earlier and never administered. I convened a committee to update its requirements.
- Religious Studies
- Comparative Literature

The last two programs deserve special attention. They point to the role that circumstance may play in the creation of interdisciplinary structures. A Department of Comparative Literature, Religion, and Film/Media Studies had been created during a previous set of budgetary-inspired administrative amalgamations. A decision was made to dissolve this department. The three programs were asked where they wished to go. Film studies opted to join the English Department (which was renamed English and Film Studies). Religious studies opted immediately for interdisciplinary status. There already existed a Network for the Study of Religion at the university, which organized occasional colloquia; it was felt that this large group of scholars should govern the program. The comparative literature group was less sure, but in the end also opted for interdisciplinary status.

These decisions had an important impact on the budget of the early OIS. Much of the old department's budget was transferred to OIS. At a time of budget cuts, it would have been hard to finance the OIS in other ways. The HuCo budget (which resulted from a governmental competition to finance new programs even while it cut funding of existing programs) was also transferred to OIS. Funding for the other OIS programs was financed on a short-term basis (year-to-year). The university's financial position has improved markedly in the last years (Alberta has oil) and the OIS has benefited from an expansion in staff and hard (permanent) funding. While OIS has had some of its short-term funding hardened into long-term funding, it still receives about a quarter of a million dollars on an annual basis to fund sessional lecturers; it is hoped that most/all of this funding will be hardened in the near future.

At present (2008), OIS administers programs that collectively serve well over 100 undergraduate majors and minors, over 100 graduate students, and offers courses each term with well over 1000 student enrollments.

Early Budgetary Challenges

The key early challenge was budgetary. An administrator was hired to run OIS, and one of the staff from the old department was transferred to OIS. In the first year they shared an office in the faculty's administrative area. The workload was intense, and much support was required from staff in the dean's office. The paperwork regarding graduate admissions into the HuCo program continued to be handled by the graduate secretary in one of the departments in the faculty until OIS had the ability to manage it. The survival of this fledgling OIS depended in no small part on the dedication of the new administrator.

As of 2008 the OIS consists of 5 staff members, has a suite of offices (which were previously occupied by a research consortium no longer located at the university) and its own mailroom and conference room (it had for years been in a different building from its mailroom). The growth has in part reflected the addition of new responsibilities (There has been only one new program — a certificate in peace and conflict studies — but the OIS no longer just administers teaching but also has responsibilities for interdisciplinary research and conferences, and may soon take on responsibility for interdisciplinary research centers.) But its growth has mostly reflected a continued series of requests to the dean's office for resources commensurate with its responsibilities. As noted above, this has proven easier as the Faculty of Arts budget has expanded.

Even in the early days of stringency, there were grumbles about this new structure taking resources from departments. The OIS is still viewed with suspicion in some departments. But its existence is largely taken for granted. It should be noted that OIS funding is similar on a per-student basis to departmental funding (this varies a great deal across departments; OIS is far from being an outlier). The OIS has justified its funding in terms of student numbers; it has not argued that its programs deserve above-average funding.

One lesson that might be drawn is that while relying on short-term funding is risky, it may allow a program to show, over time, that it deserves permanent funding. This will be especially likely if the university's financial position occasionally improves. It is critical, though, that the program attracts significant student enrollment. It is also critical that senior administrators be regularly reminded of budgetary requirements.

Cross-Appointments

As noted above, provincial legislation mandates that professors be appointed to a department. All of the professors in OIS programs thus have a cross-appointment between a department and an OIS program (or OIS itself). In some cases, these cross-appointments are such that the professor does most of their teaching in the interdisciplinary program. Nevertheless, it is always the case that it is the department chair that takes the professor's case for promotion or incrementation to the Faculty Evaluation Committee (FEC), which at present includes all department chairs and several elected faculty members but no official OIS representation. The associate dean responsible for interdisciplinarity can speak at FEC but has no vote.

The potential downsides are obvious. Faculty members have divided loyalties, and may find that administrative responsibilities in their department limit their ability to participate in collegial governance of the interdisciplinary program. More insidiously, a department chair may undervalue a professor's interdisciplinary contributions, and the professor may suffer financially as a consequence where merit pay is a factor.

The system only works if department chairs cooperate. While chairs often grumble about the OIS budget they seem not in practice to transfer this concern to the individual level. Professors carrying administrative duties in interdisciplinary programs are excused from most departmental duties (which is possible given that most of our departments are very large). And interdisciplinary contributions are generally celebrated at FEC.

Some official OIS representation at FEC would be advisable in case some "rogue" chair decided to punish some interdisciplinarian. But even in the absence of such representation, interdisciplinarians can assure that others, including the associate dean, make sure that their contribution is noted in FEC. And FEC regularly over-rules a chair's recommendation. Still the system only works if there is fairly widespread recognition of the value of interdisciplinarity, which is largely the case now in the Faculty of Arts. Indeed, while interdisciplinarity is not officially recognized as a fourth division within the Faculty of Arts, its promotional materials and website now habitually treat interdisciplinary programming as a fourth category of equal visibility to programs in humanities, social science, and fine arts.

Against the potential disadvantages, the system of cross-appointments has some critical advantages. Foremost it means that there are faculty members in several departmental councils with an investment in a particular interdisciplinary program. Even one such member can change the nature of the departmental dialogue about interdisciplinarity (and this effect is intensified by the even greater participation in interdisciplinary program governance; see below).

More surprisingly, perhaps, department chairs often find cross-appointments strategically useful. Cross-appointing an existing faculty member may increase a department's chances of hiring a new faculty member. The cross-appointment may also serve to attract students in an interdisciplinary program to the department's course offerings. And interdisciplinary courses can often be counted as options toward a disciplinary major.

I have thus come to believe that cross-appointments can be a good thing for interdisciplinary programs: both programmatically and strategically. It could be that a mix of dedicated and cross-appointments is best, at least at the present stage of development of university structures. But it is clearly quite feasible to run very strong programs entirely on the basis of cross-appointments (and the occasional short-term buyouts of interested faculty members).

Hiring and Cross-Appointments

It might be thought that insistence on cross-appointments limits the ability of interdisciplinary programs to hire new staff. Indeed, it would be hard to hire a faculty member who had no obvious disciplinary home. In practice, though, new faculty with interdisciplinary PhDs have been hired and placed without difficulty in departments. A handful of the faculty's departments have proven particularly open to this sort of appointment.

For some years now, the Faculty of Arts has held a triennial competition for new faculty positions (that is, faculty lines). Departments *and interdisciplinary programs* submit proposals for new appointments. These are ranked by a committee of the dean and associate deans. While cooperation between units is not essential to success in this competition, it has been clear from the outset that there are advantages to claiming that a new appointment will benefit more than one program. Departments thus often find it advantageous to cooperate with interdisciplinary programs in putting forth these proposals. Political science recently hired a faculty member (who studies the Middle East) cross-appointed with MEAS, for example. Less formal collaborations are also possible: Anthropology promised that it would regularly offer a course required by the STS program if able to hire in that area. In each of these cases, both the department and interdisciplinary program were represented on the hiring committee, and the person hired was wanted by both programs.

Some department chairs worried at the time of the first competition that *only* interdisciplinary positions would be allocated. Of course this was neither feasible nor desirable. Integrative research and teaching does not supplant specialized research and teaching but engages symbiotically with them. By the time of the second competition, the idea that collaboration would be encouraged but not insisted upon was broadly accepted.

Interdisciplinary programs may be granted a position where the future home department is unspecified. The hiring committee in that case does not include departmental representation. When job candidates are brought in, the chair and members of the relevant home department(s) are invited to participate in the process. Chairs of departments have proven eager to participate: if the job candidate would make a valued contribution to the department, the department is effectively gaining (some fraction of) a new faculty member above and beyond any positions they may have gained in the position allocation competition. Of course, a hire only occurs if both program and department agree on the suitability of a candidate. Disagreements are rare, and in my experience never grounded in a departmental suspicion of interdisciplinarity. I have chaired HuCo hiring committees that functioned in this manner, and found that the process worked very well. All HuCo hires have occurred in this manner. Both religious studies and STS are also involved in hires of this sort.

I thus recommend this sort of position-allocation competition to interdisciplinarians everywhere. Note that there is nothing explicit in the rules governing the competition that privileges interdisciplinarity. Yet interdisciplinarity programs can prosper within such a competition. Departmental chairs are guided to see interdisciplinary programs as potential allies. As the number of cross-appointments has multiplied in the faculty as a result of these competitions, they have come increasingly to be seen (in at least some departments) as a normal component of departmental structure and departmental hiring strategies.

Other Similar Initiatives

Interdisciplinarians need to think hard about other sorts of institutional innovations that are not explicitly interdisciplinary but serve to support interdisciplinarity. The idea of a position-allocation competition can be defended on many grounds: transparency in decision-making, encouraging discussion within and across units regarding priorities, and most importantly encouraging the allocation of scarce resources to their best uses. What other sorts of open competitions might interdisciplinarians be able to advocate on grounds of efficiency and fairness?

Interdisciplinarians generally advocate pedagogical innovations. At my university, like many others, it would be difficult to argue successfully that interdisciplinary programs deserve greater funding per student than other programs. Arguments about particular courses might work, but global arguments would be greeted with suspicion. However, the advantages of certain pedagogical innovations, such as team teaching, are widely appreciated. Many department chairs would like to encourage within their departments the sort of dialogue that team teaching inspires, but do not feel that they have the faculty resources to afford team teaching. I have long urged my faculty to sponsor a competition to fund team teaching initiatives. I would anticipate that interdisciplinary programs would fare well in such a competition. Likewise, interdisciplinarians might prosper in a competition for resources to develop new courses.

Broadly Based Governance

Each interdisciplinary program is governed by a council of interested faculty members from different departments (many programs have some representation from beyond the Faculty of Arts). Some of these councils are very large: Religious studies has seventy members and MEAS has over forty members. As a result, a quarter of faculty members in arts have some official affiliation with an OIS program. And these people are invested: they attend meetings, seminars, and social gatherings of their program. Some feel a stronger loyalty to program than to department (though admittedly they may interact more with the latter simply because that is where their office is).

Programs not only gain a dispersed body of supporters, but they encourage and learn of departmental courses that their students might want to take. In turn departments learn of interdisciplinary courses of interest. Programs and departments can cooperate with respect to certain courses. And the interdisciplinary program itself is strengthened by the diversity of insights: a small group of scholars may ignore program elements that a larger group will not.

Administrative Challenges

Academics tend to think too little about the administrative requirements of the programs they offer. Yet as noted above, OIS has prospered in large part due to the dedication of its administrative staff. A number of important points deserve mention:

- The most important decision that interdisciplinarians may make in setting up a structure such as OIS (or any new interdisciplinary program) is not the issues of curriculum or governance that may occupy most of their thoughts, but a decision about who to hire into key administrative roles. Interdisciplinary programs by necessity operate in a different fashion from disciplinary programs. And thus the procedures used by departments at a particular university cannot just be taken "off the shelf." You need an administrator who is willing and able to innovate, which requires a personal dedication to the success of the initiative.
- Interdisciplinary structures such as OIS necessarily interact with both departments and the dean's office more than departments interact with each other or the dean. OIS administrators must have the people skills to establish good working relationships with administrators in other units, and the tenacity to ensure that these other units respect the needs of OIS. Interdisciplinary professors tend to appreciate the need for people skills and tenacity at the professorial level, and need to recognize that these are at least as important at the administrative level.
- A structure such as OIS presents internal challenges as well. Each program has its own director, and these naturally have their unique priorities with regard to OIS staff. In the early days of OIS, these challenges were particularly difficult because some programs had brought resources with them to OIS and others had not. As OIS funding has increased it has become easier to satisfy everyone, but differences in priorities remain. At the start the administrative staff reported to an associate dean, who could make resource allocation

decisions. At present a former associate dean has been appointed
OIS director, and serves the same function. Yet the administrative
staff still works on a daily basis with directors and other members
of the various interdisciplinary programs. Again, a mixture of tenacity and people skills is required.

• Administrators in particular must strike a balance between on the one
hand achieving administrative efficiencies by ensuring administrative similarities across programs, and on the other hand respecting
the individuality of programs. The best balance can only be achieved
through ongoing consultation with programs.

Graduate Programming

When the OIS was first established, it was impossible to govern a graduate degree program at the University of Alberta outside of departmental
structures. HuCo was an exception, but was saddled with a program and
admission structure whereby students were first (officially) admitted to a
department (in which they would take a third of their courses) and only then
to HuCo. The religious studies program at first contemplated running its
undergraduate degree though OIS and its graduate degree through a department, precisely because it thought running the latter through OIS would be
impossible.

It turned out fortuitously that the Faculty of Graduate Studies and
Research (FGSR) — which has to approve all new graduate programs — was
quite amenable to changing its rules (in part because interdisciplinary programs were emerging in the natural sciences as well). It had legitimate concerns that a viable graduate program required a critical mass of potential
supervisors. It accepted the argument that this criterion could be met by an
interdisciplinary program drawing on the expertise of faculty members situated in many departments (whether these were officially cross-appointed to
the program or not). And thus we were able to smoothly transfer the graduate programs in both religious studies and comparative literature to OIS. (At
the time, religious studies only had an MA. It has in 2008 added a PhD which
was likely only possible because of the large group of scholars involved in governance of the program, and the dedication of several of these.) FGSR also
cooperated with us in changing the structure of HuCo. Many students applied
with non–Arts or interdisciplinary undergraduate degrees and thus fit HuCo
but not any department: we created a new (super-)interdisciplinary HuCo
option for these students.

The lesson here may be that certain barriers to interdisciplinarity prove in practice to be much less severe than they might at first appear. To be sure, we would have been stymied by an FGSR dean that merely intoned the existing rules. But a dean and associate dean who instead invoked the rationale for existing rules could easily see their way to a novel governance structure.

Symbiosis

In academia we are so accustomed to subject content being organized through disciplinary departmental structures that we may think these are the only way to organize a university. As Stuart Henry (2005) has argued, disciplinary hegemony is often unquestioned. To be sure, interdisciplinary programs are often housed in departments, and often function well there. But the departmental form was designed with disciplines in mind: it serves well a group of specialized scholars with an inward-looking set of priorities. If we accept that interdisciplinarians should have a symbiotic relationship with (many types of) specialized scholarship, then it is less clear that interdisciplinarians should best be housed in isolated departments. Interdisciplinarians should have some formalized interactions with specialized scholars. The best way of formalizing such interactions is not yet clear.

Cross-appointments and broadly based governance of interdisciplinary programs are two ways of institutionalizing collaboration and symbiosis. At their best they ensure two-way communication between disciplines and interdisciplinary programs. A structure such as OIS then allows a diverse group of scholars from different departments to *easily* govern an interdisciplinary program. The OIS staff is dedicated to its programs. Interdisciplinarians do not have to beg support from departmental administrators whose primary focus is disciplinary. OIS thus provides a support similar to that provided by departments, but one tailored to the special challenges of interdisciplinarity.

The challenge is for a body such as OIS to be recognized as both unique and equal to departments in prestige and authority. Given the prevalence and normalization of the departmental structure, this sort of acceptance will not happen overnight. At this writing, though, the OIS story is a happy one of increasing resources, reputation, and acceptance. At least one other university (the University of Saskatchewan, which flew the OIS director and senior administrator in for consultation) is explicitly using OIS as a model as it develops new interdisciplinary programming.

Creating an Internal Sense of Solidarity

One of the goals of OIS was to establish a sense of common purpose among interdisciplinary programs. This goal has been achieved only to a limited extent. The vast majority of members of OIS programs have come to value the OIS itself and its staff. Monthly meetings of program directors ensure that they at least understand some of the priorities and concerns of other programs. But it is safe to say that most program members have a loose loyalty at best to interdisciplinarity itself. If OIS was threatened, the programs would likely unite strategically in its defense. Since about a quarter of professors are involved with at least one OIS program, they would provide a powerful lobby. If only one OIS program were threatened at a time, the sense of solidarity might prove much weaker.

A number of strategies were tried to encourage a common sense of belonging. Foremost, I created (consultatively) two core courses about interdisciplinarity: what it is, its history, how interdisciplinary research is best performed. It was hoped that all programs would require one or both of these. But many programs waited to see what other programs would do, and thus this requirement was not widely adopted. The individualized major requires both. STS for a while required one, but dropped this requirement because other programs did not, ironically just as comparative literature added the requirement.

The problem here was that most interdisciplinarians could more readily understand what a course, about say, religious studies would look like than a course about interdisciplinarity itself. They worried that such a course was too meta-theoretical. They worried that there were no interdisciplinary best practices. And they worried about who (if I were not around) would teach it. Most interdisciplinarians, that is, have reflected much more on the nature of a particular interdisciplinary theme than on the nature of interdisciplinarity itself (see Szostak 2006, 2007). This limits, I believe, their effectiveness as interdisciplinarians (just as a disciplinarian unfamiliar with disciplinary best practices would be limited). In particular, it is hard to agree on what should be taught in the core courses in each interdisciplinary program without some previous consensus on the nature and purpose of interdisciplinarity. And it certainly limits the sense of common purpose across interdisciplinary programs.

This task of advocating such a course has, I think, become much easier with the publication of the first textbooks in the field (Augsburg 2006, Repko 2008). I hope that in the future it will be possible to convince these programs of both the value and practicality of these courses.

An interdisciplinary speakers' series was also initiated. But after some initial successes it proved difficult to draw large numbers together to address general topics. Individual programs found it much easier to sustain their own seminar series.

Magnetism

The OIS is a potential home for any new interdisciplinary program in the Faculty of Arts. Yet only one new program has been added since the OIS was established: a certificate in peace and conflict studies. This initiative benefited from the existence of OIS. When a group of faculty members (encouraged by an external donor) met to discuss this theme, OIS was the obvious place to house the program (though it looks like a related graduate program may end up in political science for, well, political reasons).

It has turned out that the number of faculty members who say "it would be great to have an interdisciplinary program in X" is much greater than the number of faculty members who are willing to come together and achieve consensus on the nature of such a program.

One challenge in creating a new interdisciplinary program is deciding who determines its nature. When a department creates a new program, the departmental council usually votes on it. What happens if a group of scholars from different disciplines comes together? If they achieve consensus (as happened with STS) there is no problem. But when I gathered a group together to discuss a program in environmental studies (which would have required collaboration with another faculty, and involved participation by yet other faculties), different visions emerged. It was then unclear how best to decide among these (though unfair paths forward, including the one taken, could be readily identified). This is a problem that OIS alone cannot solve, but one that requires a commitment to openness and dialogue from senior administrators.

The OIS has not absorbed all interdisciplinary programs in the faculty. Women's studies, East Asian studies, and Spanish and Latin American studies remain in departments. Some, but not all of these programs, are insular, and do not draw on all interested faculty members as OIS programs tend to do. Those who run these programs have not wished to experiment with the OIS structure.

One challenge that interdisciplinarians face today is that everyone seems to claim to be interdisciplinary. Whereas interdisciplinary programs might have been challenged decades ago on the grounds that such programs were unnecessary, they are now more likely to be challenged on the grounds that they are ubiquitous. An entity such as OIS needs to be able to argue that it is able to "do" interdisciplinarity better than departments. This should be done, not as an attack on departments, but as a statement that interdisciplinarity is best served by a distinct institutional structure. As noted above, departments have a relative advantage in teaching specialized (that is, disciplinary) courses.

The easiest argument to make in this respect is that a good interdisciplinary program seeks to integrate the insights of all scholars with relevant interest and expertise. A program that claims to be interdisciplinary but arbitrarily constrains involvement should be suspect.

The harder argument — that there are interdisciplinary best practices — is potentially more powerful. If this were accepted, then departments could not casually claim that they were interdisciplinary. A structure such as OIS is the obvious place to house courses about interdisciplinarity itself, and these might potentially be viewed as a useful component of every undergraduate student's education.

Reaching Out

Canadian universities do not face accreditation agencies, and do not have general education requirements as a rule. I have argued elsewhere that general education provides a major opportunity for interdisciplinarians. They can reasonably argue that a key purpose of general education is to guide students to integrate across their courses, and this requires a familiarity with the nature and practice of interdisciplinarity (Szostak 2003).

Interdisciplinarians in Canadian universities face a greater challenge. The Faculty of Arts has a set of core requirements. These are old-fashioned "breadth" requirements, and individual requirements are protected by the units that provide them. A recent effort to develop a thematic set of requirements failed. An effort to add to present "divisional" requirements an "interdisciplinary" requirement also failed (even though the Faculty's promotional material now effectively treats "interdisciplinary studies" as a fourth division). Both initiatives would have increased the number of students taking interdisciplinary courses. It could well be that this point was prominent in the thinking of those who opposed these proposals. It could also be that many still do not appreciate the intrinsic importance of interdisciplinarity. Alternatively, they may have thought that everyone is now doing interdisciplinarity. In any case, interdisciplinarians (and any who think there is some core purpose(s) to undergraduate education) should be ready to fight this battle again.

What If the Sky Falls?

In the 1990s (when oil prices remained lower than they had been for a few years), the government slashed the university's budget by 20 percent.

While the non-academic staff bore the brunt of these cuts, there was little academic hiring for many years. Small programs were amalgamated in the hopes of achieving efficiencies (sometimes successfully, though the word "interdisciplinary" was often thrown around to justify units that were at best "multidisciplinary"— again some sense of the true nature of interdisciplinarity might have guided better or at least more honest decision-making). What would happen to OIS in the not-entirely-unlikely event that this should happen again?

On the one hand, it might be argued that OIS is easier to eliminate than a department. Its faculty members can just be un-cross-appointed back to their departments. While true, there are several good reasons to doubt this course of action. Most obviously, there is no obvious cost saving. Those hundreds of students would still have to be serviced, and the OIS teaches and administers as cost-effectively as anyone. This is certainly true if the existing programs were maintained and would likely be true even if they were not (and those students were squeezed over time into other majors).

The diversity of OIS militates against the closure of all of its programs. As noted above, a quarter of faculty members participate in at least one of these. OIS commands greater loyalty than any single department. And OIS programs have some visibility outside the university as well. Comparative literature has one of the best high school outreach initiatives in the faculty. The faculty received some bad press five years ago when it did not immediately replace its sole expert in Islamic religion upon retirement. (The religious studies program was scheduled during 2008–9 to hire its second Islamist.) The faculty often publicly celebrates the uniqueness of HuCo. STS and MEAS may seem more useful majors in the modern day to many Alberta taxpayers than many others. The Peace and Conflict Studies Certificate has some notable external support. The (small) individualized major is a media darling: I have been interviewed several times in print and on radio about this program that allows students to design their own major.

On the other hand, there might be both economic and pedagogical rationales for rolling some of the faculty's other interdisciplinary programs under the OIS umbrella. Some of these programs would improve simply by engaging with a broader set of interested faculty members. And it could well be that OIS staff, familiar with the special needs of interdisciplinary programming, would administer such programs more easily than departmental administrators.

Conclusion

I would draw the following lessons for interdisciplinarians interested in growing a sustainable program:

- Seize opportunities.
- Take reasonable risks.
- Be prepared to build a new program over time.
- Seek institutional innovations with broad appeal that support inter-disciplinarity.
- Do not assume that barriers are real.
- Pursue a shared vision of interdisciplinarity.
- Seek a deep interaction with other departments.
- Hire staff that are dedicated, consultative, and innovative.
- Pursue a role in general education.
- Grow and be happy.

More concretely, and more controversially, I recommend cross-appointments and broadly based governance of interdisciplinary programs. These have their problems. But in my experience the advantages are greater; at least once the appropriate administrative structure is put in place. The problems in part stem from the novelty of the enterprise at least at my university. But once we appreciate that an interdisciplinary university needs to move away from the vertical model of disciplines toward an increased emphasis on horizontal linkages, then the novelty should seem less a historical accident and more a harbinger of the university of the future.

NOTE

I would like foremost to thank Barb Heagle, administrator extraordinaire, for keeping the flame alive. Barb Heagle and Ken Munro (Director of OIS) read an earlier draft and made helpful comments. Any errors or omissions or hyperbole remain the author's responsibility.

REFERENCES

Augsburg, Tanya. 2006. *Becoming interdisciplinary: An introduction to interdisciplinary studies.* Dubuque: Kendall Hunt.

Henry, Stuart. 2005. Disciplinary hegemony meets interdisciplinary ascendancy: Can interdisciplinary/integrative studies survive, and if so how? *Issues in Integrative Studies* 23: 1–37.

Repko, Allen. 2008. *Interdisciplinary research: Theory and process.* Thousand Oaks: Sage.

Szostak, Rick. 2003. "Comprehensive" curricular reform: Providing students with an overview of the scholarly enterprise. *Journal of General Education* 52:1: 27–49.

_____. 2006. Whither interdisciplinarity? *Issues in Integrative Studies* 24: 145–9

_____. 2007. How and why to teach interdisciplinary research practice. *Journal of Research Practice* 3:2, October. *http://jrp.icaap.org/index.php/jrp/article/view/92/89* (accessed November 18, 2008).

Conclusion

Tanya Augsburg, Stuart Henry, William H. Newell and Rick Szostak

Introduction

At the outset of this book the editors presented some of the challenges facing undergraduate interdisciplinary studies, not least that recently many programs have been subject to cuts, dilution, dispersion and, in several cases, complete closure; and this occurred at the very time when the concept of interdisciplinarity was in the ascendancy. We argued that undergraduate inter-disciplinary programs are at a crossroads; they can risk either disappearing as relics of educational change and experimentation, or adapt, once again to become leaders of precarious and risky uncharted educational directions. Echoing others, Newell points out that by their very nature "IDS programs are *always* at risk" which, according to Wentworth and Carp, is because of the disciplinary based, departmentally organized structure of the academy. Indeed, Henry (2005) has argued that part of the explanation for the apparent demise of several longstanding undergraduate interdisciplinary studies is "disciplinary hegemony" or the power of the disciplines rooted in the depart-mental organizational structure of the university.

As a result of this structural and organizational power, disciplines are able to marginalize those educational forms that deviate from the normal practice, especially if these forms are perceived as threatening due to their resource acquisition, student enrollment or their ideological challenge to the mainstream. Each discipline has its own distinct "disciplinary culture" and identity. Disciplines regulate how their discourses, concepts, theories, methods, and research are preserved and disseminated. While they are sup-portive or even indifferent to the importance of other disciplines, they are often disparaging about the existence of that which they deem as non-disciplines, whether these are professions, applied programs or multi- and interdisciplinary studies.

Nonetheless, by itself, disciplinary hegemony is at best a partial explanation for the recent demise of undergraduate interdisciplinary studies programs. In this concluding chapter we consider the recurring themes that have emerged from the detailed case histories reported in the previous chapters, and which have fleshed out the local and institutionally specific ways that this challenge has become manifest. Despite the uniqueness of each institutional situation it is important to situate the recurrent themes within several dimensions of the changing political-economic context of higher education. The next sections thus review five aspects of the historical evolution of interdisciplinary programs: (1) the legacy of idealist and utopian educational roots; (2) the ubiquity of multi- and interdisciplinarity; (3) the corporatization of higher education, which is in part a response to changes in student demographics; (4) the empowerment of upper administrative personalities; and (5) the shifting structural needs of interdisciplinary programs. We conclude by offering some lessons for the future. We identify what does not work and what does work for the sustainability of undergraduate interdisciplinary programming. Ultimately we base our conclusions on the findings made in the twelve case histories offered in this volume.

Idealist and Utopian Roots

As Hendra, Newell, Furtado et al., and Wentworth and Carp have shown, the roots of many interdisciplinary studies programs lie in the wider context of the experimental ideals of 1960s academic scholars who were dissatisfied with the contemporary state of undergraduate higher education and who believed that more could be accomplished than seemed evident in the increasingly research-oriented university. Newell reflects on the idealism of the time: "We were setting up an educational utopia. We were special, different, and yes, better. We were innovative, the vanguard of a curricular and pedagogical future; civil rights, women's rights, the environment." The desires here were multiple but included relevance, access, engagement, critical awareness, empowerment and agency. For many of this foundational first generation IDS era, the objective was to forge activist critical thinking from inquisitive student innocence. This objective implied collaborative learning among a community of fellow students and dedicated scholars. It required educating future citizens to address complex contemporary issues rather than replicate intellectual clones to enhance obscure fields of academic inquiry. Most of all it required a break from existing undergraduate educational norms. At its heart was a tension between interdisciplinary studies (IDS) as an abstract integrating exercise, and the need for IDS to take place in a living-learning context and be applied to real-world events. This goes to the roots of IDS in the experimental college movement, but has shifted generationally from experimentation to pragmatism. [This was partially captured by Newell's (1998) vision of the professionalization of IDS and by his observations (Newell forthcoming 2009) about its shift from the radical fringe to the liberal mainstream, to a small but normal part of a university education, to the new "in" thing.]

For some in this movement, the integrated interdisciplinary solution was less important than breaking from traditional majors, which as Hendra explains, at University of Massachusetts–Amherst partly reflected "a reaction to the strictures of the departmental major; but it was more fundamentally a shift from a faculty-centered to a student-centered instructional approach." Indeed, Hendra says that the individualized designing of one's own degree was "a form of meta-learning." While this often leads to an interdisciplinary course of study, IDS was not an explicit requirement. In this approach the degree could be narrow or broad, draw on two disciplines or many, and says Hendra, "Though not as tightly structured as an interdisciplinary degree, the individualized degree raises the same questions as to the capacity of any one discipline to comprehend adequately or address the complex, holistic nature of the subjects in life's curriculum." At its worst the individualized program can become little more than a degree completion program, emphasizing breadth over depth, without an attempt at internal coherence, no real thought about the student's education or ownership of it. Indeed, the University of Massachusetts, in fall 2008 celebrated more than 500 adult learners enrolled in its University Without Walls program: "It is the largest enrollment ever for the groundbreaking degree completion program ... and close to 80-percent of UWW students are doing online coursework" (UMass 2008). At its best undergraduate self-designed majors can be vibrant areas of academic creativity, thematically structured and rigorously evaluated. Over time advising issues and faculty workload issues become critical factors for an individualized program's sustainability — despite individualized degree programs' attractiveness to growing numbers of students.

Wakefield describes an individualized program at Emory that exists within and under the wing of the Graduate Institute of Liberal Arts founded in 1954, and modeled after it. As the graduate program has changed, so has the undergraduate program; undergrads are exposed to doctoral student research, lending legitimacy to the undergraduate program. However, as Wakefield points out, this undergraduate program is small, "amorphous by definition, and occasionally unruly in practice." Most undergraduates are attracted to the program out of frustration not with the constraints of disciplinary majors but with the absence of a major in their area of interest (often developed through personal experience). In this sense the undergraduate individualized major provides a structure and format to serve the functional needs of students who want to be creative and free to experiment. Its small size compensates for any "unruliness" as well as attributing to its sustainability.

As the academic innovators of the 1960s designed creative, student-focused programs that came to fruition in the 1970s, the view that education had intrinsic value regardless of the field of study, gave way to increasing specialization tied to professions or careers, with the pragmatism of training for employment being more resonant than the idealism of education for its own sake. The materialism of the 1980s saw a growth in professional and applied fields, particularly business, which has become the most popular undergraduate major (Donoghue 2008, 91). By the 1990s there was a decline in the value of liberal education. Yet IDS programs retained their first generation ideals.

As Davis reports the San Francisco State InterArts Center (IAC), for example, between 1992–2003 explored some seven opportunities of significance to faculty and students, one of which was "employing creative expressions as catalysts for constructive social change (this possibility emerged within almost all IAC courses)." Indeed, in this changing political economy of academia, some interdisciplinary studies programs seemed prophetically relevant for dealing with emerging complex problems, while others appeared to be increasingly ossified relics of the past. By the 1990s there had been a generational change, although this had not necessarily been reflected in the faculty of interdisciplinary studies programs who were often locked in their past, and in some cases had not hired the next generation to replace them. As Davis makes clear, the lack of tenure-track and tenured faculty can render existing interdisciplinary studies programs as extremely vulnerable (see also Burkhardt 2006).

The range of the case histories illustrate that interdisciplinary programs did not all start at the same historical time period, suffer the same trajectory, or have similar duration; some emerged and then died after a short duration, others have 30–40 year life spans, and yet others underwent metamorphoses into unrecognizable forms. If first generation interdisciplinary programs with their utopian legacy of the experimental college-based IDS programs were slow to adapt to the changing context of higher education some others, born in a later era, have proven to be more resilient. In part they have accomplished this by adapting to the changing corporate nature of the academy. Muir describes how New Century College at George Mason University embraced competency-based education, service learning, FYE, and learning communities that distinctively mark it as a second generation IDS program, although one that doesn't take a second generation approach to IDS, perhaps because they used TESC (Thomas Edison State College) as a model. Similarly Repko describes the success of IDS at Texas Arlington that has moved from a program of 200 students and two advisers to one of over 700 with four full-time, tenure track faculty lines. To the extent that they are self-conscious about their use of disciplines, as in the case of UT Arlington, interdisciplinary studies programs are starting down the road to second generation forms. In contrast NCC's proposed revisions for 2009 make no mention of IDS much less ID process and they seem to have taken the route toward inculcating students with qualities of leadership and self-direction over an explicitly interdisciplinary process.[1] It will be interesting to observe how liberal studies programs in the California State University system will negotiate between any steps toward becoming more explicitly interdisciplinary while still providing the multidisciplinary foundation necessary that is strongly recommended for teacher preparation.

The Ubiquity of Multi- and Interdisciplinarity

By the 1980s and into the 1990s it became clear that interdisciplinary studies had been impacted by the changing nature of undergraduate academic study; toward majors in multidisciplinary and interdisciplinary fields such as environmental studies, cultural studies, criminal justice studies, women's studies, varieties of area studies, communications studies, television and film studies, etc. These composite fields, often drawing on a variety of disciplines, attract many students that might previously have gone into disciplines or, for that matter, into interdisciplinary studies. This might suggest that as catalysts for change interdisciplinary studies has become redundant; the claim from some quarters was that perhaps IDS was no longer necessary since interdisciplinarity was now everywhere; "it was the air we breathe." Other, more traditional disciplines such as those in the humanities have been encouraged to recognize that "interdisciplinarity begins at home" (Menard 2005, 14). In this sense IDS has ascended, dispersed and the Interdisciplinary Diaspora has successfully permeated academia. The question of course is what kind of interdisciplinarity has been successful? For Miller and Newell the absence of clear core principles and agreed upon processes of integration in many multi- and even interdisciplinary fields is not evident, with the result that these new forms represent "weak" interdisciplinarity insofar as no real commitment to interdisciplinarity is indicated. Indeed, as Szostak observes, the challenge to IDS programs today is not that they are unnecessary but that they are ubiquitous, and the administrative structure that supports them needs to demonstrate that its programs do IDS better than those supporting weak interdisciplinarity (e.g., interdisciplinarity in name only). We also need to make the case not only for the potential of IDS but also the profession's capacity to deliver on its promises; it has to address the real-world application of ID solutions, not just the intellectual viability of IDS, since we claim to be a bridge between the Ivory Tower and the Real World. In Wentworth and Carp's terms, we need to move our field from the periphery to the core of academia. To achieve this we need to acknowledge that "recent fortunes in institutionalisation may have mainstreamed interdisciplinarity, but they have not provided material and conceptual support for its development. These factors make interdisciplinarity as a radical research or pedagogic position difficult to sustain" (Vasterling et al. 2006, 66). Indeed, these have increasingly to be negotiated in the corporate university.

Corporatization of Higher Education

As Miller, Hendra and Wentworth and Carp point out, interdisciplinary studies programs have been negatively affected by the increasing corporatization of the university and the changing role of its administrative leadership. When educational decisions are based on the bottom line, programs, regardless of their educational quality and value, are vulnerable to budget cuts. No better insight into this corporate thinking was expressed by Arizona State University Provost Betty Capaldi commenting on recent cuts to their nursing program: "They are a money-losing operation. And I know it's a horrible way to talk about it, but we are a business.... So if you have part of your operation that's losing money, you have to generate enough revenue elsewhere, and right now our revenue is being decreased" (Ryman 2008).

The shift from pedagogical experimentation to market driven trends, says Miller moves us from "strong" interdisciplinarity to "weak" interdisciplinarity. The latter chases funding and student tuition dollars rather than a genuine commitment to interdisciplinarity. This shift reflects a broader change in university funding for higher education from being a state and individual responsibility to being dependent on donors and grants. Reflecting this shift, the role of university academic leadership has changed from the promotion of good scholarship, teaching excellence and engaged service, to one bent on promoting institutional prestige, grantsmanship for federal and foundation dollars and prioritizing, above all else, development/advancement (fundraising) that places "donor cultivation" over critical deliberation. By the mid–1990s public university budgets began to look more like those of private institutions and this was not helped by a series of national economic declines in the early 1980s, again in the early 1990s and early 2000, and most recently in 2006–2008. According to a 2008 report from the Center on Budget and Policy Priorities, "at least 21 states have made cuts to public university budgets or are planning tuition increases of 5 percent to 15 percent" (McNichol and Lav 2008, 6). The impact on IDS of such cuts can be devastating. For example, as Miller and Davis explain between 1992 and 1995, almost all of the special programs at San Francisco State were eliminated when "several waves of economic hardships struck California" and this was made easier because their faculty were non-tenure track. The BA InterArts program was so decimated by resource reductions by 1995 that it was not viable, and a new dean's first step was to eliminate it. In 2001 the two MA InterArts programs were also deemed non-viable because no new resources were foreseen and they too had been starved for resources (having only one tenured faculty member between them) in spite of acknowledged high quality. Like the BA program, Davis claims, they were largely starved out of existence. Similarly, Wayne State University used the argument of economic crisis as the bases for cutting its IDS program, but as Furtado et al. point out, no money was actually saved. Clearly, at times of economic exigency interdisciplinary studies is at its most vulnerable, but as we have argued, this is not only because of its weak funding structure.

The business/corporate model of education, as Wentworth and Carp and point out, has led to the appointment of administrators inimical to IDS. This was part of the changing larger political economy of higher education attributable to the Reagan era's long-term influence on the society as a whole. The result was a growing scrutiny of the cost-inefficiency of academic programs, regardless of their educational quality. Class sizes increased (in California State Universities for example, average class size increased from 35 to 70 students) and the proportion of full-time faculty hired at universities shrank to below 50 percent as much cheaper, practicing professionals and adjuncts, were hired to fill the gap. This shift also saw the merger of departments and programs into larger organizational units, while others were cut entirely. It also saw the emergence of national concerns among legislators over measuring the effectiveness of higher education, concerns that drove accrediting agencies' requirements. Federal guidelines for student loans specified seat-time criteria that threatened the flexible scheduling and interdisciplinary approaches to adult learning of some universities, subjecting their institutions to probationary accreditation status (such as happened at the Union Institute which was subject to oversight by the Ohio Board of Regents). With increased attention to issues such as "enrollment management," "retention rates" and "graduation rates," programs increasingly have had to "prove" themselves in terms of what is increasingly deemed as "student success." No longer was it enough for a professor to grade students' course work; to the professor's charge was added outcome assessment measures designed to demonstrate how successful a program or a course was in meeting its "learning objectives." The discourse of "action verbs," through which students must demonstrate skill sets, replaced the more ethereal concepts of understanding, comprehension and awareness that were the backbone of the educational revolution of the 1960s and 1970s. As Hendra says, sadly, the bottom line for student-centered education may be that it is more profitable to teach students content than to help them learn how to learn.

Not surprisingly, faced with these political and structural forces, interdisciplinary faculty often retreated into their interdisciplinary oasis, which contributed to their isolation and marginalization. At some universities, such isolation and marginalization were imposed from above, while at others it was the result of attempts to avoid the fear of decimation from collaborating with disciplines whose faculty often held these programs in contempt. Either way, IDS programs were not in the center but on the periphery of the university, sometimes physically as well as structurally, making it all too easy, as Burkhardt (2006) points out, to inculcate "mutual othering," which Henry (2005) has argued is part and parcel of disciplinary hegemony.

Wentworth and Carp point to these programs' image on campus, to core/periphery tensions *within* the department, and tension between the missions of normalization and insurgency. This last issue goes back to the generational shift in IDS. Established IDS programs that remain must decide whether they wish to play a leadership role in the IDS of the new generation, in which case they will have to make some major adjustments (including in mission but also in conception of IDS, intentionality and explicitness of process, and grounding in recent IDS literature), or whether they feel compelled to opt for a rear-guard action fighting the good fight and going down in glorious flames.

In some cases, as illustrated by Furtado et al.'s analysis of the adult oriented interdisciplinary studies program at Wayne State University, race and class issues may have been at work in their demise. As public universities sought to raise their prestige, research standing and graduation rates, commitments to access, remediation and nontraditional programming became cost-inefficient. In 2005, for example, Temple University in Philadelphia, under then President David Adamany (the former president of Wayne State), announced that it had abandoned its urban working class students in a search for "better students" and a renaissance in research. As well as building halls of residence at this former urban commuter school, the university boasted about raising the average SAT (Scholastic Aptitude Test, used as a college admission criteria) by 111 points to 1099. President Adamany said Temple's mission should change: "Its sky-high dropout rates in the 1990s prove the folly of accepting marginal students, who would be better served by community colleges." Temple's director of admissions, Tim Rinehardt, stated, "once you become open enrollment, once you let everyone in ... that's the kiss of death" (Kerkstra, 2005). Not surprisingly Temple's percentage of African American students shrank; they found it harder to get in, and graduates from the Philadelphia public schools declined from 29 percent of the freshman class in 1996 to 10 percent in 2005. Indeed, Temple during the period 2000–2005 "has morphed from a commuter college known as "Diversity University" into an institution far more academically selective — with a 34,000-member student body that is whiter, wealthier and more suburban than ever.... To make it a truly great institution ... means ... looking for better students," stated Howard Gittis, chairman of Temple's board of trustees (Kerkstra, 2005).

These developments at Temple were reflected at Wayne State University, which abandoned its College of Lifelong Learning and its Interdisciplinary Program as well as its applied College of Labor, Urban and Metropolitan Affairs, and at the University of Minnesota which announced closing its long-standing College of General Studies and shifting the resources to enhance its honors program, among other things, in a quest to become ranked in the top three public universities in the world. These developments at public urban universities are supported by recent research. Gene R. Nichol in his commentary in the *Chronicle of Higher Education*, cites a recent report by the Education Trust, "Engines of Inequality: Diminishing Equity in the Nation's Premier Public Universities," which documents that "our flagship universities have become less accessible to low-income and minority students since 1995" (Nichol 2008, A50; see also Newfield 2008).

In many cases, the corporate structure allows ideological prejudices and historical grudges to be rationalized under the notion of saving money in tight budget times. At San Francisco State, Miller reports that the budget crisis in 2000–01 led the president (as it did at Miami) to cut entire programs instead of implement across-the-board cuts. The Interdisciplinary Social Science program was one of 10 IDS programs (out of 11 total) selected for cuts. The rationales given were that these programs were expensive, out-of-date and that "its interdisciplinary mission was being fulfilled in other programs" (so it was no longer a "distinguishing characteristic"). (These same rationales were also used for closures at Miami University and at Wayne State University). Miller also argues, as does Newell and Furtado et al., that no money was actually saved. Regarding the mission-fulfilled-by-others argument, Miller insists "this inadequate understanding of interdisciplinarity is shared by most other faculty, including members of ostensibly interdisciplinary departments."

With regard to the views of the administrators making these decisions
Archibald says, "Interdisciplinary studies programs are often seen as expendable, as a nice add-on but not rigorous or academic enough to warrant any
real commitment from the institution, especially when budgets are being
slashed." However, there is often more involved than a perception of peripheral value.

In the context of the corporate university it is important to recognize
that, as education has become commodified, students have become "con-
sumers of education." As education is viewed instrumentally, as a credential
toward their future careers or promotion, students' orientations to higher education have changed, thus necessitating both curricular and structural changes
in IDS programs. Among first generation IDS programs, students majoring
in IDS were described as left of mainstream. Newell reports, "Western students invariably talked in class, acted self-assured, and seemed intellectual
engaged. On the other hand, a few Western Program students ... were highly
visible at the University: student body presidents or other leaders in student
government; leaders of social justice, political, community service, or environmental organizations." Wentworth and Carp note that at Appalachian
State "students have always been risk-takers; they seem to be generally bright
and willing to work, somewhat rebellious or distrustful of authority, more
"left" than "right"; they tend to see themselves as "different."

As Newell, Wentworth and Carp attest, such students still exist, but
their numbers have dwindled nationwide with the increased emphasis on
career development and preparation. Exponentially rising tuition and living
costs have transformed students' lives — not only have students become more
vested in their education, they need to work more to pay for it. In 2001, 82
percent of all college students worked — 32 percent full-time. Consequently,
students are taking more than four years to complete their degree. There has
also been a change in student demographics. With the increases of transfer
and returning students the majority of college students are now over 24 years
of age (Donoghue 2008, 90). Indeed, in 1970, when many of the longstanding IDS programs were founded, only 28 percent of all college students were
25 years of age or older. By 1998 the proportion of adult learners in college
had increased to 41 percent. Moreover, by 2001 19.2 percent of college students were age 35 and older up from 9.6 percent in 1970. While some interdisciplinary studies programs such as those at San Francisco State, Wayne
State and UMass Amherst have served adult students since their inception,
and there are arguments why interdisciplinary pedagogy dovetails with adult
learning styles, these students also bring pressure to elevate degree completion over strong interdisciplinarity, as each of these programs experienced.
Indeed, although most university IDS programs were not conceived as degree-

completion programs, the reality is that these are programs serving students who would not be able to obtain degrees elsewhere within the same institution.

Administrative Personalities and Academic Politics

The field of interdisciplinary studies has been significantly affected both positively and negatively by the personality and academic, political and ideological leanings of academic leaders. Why personalities count so much in the politics and survival of IDS units but not say in physics is an interesting question. Presumably this is because physics as a prestigious discipline has a prima facie case for survival irrespective of personalities that IDS has not had. This lack of prestige makes IDS vulnerable. In an era when it is very difficult to make innovations within established disciplines, the idea of bringing together isolated and specialized disciplines in a cross fertilizing dialogue was at once attractive, creative and deliverable, especially for aspiring provosts, presidents and deans. Moving around peripheral pieces of the university to show change has been made, looks good on the senior administrator's résumé, especially since it is often done at relatively low or no political cost, and often at least *claims* some economic saving. Ironically, the same forces that facilitated some administrators to demonstrate their creativity through innovating interdisciplinary units, programs and linkages, allow others to show their administrative mettle by merging, dissolving or closing these same units, again with the claimed effect of saving money and without disrupting the structure of power in traditional disciplinary departments.

Unfortunately, the analyses of Newell, Furtado et al., Muir, Wakefield, Davis, Miller, Wentworth and Carp, and Archibald all seem to suggest that the cost to interdisciplinarity of this window of administrative megalomania is that undergraduate IDS programs are often dependent on the "kindness" of administrators (see also Burkhardt 2006). As Davis says, "The necessity for a dean's understanding, appreciation, and support of an interdisciplinary [program] cannot be overestimated." Yet as administrators change so, too, can the support for these programs. Indeed, deans with IDS programs in their schools are rarely vetted for insight into and appreciation of interdisciplinarity when hired; if IDS is valuable to an institution this may need to change. We ought to emphasize that "rarely" does not mean "never": indeed, a recent example where both familiarity with, and commitment to interdisciplinary studies programs were important criteria was the search for the dean of undergraduate studies at San Francisco State in 2007–2008.

One of the ambivalent roles into which IDS programs can be cast by administrators is as catalysts for innovation. IDS programs, such as those at George Mason, Arizona State, San Francisco State, Wayne State and Emory can find that they are often asked by senior administrators, on whose goodwill they depend, to develop new initiative, perhaps distance learning, programs for working adults, or for remedial students, or as degree completion initiatives, which don't fit easily in more focused departments but can be conveniently housed in IDS programs to see if they can gain traction. In some cases, as Wakefield reports, the IDS unit "itself has served in different capacities as an incubator for a number of forms of intrinsically interdisciplinary inquiry that now have their own departments." In other cases, the infusion of such initiatives and the lure of student FTEs that they may bring, tend to divert the program from its interdisciplinary focus, stretch often already-extended resources, and force numerous compromises in order to accommodate the new initiative. As Davis says of San Francisco State, "the Dean of the School (now College) of Creative Arts assigned a group of non-degree functions between 1986–89. Again we see the role of an administrator who seeks a home for a variety of activities that don't fit into departmental structure; IDS then can become a collection of organizationally and conceptually non-conforming units drawing resources away from and diluting its main mission. At San Francisco State "these 'Special Programs' were to be fulfilled within the limited resources assigned to IAC." The dean "had come to perceive the primary function of the CEIA/IAC as a service organization for the School."[2]

In this changing macro-academic context then, the survival and sustainability of interdisciplinary studies programs depends upon a number of interconnected elements. Indeed, while significant long-standing programs have either been closed and in many cases radically transformed, others such as that at Evergreen University and the Liberal Studies program at San Francisco State, have played central roles in their respective universities. As can be seen from the case studies, a significant factor in sustainability is the structure and administration of undergraduate interdisciplinary studies programs, which makes them particularly vulnerable to budgetary changes, and to the whims and creativity of administrative innovation in the political economy of higher education.

Administrative Structures: On Bridge Building and Dangerous Liaisons

The sustainability of interdisciplinary studies depends, in many ways, on the nature of the relationships it has with faculty in other departments and across the university, and not least on their place in the university administrative structure. The form of administrative structure in which these programs are housed can, in turn, significantly affect these relationships, as can the understanding of interdisciplinarity by deans and provosts, and the priority they place on it. While there are numerous organizational structures through which interdisciplinary programs have been administered, some are more evident than others. Among those more frequently occurring, and that have existed at various times are: (1) as a separate college (Western College at Miami University of Ohio, New College at Alabama, Tuscaloosa; New Century College at George Mason, Arizona International); (2) as a school at Miami University and, briefly, at Arizona State University, (3) as a department in another College, e.g., WSU from 2003–2007; Appalachian State University, and University of Texas at Arlington; and (4) as a program, either in a college or under the provost, as at UT Arlington pre–2002. The history of IDS organizational location within the university provides important lessons in resistance and agency. For example, in its relatively short life the Bachelor of Interdisciplinary Studies program at Arizona State has been an undergraduate program housed inconveniently in the graduate school, a program within the Division of Undergraduate Academic Services, a school within a university college, and a program in the School of Letters and Sciences within a university college. Others, like INTS at UT Arlington, have gone from being a program in the provost's office to being a department in the School of Urban and Public Affairs. At Wayne State, the administrative decision to close Montieth College, gave instant birth to the College of Lifelong Learning as administrators feared attempts by Michigan State University to open a branch campus serving adult students in nearby downtown Detroit. When, after 30 years the college was slated for closure under then Provost Charles Bantz, who had been a supporter of IDS since his Arizona State days, its then director negotiated with the dean of the College of Urban, Labor and Metropolitan Affairs (CULMA), an interdisciplinary applied social science college, to house it as a department, rather than have the unit relocate within the explicitly hostile (to CLL and CULMA) College of Liberal Arts. But WSU's new Provost Nancy Barrett, who previously had moved the IDS New College at the University of Alabama–Tuscaloosa into its College of Arts and Sciences, closed down CULMA. Interdisciplinary studies was now faced with becoming a remediation program under the provost's office or joining the now College of Arts and Sciences. It reluctantly chose that latter, but despite assurances to the contrary, it was closed completely within two years and its 18 faculty dispersed to disciplinary departments. Similarly, though with less dramatic effect, conservative political administrative appointments contributed to moving George Mason University's New Century College into its College of Arts and Sciences, which undercut faculty exchanges with disciplinary departments, yet the move was seen as a major initiative to weave the program into the fabric of the university ("build relationships across campus"). Ironically, the faculty was then asked to "make greater university connections." Yet another structural change however, ultimately proved beneficial to NCC since it aligned them with a more resonant structure and supportive dean. This involved a split of the College of Arts and Sciences into a College of Science (COS) and College of Humanities and Social Science (CHSS). Muir reports that the latter proved a much more congenial home for NCC; a supportive dean, structural clustering of 11 IDS programs and a governance system that permitted NCC faculty to play leadership roles, all combined to prove that an IDS program can thrive within a larger liberal arts division. Indeed, the new associate dean for NCC's "portfolio has expanded to working with more interdisciplinary degree programs within CHSS." Why then is IDS so subject to structural organizational change?

As we indicated above, it is important to recognize that interdisciplinary studies programs do not easily fit into the existing structures of a university. The necessity of them becoming a department has more to do with how a university's resources, particularly budgets and tenure homes, are allocated, than to do with whether something that is interdisciplinary can be departmentalized. As Davis points out, San Francisco State's "choice of a 'center' rather than a 'department'" reflected a desire to have "more flexible relationships" with the various departments in creative arts. Those flexible relations were in tension with the organizational normalization afforded by a departmental designation. We face the same issue today in deciding on the most appropriate organizational relationship between IDS and the disciplines. Indeed, Wentworth and Carp, in their analysis of the transformation of Appalachian State's Department of Interdisciplinary Studies into a program within the College of Undergraduate Studies, argue that there is an essential incongruity between the very conception of IDS and the structure of the core of the institution: "[W]e now think that stable institutional forms capable of sustaining open-ended, disciplined, interdisciplinary inquiry are to some extent incompatible with those that currently sustain disciplinarity, and that interdisciplinary units are, for that reason, inherently unstable in the Academy." This incongruity has partly to do with essential differences between IDS and disciplines.

Disciplines focus on a distinctive subject matter, whereas IDS is content-neutral; IDS represents an approach to knowledge, a method of treating knowledge about any subject, rather than knowledge about a particular subject. While both disciplines and interdisciplines engage in the analytical process, IDS also synthesizes. Whereas the disciplines are capable of operating in isolation (though increasingly they choose not to do so), IDS can only function by drawing on the work of the disciplines. IDS is clearly not just another discipline, requiring its own parallel niche, although some such as Rogers, Booth, and Eveline (2003) argue that is the only way it will survive. In some senses, IDS may be more on a par with the disciplines as a whole, yet it is dependent on them as well. At the same time IDS is so much less than the disciplines as a whole since it seeks their connections and only draws on aspects of their depth. Thinking of the two parts of the IDS process — drawing on insights of various disciplines, and integrating their insights utilizing a fundamentally and radically different approach from the disciplines — one could argue that IDS simultaneously goes beyond and falls short of the disciplines. Thinking in terms of the reciprocal relationship between IDS and the disciplines, in which the disciplines arguably need IDS for real world relevance and for the chance to contribute to the understanding of complex issues that transcend individual disciplines, as much as IDS needs the disciplines for depth of insight into individual aspects of complex and/or real world issues, IDS should be in a relationship of mutual respect, if not full parity with all the disciplines combined. What do these differences suggest about how and where IDS fits in the structure of a university?

Wentworth and Carp view this as a conundrum or a tension. Indeed, they conclude that "interdisciplinary practices that are institutionally, culturally, and individually transforming" can survive only through individual ad hoc practice and through "networks of faculty relationships," not through "creating enduring entities." We may wonder whether 37 years (for Appalachian State) and 34 years (for Miami) and even longer for Wayne State (if Monteith College is included), do not constitute "enduring." Indeed, the majority the universities in the U.S. are less than four times that old. We might even speculate that many institutions of higher education, let alone individual disciplinary departments within them, may themselves go out of business or be radically transformed in the decades ahead because of developments in "the for-profit revolution" that includes online education, and for-profit schools symbolized by the University of Phoenix, Walden University and DeVry (Donoghue 2008, 93).

However, it might be more productive to think in terms of other areas of the academy that draw on disciplines yet transcend them in some way, rather than thinking in terms of existing administrative arrangements. Perhaps IDS belongs in a separate professional school or college alongside the School of Architecture, the School of Public Affairs, the College of Business, and the School of Public Health. Indeed, maybe IDS itself should be thought of as a profession, not as a field or specialty or approach within the liberal arts. Even if one accepts this radical position, IDS would still be unique among the professions in its close reciprocal relationship with the arts and science disciplines. Further, the applied focus of the professions would suggest that transdisciplinary (in the European sense), rather than interdisciplinary studies, would be the more suitable choice for a profession. Within a generation, it may be that transdisciplinarity and interdisciplinarity merge, since each really needs the expertise of the other to be complete, in which case that merged field could legitimately claim to be a profession (again, a unique one given its closed ties to the disciplines) and thus deserving of a separate college or school. Even so, that still leaves a gap of a generation in which we need to find a structural home for IDS. In light of the diverse ways one can infer the appropriate location in the university structure from the nature of interdisciplinarity it is not surprising that some administrators might decide that IDS does not belong in an administrative structure at all. This might lead to the conclusion to disband IDS programs and let everyone participate to the extent they want, in the way they want, as long as they want. In some ways this is the implicit vision behind the Duke University's Promotion and Tenure (PT) revision to facilitate IDS: let each faculty member select how, when, and how much to be involved in a variety of ID activities, and then ask each individual to identify who needs to be involved in that person's PT decisions as a result. What the Duke strategy may ignore is the concomitant need to free up the location of faculty within the institution so that they are able to move through the structure; why shouldn't a faculty member's location within the structure of the institution shift as that person's activities evolve?

Where interdisciplinary developments come from top-down administrative initiatives there can be advantages and disadvantages to having links with disciplinary departments. As Szostak points out departments, and even skeptical chairs, may choose, particularly during administratively driven reorganizations, to affiliate themselves with an interdisciplinary unit (i.e., opt for interdisciplinary status) for political reasons rather than because of any commitment to, or even interest in, interdisciplinarity. They then have a stake in a weak definition of interdisciplinarity and an unfocused mission for the unit, which can be counter productive toward any attempt to achieve genuine disciplinary integration.

However, if these weak affinity models are pursued, do they lack sufficient formality and rigor needed to drive disciplines to search outside of themselves? Do we not need to formalize interdisciplinarians' interactions with each other and with specialized disciplinary scholars in something more than a departmental structure (which serves only disciplinarians well) and if so, what kind of structure might serve it best?

Davis argues that "it is imperative for those teaching within interdisciplinary programs to pursue frequent dialogue, and even pursue collaborative efforts, with faculty in related fields outside their academic unit in order to nourish" their understanding and appreciation of "authentic forms of inter-disciplinary expression." He says: "there must be meeting points between the events and interest within an interdisciplinary program and those occurring within [affiliated] traditional departments." The challenge is how to achieve this dialogue without diluting interdisciplinarity and without threatening to undermine the value added by interdisciplinary integration. Davis believes that one way of securing protection from the disciplines is "to place interdisciplinary programs within an academic unit that is the equivalent to that of a department, and preferably independent of a traditional discipline." However, there is no guarantee that these multi- and or interdisciplinary structures are not themselves ultimately vulnerable to the forces of disciplinary rationalization, as faculty at Wayne State found in their futile and short-lived attempt to find protection in a multidisciplinary college that itself was subsequently closed.

Beyond the free affinity model it might be that formal linkages between disciplinary departments and IDS could be established in some form of administrative superstructure; however, this too is fraught with danger. One form of administrative super-structure supporting interdisciplinary programs is the governing council drawn from across the college, division or even the institution, such as that operating at Oakland University in Michigan. Szostak says these kinds of structures can provide an official affiliation, a sense of investment, and even feelings of loyalty to the program — and Goldsmith would agree. Their meetings can reveal courses of interest to departments and vice versa, and "a small group of scholars may ignore program elements that a larger group will not." In addition, such an affiliation provides an administrative layer of protection between the disciplinary departments and the interdisciplinary program.

A governing council can also facilitate joint (or cross) appointments and these give faculty members from several departments a stake in an IDS program. Even department chairs may see joint appointments with IDS programs as a way to hire an additional faculty member, and a way to attract students to the contributing discipline. Moreover, the courses offered by IDS programs can be accepted as options that count towards a major in that discipline. Szostak says that a mix of dedicated (faculty whose course load requires them to teach in interdisciplinary studies) and joint-appointments may be ideal, but (given changes in the institution's promotion, tenure, annual salary increment policy) a program can function with only joint-appointments. San Francisco State interdisciplinary arts programs between 1970 and 1985 tried a model in which they brought in program associates from disciplinary departments to serve as mentors. As Davis says, "One goal of this approach was the hope that the experimental and interdisciplinary nature of the project would inspire students majoring in that discipline to think and work in a more interdisciplinary manner." However, he points out that two significant problems arose from this system: (1) the faculty mentors were generally not interdisciplinary artists/theorists, and (2) it was extremely difficult to convince instructors, whom students barely knew, to consent to spend the considerable extra time with someone who wasn't in their own department." The former was a professional development problem, i.e., lack of preparation for faculty to teach interdisciplinary arts, whereas the latter was a faculty incentives problem — what counts for professional rewards, status, and advancement? Indeed, the latter problem raises important questions for any faculty member having joint responsibilities to IDS and a disciplinary department.

There is a clear disadvantage for IDS faculty whose tenure is in a disciplinary department, especially those doing most of their teaching in IDS programs. This relates to how committed their disciplinary department chair is to present their case for promotion or salary increment, and if the person charged with administrating IDS programs has voice but no vote in the decision. Even more problematic may be making the case for tenure for someone who is expected to teach for more than one department or one who resides in an interdisciplinary department. It can often seem to faculty members that they are expected to be full-time in each department with which they are affiliated, and that they have to demonstrate expertise and depth in each, as each will be judging them for tenure and promotion. This problem is compounded as the faculty member's case goes to committees of the college or university that are dominated by disciplinarians and whose tenure application will be judged against those of specific disciplines.

Cross-appointments and broadly based governance of IDS programs help but may require some sort of super-structure (which must be recognized as unique yet on a par with departments). Without additional steps, solidarity within the super-structure is likely to be weak. Clarity/precision of agreement on the conception of interdisciplinarity among representatives of the superstructure may help strengthen the relationships, since they would then share more of a commitment to interdisciplinarity itself. Also helpful would be a set of core courses on IDS in which that conception is spelled out, especially if individual IDS programs require them. The best order for these steps is unclear. Textbooks by interdisciplinarians, such as those by Augsburg (2006) and Repko (2008) should help consolidate the definition. Once these steps have been taken, a speaker series or lecture series on interdisciplinarity might strengthen them.

Once a super-structure is in place, and some internal solidarity is established, a procedure needs to be put in place for establishing new programs.
The argument needs to be made that the administrative super-structure that
transcends departments facilitates IDS better than does a departmental structure because it draws most widely on the available perspectives. IDS programs housed in insular departments are more prone to seeking to construct
a new orthodoxy, i.e., an interdiscipline, not an interdisciplinary program
(women's studies, for example, is increasingly viewed as an interdiscipline).
Once there is agreement on best practices, then it becomes a matter of determining which programs employ those practices. If the super-structure contributes to cost-effective teaching and administration, then the diversity of
faculty militates against its elimination.

A variation of the superstructure is suggested by Archibald that involves
creating a hub for interdisciplinary and integrative activity to coordinate,
connect, and enable IDS through resource management, programming, and
assessment and progress monitoring. She advocates forming an IDS Programs
Committee that can provide a forum for IDS programs to communicate concerns, identify needs, share expertise and/or materials, seek collaboration, and
work together to improve the quality of interdisciplinary teaching and learning. As Miller points out, the University Interdisciplinary Council (UIC) at
San Francisco State has performed many of these functions since 1981.

What Doesn't Work?

It is of central importance to the future of IDS that the discourse shift
from the creation, survival, and success of interdisciplinary programs to their
sustainability. How can what we do today in interdisciplinary programming
serve present needs, without compromising those of future students of IDS?
The purpose of the next two sections is to describe what strategies seem to
not work and what strategies seem to work in the support of interdisciplinarity. As the preceding historical/contextual sections should make clear, we do
not live in a perfect world. Much of what did not work for interdisciplinary
programs should have worked. Some may feel likewise that some of what does
work should not be necessary. The next two sections, then, are designed with
practical use in mind. What can interdisciplinarians do (and not do) to ensure
program sustainability? But we would also guide interdisciplinarians not to
lose sight of the broader picture: while strengthening interdisciplinarity within
existing structures and mindsets we can continue the battle to change those
very structures and mindsets. Our foremost concern is for the present and
future students that IDS programs are intended to serve. In protecting the

intellectual legacy of the first generation programs we need to facilitate the second generation goals and ideals while preparing the intellectual and structural ground for the third generation of interdisciplinary programs.

So what doesn't work? It is obvious from various chapters, but deserves to be stressed, that having a national or international reputation as a cutting-edge interdisciplinary program does a program little good. In the cases of Miami of Ohio, Wayne State, and Interdisciplinary Arts at San Francisco State, one could hardly wish for a more esteemed place in the national academy than these programs possessed. Every program discussed in this book can point to national and international acclaim. However, it is not the national or international bodies of hard-core interdisciplinarians that make budgetary decisions on a particular campus. It is the denizens of disciplinary and superficially interdisciplinary programs that do so. And they will simply dismiss outside accolades from bodies with which they are unfamiliar. New Century College at George Mason has made a greater effort at achieving objective external commendations (such as its 18th place ranking among learning communities from *US News and World Report*) than other programs; the lesson from other programs is that it is best not to rely exclusively on these accolades to maintain institutional viability.

Likewise, grateful and laudatory alumni are much less useful than one might have expected. Every program in this book has alumni who think the program changed their lives for the better. Again, their praise is too readily dismissed by those suspicious of the idea of self-conscious interdisciplinarity. Muir is confident that objective evaluation of student progress and the leadership role played by interdisciplinary students on campus will enhance the viability of New Century College; Newell reports instead that student success and visibility on campus can be perceived by others as a threat. Wentworth and Carp disagree about whether a letter-writing campaign from their alumni would have worked for ISP at Appalachian; the experience of Wayne State, where alumni spoke forcefully to the media and the Board of Governors, invites pessimism. Providing a high-quality student experience is not sufficient for program viability but might be necessary; it needs in any case to be combined with other program characteristics if viability is to be assured.

Complacency does not help either. Few saw it coming. They knew they were doing good work. They knew they were celebrated. They did not think they had to educate each new administrator. Newell perhaps makes this point most forcefully.[3] The lesson is clear: eternal vigilance is the price of interdisciplinarity. Those institutions that at present boast of supportive senior administrators had best beware.

Over and over we are told of deans and faculty members in other programs who just did not understand interdisciplinarity. Davis draws this as one of his key lessons. Miller reports that administrators at San Francisco State explicitly stated that interdisciplinarity now infused the entire curriculum and thus a specific IDS program was no longer necessary. He reports: "Unfortunately, this inadequate understanding of interdisciplinarity is shared by most other faculty, including members of ostensibly interdisciplinary departments." These other programs do not consciously focus on integration. Miller makes a strong case that "weak interdisciplinarity" is thus the greatest enemy of "strong interdisciplinarity." Furtado et al. echoes this concern. The answer would seem to involve making the case for "strong interdisciplinarity" both locally and globally. As Newell has argued, the most viable strategy for preserving these interdisciplinary programs is for them to get serious about interdisciplinarity. They need to become self-conscious and intentional about the integrative process — or, at the very least, about being interdisciplinary. Muir describes how New Century College faculty members use their positions on university committees to educate about the nature of interdisciplinarity. Conversely, Wentworth and Carp report that the unwillingness of interdisciplinarians to volunteer even for internal administrative jobs was a key factor in the elimination of their program.

Wentworth and Carp also note that even the interdisciplinarians *within* their program often queried the need for courses about interdisciplinarity itself rather than the thematic interdisciplinary courses they preferred. Wakefield likewise reports on the difficulty of defining the essence of interdisciplinarity in a program where most faculty have interests elsewhere: the program is creating core courses, but they are conceived in a way that may not answer the call to distinguish real interdisciplinarity from its imitators. The first line of battle then is internal: our own programs need to be self-consciously interdisciplinary if we hope to convince senior administrators that we do a more complete and better sort of interdisciplinarity than others. Szostak reports this as the major failing of interdisciplinary initiatives at Alberta: even with the appropriate administrative structure in place, and support from senior administrators for the idea, thematic interdisciplinarians balked at the idea of requiring their students to learn about interdisciplinarity. Alternatively, Repko reports that the program at Arlington has a guiding principle that students need to be taught about interdisciplinarity itself. The faculty survey conducted at Lowell suggests that there is widespread faculty interest in interdisciplinary faculty development; this interest might be harnessed (perhaps with external funding) to the task of creating a body of scholars with a shared understanding of the nature of interdisciplinarity.

Burkhardt (2006) has discussed the challenges of convincing the disciplinarily trained of the values of interdisciplinarity. He concurs with Szostak that this task may be easier if we speak of integrative and specialized research instead: it is then easier to suggest that these two types of research and teaching are inherently complementary. Indeed, fully integrative work can be highly specialized even narrowly focused.

Archibald's committee at Lowell collected a host of useful information: on the value of interdisciplinarity to students and faculty at Lowell, on the potential for interdisciplinarity to enhance student employment outcomes, on the potential for interdisciplinary research grants, and so on (see Appendix II). This information served to strengthen faculty support for interdisciplinary initiatives, but was not enough to overcome administrative resistance.

Szostak suggests one standard by which an interdisciplinary program might be judged: all interested faculty members on campus should have an opportunity to participate. However, there is a fundamental tension between the value of inclusion and the value of consensus on a rigorous definition of IDS. Disciplines that pretend to interdisciplinarity generally fail this simple test. But if we will impose this standard on others we must impose it on ourselves.

Another recurring factor that occurs in program closures involves being visibly expensive (or just appearing that way). The individualized major at Massachusetts–Amherst proved to be expensive as it became popular. (The somewhat similar program at Emory seems to survive because it is kept small, the students it accepts are easy to advise, and the institution has a healthier budgetary outlook *for now*.) More generally, team teaching and small class sizes are expensive. If interdisciplinarians wish to fight for greater per-student funding than other programs they can expect not to be universally loved. Worse, they may be setting themselves up to be axed in a future round of budget cuts. If programs want to advocate team-teaching or small class sizes, this needs to be an institution-wide innovation not just for the IDS program (and they need to be prepared to identify commensurate cuts they are prepared to advocate elsewhere in the institution). Arguing that IDS *requires* small classes and team-teaching is tantamount to making the case that the institution cannot afford the luxury of IDS in times of tight budgets. IDS that successfully competes should not come to *rely* on those luxuries, since they will likely disappear with the next budget crisis.

Szostak suggests a possible strategy: encourage university- or college-wide competitions for team teaching or faculty lines and then excel in these competitions. Newell emphasizes the importance of accurate accounting: it should not matter whether one's faculty is old or one's buildings need repair, as comparison should be based on the long-term cost of programs. Miller argues that interdisciplinary programs at San Francisco State were wrongly accused of being expensive. He also shows how external funding can (albeit temporarily) allow team teaching to gain institutional support. Wayne State's program also seems to have suffered from questionable calculations. Notably, their pledge to cut costs had no effect on the decision to close: interdisciplinary programs it seems must be clearly perceived as cost-effective *before* their existence is challenged. At Appalachian State, efforts to bring the program's expenses precisely in line with those in other programs came too late to stem the tide of criticism. In contrast, Repko reports that the interdisciplinary studies program at Texas Arlington is *both* cost-effective and data-driven.

Alternatively, some interdisciplinary programs suffer from under-funding. Under-funded programs are unsustainable in the long run; they may survive for a while due to the dedication of a few faculty members but will die when these retire or move on. Still, the Szostak article, among others, highlights the fact that such programs may be able to attain reasonable budgets over time if they maintain visibility, especially if the institution's budget from time to time increases. However, Burkhardt (2006) reminds us of the importance of timing: Arizona International was pressing for budgetary increases while others had already begun to question the need for its existence.

Interdisciplinary programs often suffer from being too different. Interdisciplinary programs by their nature are different. They stress different learning outcomes and attract a different student body. We need to work hard nationally and internationally to stress the importance of the skills we strengthen and the societal goals we support. But in the meantime we have to fight internally to justify ourselves in large part in terms of the criteria by which disciplines judge themselves. This is unfair to be sure but it is political reality. Wayne State's experience provides a powerful example. Its service to adult African-American learners more closely fit the University's stated mission as an urban university than the programs of traditional departments, but it was not that mission but rather disciplinary understandings of what a student career should look like which prevailed; the interesting question is why. One reading is that it was high-level administrators, bolstered by powerful disciplinary departments, whose understanding prevailed. The attack was based partly on a desire for prestige, and partly on a desire among some disciplinarians to restore the pre–Adamany (former president) disciplinary structure of the university. Part of the Adamany era's legacy was to weaken the disciplines by creating applied interdisciplinary colleges. So it was not specifically a prejudice against IDS that brought its demise at Wayne State, but an opposition against its use to micro-manage and undermine the power of traditional disciplinary departments by weakening them though interdisciplinary innovations. The "mistake" of IDS was compounded by identifying itself with the "wrong" kind of students for the new de facto mission of the institution. Whether the program could have prevented its demise by reading top-level administrators' intentions accurately (and quickly enough), combined with their case that IDS is even more necessary for the most academically advantaged students as they prepare to assume positions of leadership in a complex, globalized world (Ntiri, Henry and Schindler 2004), is arguable. However, with disciplinary institutional forces perceiving interdisciplinarity as the vehicle of their subordination by the former president, pedagogical arguments carried little weight.

While student assessment is grounded in an understanding of interdisciplinary outcomes (in part to prevent pseudo-interdisciplinary programs from claiming that they are doing real interdisciplinarity), the types of assessment used are still easily appreciated by disciplinarians.

Lack of dedicated administrative support is a component of some of the problems faced by interdisciplinary studies programs trying to get serious about interdisciplinarity. After all, it's what can and should most distinguish a genuine interdisciplinary program from others that casually call themselves interdisciplinary.

Miller shows how interdisciplinary programs were marginalized at San Francisco State once they were robbed of a centralized and shared administrative support structure. Interdisciplinary programs reliant on the sacrifices of overburdened faculty members or the kindness of strangers in departmental or decanal administration will eventually fail as personalities change. Interdisciplinary programming was strengthened immeasurably at Alberta through provision of dedicated administrative support; Szostak details the many benefits that this simple innovation brought. Szostak also highlights the importance of hiring the right type of administrator: these need to be dedicated, innovative (because interdisciplinary programs cannot just copy disciplinary administrative practices) and consultative (because regular interactions with departments and deans are so important). Interdisciplinary programming at George Mason has waxed and waned as independent administrative support has been provided or withdrawn. The lack of administrative support was cited in a faculty survey as the third most important barrier to interdisciplinarity at Lowell — and likely also contributes to the first (the time demands of being interdisciplinary) and the second (the lack of cross-departmental structures). Archibald sums up the Lowell problem thus: "Interdisciplinarity does not have a home."

Yet a common answer to the need for dedicated institutional support — some sort of departmental structure — is itself problematic. Wentworth and Carp make the point most clearly: the departmental structure serves disciplines well but was not designed with interdisciplinarity in mind. If interdisciplinarians are to perform the tasks of integrating specialized understandings and reminding disciplinarians of what their narrow focus leaves out, being housed in a separate department is far from the obvious institutional structure for doing so. Szostak concurs, and explores the possibilities of alternatives such as cross-appointments and broadly based program governance.

Last but not least, Burkhardt's (2006) sobering analysis of Arizona International College suggests the unsurprising potential downside of relying on non-tenure track faculty members. These can be let go too easily in a budgetary crisis. While non-tenure track faculty are a growing proportion of most types of academic program, they are often especially favored in "experimental" programs, and interdisciplinary programs start out as experimental much of the time. Faculty members in such programs are urged to push for tenure-track status as soon as student numbers warrant this. Burkhardt (2006) stresses that the non-tenure track model had its pluses, and was not necessarily associated with lack of job security, but became so once closure was on the table.

What Does Work?

We close with some more positive lessons. The various case studies support a set of powerful recommendations for enhancing the sustainability of interdisciplinary programming. Foremost among these involves the importance of being self-conscious about interdisciplinarity and integration. Students need to be able to articulate what interdisciplinarity means and they need to understand what is meant by integration. Interdisciplinarians who believe there is a symbiotic relationship between specialized and integrative research or those who see the two as interrelated, need to live this vision by interacting regularly with specialized researchers.

Interdisciplinary programs that wish to survive need to integrate their activities with those of more traditional disciplines. An interdisciplinary program seen as "the other" by disciplines—and by the superficially interdisciplinary programs these disciplines may spawn — is at risk the moment the budget turns sour or a skeptical administrator takes power. Burkhardt (2006) reports that disciplines at the University of Arizona and interdisciplinarians at Arizona International each viewed the other as "the other"; only one of them had the power to act on this perception. The Wayne State program had limited contact with departments in the College of Arts and Sciences. Ditto at Miami. The San Francisco State InterArts program did not get buy-in from the departmental "mentors'" who it was hoped would play an important but subsidiary *and unrewarded* role in interdisciplinary supervision. Integration is successful when members of traditional departments feel invested in quality interdisciplinary programming. Wentworth and Carp report, "We had become insular as a way of protecting ourselves and because we were so busy with recruiting, designing curriculum, learning new subjects, working with students, etc., we tended to be arrogant in our view of our own accomplishments and as ignorant of others' work as they were of ours." They urge interdisciplinarians to provide regular and visible support to the rest of the university. Alternatively, Miller hails the University Interdisciplinary Council at San Francisco State for encouraging broad support for a range of interdisciplinary programs. At Alberta, cross-appointments and broadly based governance structures ensure that a sizeable minority of faculty members feel an attachment to at least one interdisciplinary program (but interdisciplinary programs have a separate administrative support structure despite lacking departmental status). Interdisciplinary faculty at Emory often teach courses for departments. Davis suggests a range of 'meeting points': shared courses and seminars and other activities.[4] Muir reports how budget cuts limited the ability of New Century College to financially attract teachers from departments and thus led to a loss in both program quality and program support.

One challenge here is to be seen as essential without being seen as a threat. The ISP program at Wayne State created general education courses for its own students; departments came to fear that their students would prefer ISP's offerings to their own. General education is a place where interdisciplinarity can thrive — after all, what is the use of exposing students to a wide range of material if they lack the tools to integrate? — but efforts to do so must take political realities into consideration while advertising the pedagogical advantages of reflective and self-conscious interdisciplinarity. There is probably no more contested terrain in universities than the contest to have classes included for general education credit.

What about Arlington? The strong ISP program there has been seen as a threat by departments in the College of Arts and Sciences, and has little formal contact with them. The Wayne State experience suggests that in the longer term it is these departments that matter, not the college in which one is housed. Repko reports that he collects data on the different sources from which his program draws students than these liberal arts disciplines. Again, the Wayne State experience suggests that this is a double-edged sword.

Another important strategy is experimentation. It would be a mistake to focus only on the death throes; these chapters speak volumes about the process of creating quality interdisciplinary programming. Rarely do such programs emerge fully mature. They develop through time as different opportunities arise, challenges are faced, and solutions appreciated. Even the relatively new New Century College at George Mason has undergone many changes, and these have not gone unnoticed by the wider university community. It is clear from the New Century College model that one of the main elements in their sustainability is that continued innovation is essential, and complacency is dangerous in a "rapidly changing educational environment."

Note here that the broader the community of supportive scholars involved in experimentation, the better the result is likely to be and the more solid the institutional support for it. The explicit strategies for program evaluation and experimentation pursued by New Century College at George Mason are particularly notable.

However, experimentation has its bounds as well. A point made clearly in the Wayne State chapter is that faculty members cannot sustain experimentation forever. (Wentworth and Carp also note that ongoing curricular discussions weakened the attractiveness of interdisciplinarity for young faculty struggling toward tenure.) Interdisciplinary faculty members have to research and teach and meet university-wide standards for promotion and tenure, and cannot devote their entire lives to curricular revolution.[5] At some point we must reach a level of satisfaction with interdisciplinary curricula such that permanent revolution becomes unnecessary. It is likely that senior administrators expect such an outcome (though administrators at Miami at times expressed frustration that the Western College program was not a continual source of innovation for the whole university). And we can hardly expect to overwhelm administrators with arguments for the necessity of our type of interdisciplinarity if we cannot agree what this is among ourselves. As Repko notes, "Developing a sustainable interdisciplinary studies program begins with having a clear notion of the nature of interdisciplinarity."

Broadly based governance appears also to be a winning strategy. As noted above, Miller celebrates the value of a campus-wide interdisciplinary council. Szostak likewise celebrates the value of large governing bodies for thematic interdisciplinary programs (while worrying that they are not self-conscious enough about interdisciplinarity itself). If faculty members from departments are invested in interdisciplinary programming, the sorts of disciplinary conversations about the "otherness" of interdisciplinary programs detailed in many chapters becomes impossible. However, Goldsmith notes that faculty members with primary responsibilities elsewhere may not have sufficient time or energy to devote to the program; some faculty members with a primary loyalty to the program are necessary. The experience at Lowell is cautionary: broadly based consultation by a carefully picked committee of leaders could not guarantee that embryonic interdisciplinarity was not aborted (with much support from non-interdisciplinarians); one nevertheless gains the sense that if they had been able to put in place some of their recommendations they would have created the sort of ambience in which these could thrive. One of the key recommendations was to institute a permanent council(s) of the form that Miller and Szostak celebrate.

If departments are problematic, can we point to a superior structure? While the ideal institutional home for interdisciplinarity may still escape our imagination, it would seem that there is a place for certain practices: cross-appointments (hailed by Wentworth and Carp, and by Szostak, though not without misgivings), incentives for disciplines and interdisciplinarians to work together (as in the competition for faculty lines reported by Szostak, or in team teaching), and instituting self-conscious interdisciplinarity within general education. Archibald lists a number of basic administrative desiderata: interdisciplinary courses should have their own course prefixes; interdisciplinary program directors should be included in many/most/all administrative bodies where chairs are represented; interdisciplinary programs need a physical presence (website, bulletin board, meeting place) and control over information on such things as course enrollments; notably none of these require a departmental format. Of course many of the now defunct programs had all of these things in place.

A stress on skills also appears useful. New Century College at George Mason stresses the skills that its students master and provides individual measurement of these. Wentworth and Carp urge us to "do excellent assessment regularly and keep it in front of your chief academic officer." Repko has embedded arguments about the special skills associated with interdisciplinarity into the basic governing premises of Arlington's INTS program.

External financing can also be beneficial. Many programs received temporary support from external grants. Interdisciplinarity is potentially attractive to a range of granting agencies. The challenge is planning for the period after the grant ends. More generally, Repko urges interdisciplinary programs to be seen as a financial asset: "By 'financial asset' is meant that the program attracts tuition dollars that might not otherwise flow to the university, retains tuition dollars that might otherwise leave the university, and secures grants and scholarship funds from sources that are supportive of interdisciplinary work."[6]

Last but not least, we could stress the importance of asking for more. Goldsmith underlines an important fact: you do not get faculty lines devoted in whole or in part to interdisciplinarity unless you ask for them. Szostak also highlights the importance of continually asking for additional resources; the interdisciplinarian should always be ready to seize new opportunities, and may often find that seeming barriers can be overcome. At the same time, caution needs to be exercised here. One of the key lessons Newell gleaned from the demise of the Miami program is the importance of remaining cost effective. He unsuccessfully urged their dean *not* to ask for additional faculty lines, lines that they were granted and that made them too expensive. Archibald admits that the whims of senior administrators are paramount, but argues that the best hope for interdisciplinarity is to make a well-argued case for it within your institution.

In the final analysis, we need to get serious about interdisciplinarity. After all, it's what can and should most distinguish our programs from others who casually call themselves interdisciplinary. Without holding true to these principles, interdisciplinarity will be diluted into obscurity and will no longer remain sustainable.

NOTES

1. Muir also describes how the "incubator problem" at New Century was dealt with creatively. She says when IDS programs were, from time to time, shifted into NCC, they used several strategies to integrate them: "New curricular designs, re-envisioned websites, inclusive governance and shared teaching philosophies were ways that these programs began to build synergy." The sustainability of NCC is built on the principle that the quality of students matter, and NCC filtered students positively interested in integration and interdisciplinarity and channeled others into degree completion-type programs, retaining the integrity of its IDS commitment (distinctive students attracted, leaders emerged, intellectually engaged, loyal alums — which was much like the Western College program at Miami, although whereas NCC had close to 850 student enrollment, Miami had 140).

2. Miller too is wary of structural relationships that not only compromise IDS but place it in a dependent and vulnerable relationship to others in the university. Of four generic IDS programs at San Francisco Sate, the only one left standing is humanities, which says Miller was the only one to "follow a self-contained curriculum strategy for its majors." They weren't dependent on other departments and they had a larger tenure-track faculty, which gave them more political clout.

3. The Lowell case study provides a time-condensed example of how the fortunes of interdisciplinarity can wax and wane with changes in senior administrators.

4. Davis is though skeptical of taking on too many service responsibilities. While all programs need to ensure that responsibilities are in line with resources, visible service functions *that benefit faculty members elsewhere in the university* can be an important source of program strength.

5. That chapter suggests that interdisciplinary teaching and research may by their nature be more time-consuming than disciplinary; this is a suggestion worthy of further study; one key question is whether the articulation of guidelines for teaching, research, and curriculum development, among other things, can lessen the load significantly.

6. Interdisciplinarity likely also has a symbiotic relationship with community service learning. NCC at George Mason again provides a useful example. But community-service learning is expensive. It may best be funded externally.

REFERENCES

Augsburg, Tanya. 2006. *Becoming interdisciplinary: An introduction to interdisciplinary studies.* 2nd ed. Dubuque, IA: Kendall/Hunt Publishing.

Burkhardt, Paul. 2006. Administering interdisciplinarity and innovative programs: Lessons from the rise and fall of Arizona International College. *Issues in Integrative Studies 24:* 159–172.

Donoghue, Frank. 2008. *The last professors: The corporate university and the fate of the humanities.* New York: Fordham University Press.

Henry, Stuart. 2005. Disciplinary hegemony meets interdisciplinary ascendancy: Can interdisciplinary/integrative studies survive, and, if so, how? *Issues in Integrative Studies* 23: 1–37.

Kerkstra, Patrick. 2005. A tale of two Temples. *The Philadelphia Inquirer.* June 5, 1.

McNichol, Elizabeth, and Iris J. Lav. 2008. State economic budget troubles worsen. Washington D.C.: Center on Budget Priorities. *http://www.cbpp.org/9-8-08sfp.pdf* (accessed December 13, 2008).

Menard, Louis. 2005. Dangers within and without. In *Profession,* 10–17. New York: Modern Language Association of America.

Newell, William H. 1998. Professionalizing interdisciplinarity: A literature review and research agenda. In *Interdisciplinarity: Essays from the literature,* ed. William H. Newell, 529–563. New York: The College Board.

_____. Forthcoming, 2009. Interdisciplinarity in undergraduate general education. In *The Oxford handbook on interdisciplinarity,* ed. Robert Frodeman, Julie Klein, and Carl Mitcham (Chapter 41). Oxford: Oxford University Press.

Newfield, Christopher. 2008. *Unmaking the public university: The forty-year assault on the middle class.* Cambridge, MA and London: Harvard University Press.

Nichol, Gene R. 2008. Public universities at risk abandoning their mission. *Chronicle of Higher Education,* October 31, A50.

Ntiri, Daphne W., Stuart Henry, and Roslyn Abt Schindler. 2004. Enhancing adult learning through interdisciplinary studies." In *Degrees of change: developing and delivering adult degree programs,* ed., Jerry Jerman and James P. Pappas, 41–50. San Francisco: Jossey-Bass.

Repko, Allen. F. 2008. *Interdisciplinary research: Process and theory.* Thousand Oaks, CA: Sage Publications.

Rogers, Steve, Michael Booth, and Joan Eveline. 2003. The politics of disciplinary advantage. *History of Intellectual Culture,* 3(1). http://www.ucalgary.ca/hic/issues/vol3/6 (accessed, September 30, 2005).

Ryman, Anne. 2008. ASU's cuts worry nursing community. *Arizona Republic* (Dec 7). *http://www.azcentral.com/community/phoenix/articles/2008/12/07/20081207nursing1207.html* (accessed December 7, 2008).

UMass. 2008. University Without Walls. UWW stature grows online and in the community. University of Massachusetts Amherst. http://www.umass.edu/uww/news_events/news.html (accessed December 13, 2008).

Vasterling, Veronica, Enikő Demény, Clare Hemmings Ulla Holm, Päivi Korvajärvi, and Theodossia-Soula Pavlidou. 2006. *Practising interdisciplinarity in gender studies.* York, UK: Raw Nerve Books.

Chapter 3 Appendices

(From Maruca, Lisa. "Re: Review of IS General Education Courses."
Memo to Roslyn Schindler, Acting Chair,
Department of Interdisciplinary Studies. March 29, 2006.)

[The] Associate Dean ... requested that we forward the attached collection of syllabi which includes one syllabus for each of the General Education requirements. As a new department in the college, we welcome the chance to interact with the CLAS Curriculum Committee and acquaint our colleagues with our student-centered program of interdisciplinary general education.

The Department of Interdisciplinary Studies prides itself in being an integrative learning community for working adults. As such, our general education offerings do stand as distinct courses, but are also fully integrated into the curriculum of our major across the entire educational career of our students. We accomplish this goal in a variety of ways and places:

• **First-year Seminar/Introductory Course:** ISP 2030 (a non–General Education course) introduces students not only to their major through an introduction to the theory and practice of interdisciplinarity, but also to university education in general, including the Gen Ed program requirements. Because this class is writing-intensive, informal connections are forged between this class and ISP 1510, the Basic Composition (BC) requirement most students are taking contemporaneously.

• **Divisional Offerings:** Our Gen Ed courses are spread out among all the four divisions of our program: Critical Literacies, Humanities, Social Sciences, and Science and Technology. Students must take both Gen Ed and IS courses from all four areas in order to graduate.

• **Course Linkages:** In keeping with our overall commitment to fostering greater coherence and connectedness in the undergraduate curriculum, students have the option of clustering and linking courses in particular thematic areas. Many of our General Education courses are thus offered with an optional related course that is part of the IS major. For example, students taking IST 2310: Living in the Environment (Life Science) are given the option to enroll in a coordinated course, IST 1990: From

Silent Spring to *Our Stolen Future*, which provides them the opportunity to read three classic texts in environmental science studies.

• **Integrated Learning Across the Curriculum:** The writing-intensive nature of our major means not only that the BC, Intermediate Composition (IC) and Writing Intensive (WI) competencies required by Gen Ed are crucial to our program, but that students must continue developing their skills beyond these. Thus the majority of our Gen Ed courses include significant paper-writing requirements. To foster faculty support of student writing in these classes, our Critical Literacies division offers a Writing Across the Curriculum program supporting faculty through brown bag training and a newsletter, *Writing Matters*. Critical Literacies also collaborates with Science and Tech to foster math across the curriculum. Finally, the Science and Technology division stresses the scientific method across their courses, including Critical Thinking (CT).

• **Interdisciplinarity:** Although courses are divided among divisions, all divisions bear the responsibility of teaching students, even in discipline-based Gen Ed courses, to be good interdisciplinarians. Each course in our program provides interdisciplinary content, offers readings from a variety of disciplines, and/or stresses inquiry-based multi-disciplinary research skills. As students advance through our curricular "spine" of core courses, they are working progressively on refining these skills, which culminate in our two-semester senior capstone requirement, Senior Seminar or, for qualifying students, Senior Essay (both of which fulfill the WI requirement).

• **Adult Learning:** As an urban university, Wayne State attracts a large number of non-traditional students to every program. However, in a program specifically designed for this unique population, faculty are able to concentrate on meeting the learning needs of adult students — whether this means meeting the logistical challenges of those with full-time jobs and families or adjusting pedagogically to the strengths and weaknesses of those with life experience — in all our classes, including our General Education offerings. Because we are an adult learning community, it is crucial that our students have Gen Ed offerings that are available at night and on weekends as well as online, options that are not readily or widely available to them otherwise. In keeping with the urban mission, flexibility of delivery system is essential.

• **Assessing Learning and Curriculum:** Because we are a residential faculty offering a full panoply of General Education courses within a degree program, we are able to link our major outcomes with those of Gen Ed, and continually — within our divisions, faculty workshops and retreats, and through our interaction with Academic Staff— monitor courses and provide constructive criticism to continually implement and revise our best practices. Recently, we have begun piloting a program of more formal entry and exit assessment, using a variety of instruments and methods, from testing to portfolios of student work. We look forward to using both quantitative and qualitative evidence to create an even more effective feedback loop into curricular development and improved pedagogical strategies. We are also using assessment (triangulated data) in our introductory course to place students in an appropriate writing course, further linking our BC course into the major.

A representative from each of our divisions will be happy to meet with the CLAS Curriculum Committee to discuss our integrated program of General Education or individual courses.

APPENDIX 2: EVIDENCE FOR IS
AFRICAN-AMERICAN GRADUATION RATES

To understand retention rates, it is first useful to realize how many African American students the Interdisciplinary Studies Program graduated over the years. Table 1 compares the IS graduation profile by ethnicity with selected majors where the African-American enrollment is relatively high either on a percentage or on an absolute basis.

**Table 1. Graduation Profile by Ethnicity
with Selected Majors, 1998–2007**

Undergraduate Degree	*IS*	*Criminal Justice*	*Journalism*	*Psychology*	*Elementary Education*	*WSU (All)*
	565	693	250	1391	1787	21218
% total graduates from each major	2.66	3.27	1.18	6.56	8.42	100.00
% African-American	45.1	33.3	36.4	26.2	17.4	19
% Asian origin	1.2	1.6	4.4	5.7	2.3	6.2
% Caucasian	40	53.5	49.1	54.9	71.2	61.1
% Hispanic	1.2	3.2	3.2	3.1	2	2.2
% Native American	0.5	0.4	0	0.5	0.4	0.4
% non-resident alien	0.3	0.7	2.4	2.6	0.2	4.5
% unknown	11.7	7.2	4.4	7.1	6.4	6.6

Interdisciplinary Studies graduates almost 12 percent more African-American students than its closest competitor.

The rates of graduation of these students also shed favorable light on the program. IS compiled it own evidence to track both White and Black graduation rates within six years, a more appropriate measure for adult, part-time students (though many students take longer). Much data could be extracted from Wayne's Student Tracking Advising Retention System (STARS). However, the databases installed in the system, for the most part, originate in Fall 2002, making it impossible to calculate six-year graduation rates from the system to date. Student data contained in a now outmoded tracking system prior to this date are difficult to access. Therefore, for the cohort staring in Fall 1998–Winter 1999–Spring/Summer 1999 we rely on hand calculated data prepared by Stuart Henry, former Chair of the Department of Interdisciplinary Studies (1999–2006), and summarized in Table 2 below.

Table 2. Graduation Rates for Students Entering 1998-1999

	IS 1998-1999 Cohort		WSU 1998-1999 Cohort
Total cohort population admitted but not necessarily registered	249		
Median GPA on Admission*	146	2.82	
GPA on admission <2.0	63	43.2%	
Regular Admits	167	67.1%	
Special Admits	82	32.9%	
Six year graduation rate for students with at least 8 credits in the program	116	16.3%	31.70%
White student subset graduation rate	24	37.5%	43.60%
Black student subset graduation rate	80	12.5%	10%
Black-White graduation gap		25.0%	33.60%

*Only 146/249 of those admitted provided transcripts with this information

As noted above, we also only include students who have completed 8 credits, which again, is appropriate for our specific population. Students were often attracted to the program due to scheduling conveniences with respect to time and location, and the possibility of interacting with other adult students, but its philosophy and content might escape them until they are closer to enrollment or actually enrolled. For example, of 249 students who were admitted in the Fall 1998–Winter 1999–Spring/Summer 1999 cohort, some did not enroll, and only 116 remained to enroll beyond 8 credits in the IS program.

Another interesting point of comparison is that, although IS was considered an open admission program, over 67 percent of enrollees with transcripts were "regular admits," with a median GPA on admission of 2.82. For the purposes of comparing IS graduation rates to those of the university overall, however, we did not separate out "regular" vs. "special" admits.

At first reading, the six-year IS graduation rate of 16.3 percent overall does not compare favorably with the equivalent WSU graduation rate of 31.7 percent. However, it must be noted that the particular IS cohort examined is 69 percent Black vs. about 28 percent for the Wayne cohort as a whole. A more telling contrast is revealed when we break down the IS graduation rate into Black and White subgroups and then compare the subgroup performance. The WSU graduation rate for Black students is only 10 percent compared to IS's 12.5 percent for the 1998-99 cohort year.

Retention data for the IS and WSU Black population in the Fall 2002 cohort was extracted from the STARS system and is tabulated below.

Table 3. Retention Rates for Black Students Entering 2002
(Fall 2002 Undergraduate Cohort;
Black subpopulation retention compared
[IS 71.8% Black, WSU 31.6% Black])

Subgroup	Cohort	N	% Full time	*% retained or graduated in Winter 2003 (First term retention)*	*% retained or graduated in Fall 2007 (Five year retention)*	*% of cohort retained or graduated from Winter 2003 to Fall 2007 (Second semester used as starting point)*
First Time in College	IS*	36	52.8	66.7	5.6	8
	WSU	765	74.8	72.1	21	29.2
Transfer Students	IS	58	39.7	56.9	25.9	45.4
	WSU	657	35.8	62.4	21.04	21.2
Overall	IS	94	44.7	60.6	18.1	29.8
	WSU	1422	56.8	67.7	17.4	25.8

*This counts those registered for the BIS degree alone and does not include data for students in the BTIS program.

As before, this comparison is best made if we start tracking retention from the second semester (Winter 2003)—note that only about 2/3 of black students overall decide to stay in the IS Program or WSU after one semester. For the students who do stay, however, the Black sub-population in IS is better retained than the same subpopulation in WSU, for those who have transferred college credits prior to entry (45.4 percent vs. 21.2 percent), and for the Black subpopulation as a whole (29.8 percent vs. 25.8 percent). When these numbers are compared to those in Table 2, they also show that the gap between IS and WSU's Black graduation rate was widening—though whether this is because of IS's continuing efforts in this area or WSU's lessening interest in this population would be difficult to determine.

The first time in any college Black subpopulation retention (8 percent) is, however, significantly worse than that for WSU as a whole (29.2 percent). This can probably be attributed to the special needs of open admissions students. The mean High School GPA for the ten first time Black students in IS whose transcripts were received is 1.98 vs. a mean of 2.58 for the 326 first time Black students from the WSU cohort as a whole and may contribute to the significant difference in performance. At the time of its closure, IS was working to address this gap. In 2005 it added a new reading and writing assessment for first-year students resulting, for about 2/3 of test takers, in placement in a new developmental reading-writing course designed specifically for adult students. Unfortunately, the effect of these enhancements on improving graduation rates for the least-prepared students will now never be known.

Chapter 11 Appendix

2006 UML Faculty Survey Results, Interdisciplinary Questions Only

32. There are already a number of interdisciplinary **teaching and learning** activities going on at UMass Lowell. Would you characterize the current amount of this work as...

	Percent
Too much	7
About the right amount	54
Too little	32
N.S./D.K.	6
D.K.	1
Total	100

33. There are already a number of interdisciplinary **research** activities going on at UMass Lowell. Would you characterize the current amount of this work as...

	Percent
Too much	4
About the right amount	56
Too little	30
N.S./D.K.	7
D.K.	3
Total	100

34. There are many different definitions of the word "interdisciplinary." What definition do you use. Please be as brief as possible.

	Percent
Collaboration / two or more departments / two or more disciplines (Collab.)	89
Problem-solving (Prob.)	8
Integration (Int.)	7
Collab. + Prob.	6
Collab + Int.	6
Collab. + Prob. + Int.	1
Other / non-sequitur	5
TOTAL	100

35. According to your definition, how much interdisciplinary **teaching** do you do?

	Percent
A great deal	14
Quite a bit	16
Something	32
Not much	19
Nothing at all	18
D.K.	0
TOTAL	100

Question #35, interdisciplinary teaching, cross-tabulated by academic rank:

	Assistant Professor	Associate Professor	Professor	Other	All
A great deal	15	18	14	7	14
Quite a bit	19	10	14	36	16
Something	35	28	30	29	31
Not much	25	13	23	0	20
Nothing at all	6	31	20	29	19
A great deal + quite a bit	35	28	27	43	30
Something	35	28	30	29	31
Not much + nothing at all	31	44	43	29	39
TOTAL	100	100	100	100	100

Question #35, interdisciplinary teaching, cross-tabulated by college:

	College of Management	College of Engineering	CAS-Sciences	CAS-FAHSS	Health and Env.	G.S. Education	D.K.	All
A great deal	4	12	14	18	19	11	0	14
Quite a bit	13	12	22	18	6	22	25	16
Something	9	26	33	46	32	11	25	32
Not much	30	26	22	10	16	22	25	19
Nothing at all	43	24	10	8	26	33	0	18
D.K.	0	0	0	0	0	0	25	0
A great deal + quite a bit	17	24	35	36	26	33	25	30
Something	9	26	33	46	32	11	25	32
Not much + nothing at all	74	50	31	18	42	56	25	38
TOTAL	100	100	100	100	100	100	75	100

(CAS = College of Arts & Sciences, FAHSS = Fine Arts, Humanities, & Social Sciences, GS= Graduate School)

36. According to your definition, how much interdisciplinary **research** do you do?

	Percent
A great deal	22
Quite a bit	22
Something	27
Not much	16
Nothing at all	13
D.K.	1
TOTAL	100

Question #36, interdisciplinary research, cross-tabulated by academic rank:

	Assistant Professor	Associate Professor	Professor	Other	All
A great deal	19	23	22	21	21
Quite a bit	25	21	21	7	21
Something	23	36	26	29	27
Not much	17	8	19	21	16
Nothing at all	13	13	13	21	13
A great deal + quite a bit	44	44	43	29	42
Something	23	44	45	50	44
Not much + nothing at all	31	13	13	21	13
TOTAL	98	100	100	100	100

Question #36, interdisciplinary research, cross-tabulated by college:

	College of Management	College of Engineering	CAS-Sciences	CAS-FAHSS	Health and Env.	G.S. Education	D.K.	All
A great deal	9	24	25	23	26	11	0	22
Quite a bit	13	15	20	28	29	11	50	22
Something	35	24	24	31	26	22	0	27
Not much	22	29	18	7	3	44	25	16
Nothing at all	22	9	12	11	16	11	0	13
D.K.	0	0	2	0	0	0	25	1
A great deal + quite a bit	22	38	45	51	55	22	50	44
Something	35	24	24	31	26	22	0	27
Not much + nothing at all	43	38	29	18	19	56	25	29
TOTAL	100	100	98	100	100	100	75	99

37. How much do you agree with the following definition of "interdisciplinary?" "Temporarily and openly integrating the knowledge, tools, or insights of more than one discipline and bringing it to bear on an issue or problem too broad or complex to deal with adequately within a single discipline or profession."

	Percent
Very strongly agree	48
Somewhat agree	43
Somewhat disagree	6
Very strongly disagree	1
D.K.	1
TOTAL	100

38. As you see it, what is the biggest problem with or barrier to interdisciplinary **teaching and learning**? Please be brief.

	Percent
Administrative Issues	**25**
Administrative Structure	8
Degree Requirements	2
Department Rigidity	9
Tradition	6
ID Issues	**30**
Student Background/Preparation	4
Knowledge of ID Approach	8
Coordination / Separation between Disciplines	18

	Percent
Resources	**30**
Funding/Resources	4
Rewards/Incentives (Tenure)	5
Space	0
Time / Workload	21
Faculty Willingness	**6**
Faculty Willingness	4
Politics (Personalities/Egos)	2
None/Don't Know	**5**
Other	**3**
TOTAL	**100**

39. As you see it, what is the biggest problem with or barrier to interdisciplinary **research**?

	Percent
Administrative Issues	**10**
Administrative Structure	3
Degree Requirements	1
Department Rigidity	5
Tradition	2
ID Issues	**28**
Student Background/Preparation	1
Knowledge of ID Approach	8
Coordination / Separation between Disciplines	19
Resources	**40**
Funding/Resources	16
Rewards/Incentives (Tenure)	7
Space	2
Time / Workload	15
Faculty Willingness	**9**
Faculty Willingness	6
Politics (Personalities/Egos)	3
None/Don't Know	**10**
Other	**3**
TOTAL	**100**

40. As you see it, what is the biggest advantage of interdisciplinary work?
    (no compilation of responses available)

41. How interested are you in increasing your engagement in interdisciplinary work?

	Percent
Very interested	46
Somewhat interested	39

	Percent
Not very interested	10
Not at all interested	5
D.K.	1
TOTAL	100

Percent Interested in Increasing Interdisciplinary Work, by Rank:

	Assistant Professor	*Associate Professor*	*Professor*	*Other*	*All*
Very interested	60	36	38	71	45
Somewhat interested	33	49	41	29	39
Not very interested	6	8	15	0	10
Not at all interested	2	8	6	0	5
D.K.	0	0	1	0	0
Very interested + somewhat interested	92	85	78	100	85
Not very interested + Not at all interested	8	15	21	0	15
D.K.	0	0	1	0	0
Total	100	100	100	100	100

Percent Interested in Increasing Interdisciplinary Work, by College:

	College of Management	*College of Engineering*	*CAS- Sciences*	*CAS- FAHSS*	*Health and Env.*	*G.S. Education*	*D.K.*	*All*
Very interested	30	44	47	46	55	56	25	46
Somewhat interested	65	38	41	33	29	33	50	39
Not very interested	4	9	10	11	13	11	0	10
Not at all interested	0	6	2	10	3	0	0	5
D.K.	0	3	0	0	0	0	25	1
Very interested+ somewhat interested	96	82	88	79	84	89	75	85
Not very interested + not at all interested	4	15	12	21	16	11	0	15
D.K.	0	3	0	0	0	0	25	1
Total	100	100	100	100	100	100	100	100

42. What incentives could the University offer that might increase your level of interest in or satisfaction with pursuing interdisciplinary work?

	Percent
Funds	22
Time	28
Infrastructure	19
Credit (tenure, promotion)	10
N.A. or "not needed"	21
TOTAL	100

About the Contributors

Diana C. Archibald, Ph.D., is an associate professor of English and the past director of gender studies at the University of Massachusetts–Lowell. She served as an administrative fellow and the chair of the Interdisciplinarity Transformation Team at UML and was lead writer for their final report.

Tanya Augsburg, Ph.D., is an assistant professor in liberal studies at San Francisco State University. Her areas of expertise include contemporary feminist performance and interdisciplinary studies pedagogy. She is the author of the first textbook in interdisciplinary studies, *Becoming Interdisciplinary: An Introduction to Interdisciplinary Studies* (2nd ed., 2006). She is curator of the first retrospective exhibition on the work of Joanna Frueh and editor of its accompanying exhibition catalogue, *Joanna Frueh: A Retrospective* (Nevada Museum of Art, 2005), and is an Executive Board member of the Association for Integrative Studies (AIS).

Richard M. Carp, Ph.D., is a professor in and chair of the Department of Interdisciplinary Studies at Appalachian State University. He works in the interstices of the academic study of religion, performance, semiotics, anthropology, cognitive science, material culture studies, and visual art and design. Recent publications include "Seeing Is Believing, but Touching's the Truth: Religion, Film, and the Anthropology of the Senses," in *Teaching Religion and Film*, Gregory Watkins, ed. (Oxford University Press, 2008); and "Art, Education, and the Sign(ificance) of the Self," in *Semiotics and Visual Culture: Sights, Signs, and Significance*, Debbie Smith-Shank, ed. (National Art Education Association, 2004).

James W. Davis, M.F.A, M.A., is a professor of creative arts at San Francisco State University. He is the former acting associate dean and director of the Inter-Arts Center and Special Programs, College of Creative Arts (1989–2002).

Andre Furtado, Ph.D., has his doctorate in chemical engineering from the University of Michigan and is an assistant professor of mathematics at Wayne State University. For over thirty years, his focus has been on mathematics education and nontraditional student retention.

Helen Goldsmith, J.D., has worked at San Francisco State University since 1983. She has been involved with the liberal studies program since 1985, holding a variety of roles and responsibilities. Currently she serves as associate dean of undergraduate services and former acting director of the liberal studies program.

Rick F. Hendra, Ed.D., is retired to occasional teaching and consulting after 30 years as an instructor, advisor, and community/program developer with the University Without Walls (UWW) at the University of Massachusetts–Amherst. He is writing a history of UWW at UMass and leading a research effort to gather the histories of all fifty Universities Without Walls across the country.

Stuart Henry, Ph.D., is a professor in and director of the School of Public Affairs at San Diego State University. Previously he served seven years at Wayne State University as chair of the Department of Interdisciplinary Studies. He is the author/coauthor or editor of 23 books, including *Constitutive Criminology* (1996), *Essential Criminology* (2004), and *Criminological Theory* (2006), as well as more than 100 articles in professional journals. He is a member of the board of AIS.

Linda Lora Hulbert, M.Ed., has over 30 years' experience in university teaching and administration, with her latest position being project coordinator in the College of Education at Wayne State University. She has won two excellence in teaching awards and has participated in more than 75 presentations, workshops, and institutes at national and international conferences, and has had many publications and consultancies in areas such as interdisciplinarity, developmental composition, adult learners, and student success strategies.

Julie Thompson Klein, Ph.D., is a professor of humanities at Wayne State University and is the author of numerous articles, chapters, and books on interdisciplinary research and education including *Interdisciplinarity: History, Theory and Practice* (1990), *Crossing Boundaries: Knowledge, Disciplinaries and Interdisciplinarities* (1996), *Humanities, Culture and Interdisciplinarity: The Changing American Academy* (2005), and *Creating Interdisciplinary Campus Cultures* (forthcoming). She has consulted and lectured widely throughout North America, Europe, Asia, Latin America, Australia, and New Zealand. She also received the Kenneth Boulding Award for outstanding scholarship on interdisciplinarity.

Lisa Maruca, Ph.D., an associate professor in the Department of English at Wayne State University, researches the history of writing technologies, authorship, and intellectual property. She has published *The Work of Print: Authorship and the Text Trades in England, 1660–1740* (University of Washington Press, 2007) as well as articles on print culture, digital literacy and plagiarism.

Caroline Maun, Ph.D., is an assistant professor in the Department of English at Wayne State University. She is the editor of *The Collected Poems of Evelyn Scott*, the author of a book of poems, *The Sleeping*, and co-editor of *Virtual Identities: The Con-*

struction of Selves in Cyberspace, forthcoming from Eastern Washington University Press. She has published articles on Emily Dickinson, W. B. Yeats, and Evelyn Scott.

Raymond C. Miller, Ph.D., has been president of two national professional associations: the Association for Integrative Studies and the Society for International Development. He was the founding editor of *Issues in Integrative Studies*. Professor Miller served as a member of the faculty at San Francisco State University for 43 years, where he is now professor emeritus of international relations and social science. He is author of *International Political Economy: Contrasting World Views* (Routledge, 2008).

Janette Kenner Muir, Ph.D., is an associate professor of interdisciplinary and integrative studies at George Mason University. She holds an M.A. from Wake Forest University and a Ph.D. from University of Massachusetts–Amherst. She is the immediate past associate dean of New Century College. She served as editor of *Communication Quarterly*, 2007–2009, co-editor of *Readings in Political Communication* (Strata, 2007), and contributing author to *Inventing a Voice: The Rhetoric of American First Ladies of the Twentieth Century* (Rowman & Littlefield, 2004), *Hate Speech* (Sage, 1995), and *The Clinton Presidency: Images, Issues and Communication Strategies* (Praeger, 1993). She received the Distinguished Service Award of the Eastern Communication Association and the Teaching Excellence Award from George Mason University.

William H. Newell, Ph.D., is a professor of interdisciplinary studies at Miami University, and was a founding faculty member of the Western College Program. Previously he taught at the Paracollege at St. Olaf College during its first four full years of operation. He has published two books and 35 articles and chapters on interdisciplinary studies. He is the executive director of the Association for Integrative Studies.

Daphne W. Ntiri, Ph.D., is an associate professor of Africana studies at Wayne State University and has served as educational consultant to UNESCO in France, Senegal, and Somalia. She has published numerous academic articles and books on adult education/literacy, gender, and Third World studies. Her forthcoming book is *Literacy as a Social Divide: African Americans at the Crossroads* (WSU Press).

Allen F. Repko, Ph.D., directs the 600-student interdisciplinary studies program at the University of Texas–Arlington where he has developed the program's required three-course core and is working with new tenure-track faculty to expand its curriculum and build partnerships with other academic units on campus. His research interests include assessment, the interdisciplinary research process, and theory. He is the author of *Interdisciplinary Research: Process and Theory* (Sage, 2008).

Roslyn Abt Schindler, Ph.D., is the former department chair and current associate professor in the Department of Classical and Modern Languages, Literatures and Cultures at Wayne State University. She has published articles and book chapters on interdisciplinary studies, adult learning, and Holocaust studies and co-edited *University Governance and Humanistic Scholarship: Studies in Honor of Diether Haenicke* (2002) and the 25th anniversary issue of *Issues in Integrative Studies* (2004). She is a past president of the AIS.

Rick Szostak, Ph.D., is a professor of economics at the University of Alberta. He is the author of nine books and 30 scholarly articles, all of an interdisciplinary nature. His most recent article is "How and Why to Teach Interdisciplinary Research Practice" (2007) in the *Journal of Research Practice*. He created the Office of Interdisciplinary Studies, and many of its programs, during a term as associate dean, and remains closely involved with the enterprise.

Peter W. Wakefield, Ph.D., Brown University (philosophy), is a senior lecturer and the director of undergraduate studies for interdisciplinary majors in the Graduate Institute of the Liberal Arts at Emory University. Wakefield's research interests focus on ancient Greek philosophy, the philosophy of teaching, and critical pedagogy. Much of his writing has focused on the problem of designing pedagogies for women, African American students, and others who have been excluded from dominant intellectual histories and dialogues.

Jay Wentworth, Ph.D., is a professor of interdisciplinary studies and the interim director of the Interdisciplinary Studies Program at Appalachian State University. He is a former editor of the AIS journal *Issues in Integrative Studies*.

Index